D0992574

THE ETERNAL MOMENT

THE ETERNAL MOMENT

THE POETRY OF CZESLAW MILOSZ

ALEKSANDER FIUT

Translated by Theodosia S. Robertson

University of California Press

Berkeley · Los Angeles · Oxford

Originally published as
Moment wieczny: Poezja Czesława Miłosza
© 1987 Libella, Paris

The Publishers wish to acknowledge the generous assistance of
the Alfred Jurzykowski Foundation, Inc., in funding the translation of
this book.

University of California Press
Berkeley and Los Angeles, California

University of California Press, Ltd.
Oxford, England

Fiut, Aleksander.
  [Moment wieczny. English]
  The eternal moment : the poetry of Czeslaw Milosz / Aleksander
Fiut ; translated by Theodosia S. Robertson.
    p. cm.
  Translation of: Moment wieczny.
  Bibliography: p.
  Includes index.
  ISBN 0-520-06689-8 (alk. paper)
    1. Miłosz, Czesław—Criticism and interpretation. I. Title.
  PG7158.M5532F5813 1990
  891.8'517—dc20   89-5150
                                                                 CIP

Poems from *The Collected Poems, 1931–1987* © 1988 by Czeslaw
Milosz Royalties, Inc. First published in the U.S. by The Ecco Press and
in the U.K. by Penguin Books Ltd in 1988; used by permission.

Parts of chapter 6 appeared in slightly different form in Aleksander
Fiut, "Czeslaw Milosz's Search for 'Humanness,'" *Slavic and East
European Journal* 31, no. 1 (1987): 65–75. © 1987 by *Slavic and East
European Journal;* used by permission of AATSEEL of the U.S., Inc.

The paper used in this publication meets the minimum requirements of
American National Standard for Information Sciences—Permanence of
Paper for Printed Library Materials, ANSI Z39.48-1984. ⊚

Printed in the United States of America
1 2 3 4 5 6 7 8 9

A NOTEBOOK: BON BY LAKE LEMAN

Red beeches, shining poplars
And steep spruce behind the October fog.
In the valley the lake smokes. Already snow
Lies on the hillsides of the other shore.
Of life, what remains? Only light,
So that the eyes blink in the sunny
Noon of such a season. You say: this is,
And no capacity, no artfulness
Can reach beyond what is.
And memory, useless, loses power.

Kegs smell of cider. The vicar with a spade
Mixes lime in front of the school.
My son runs there on a path. Boys carry
Sacks of chestnuts gathered on the slope.
If I forget thee, Jerusalem,
Says the prophet, let my right hand wither.
Underground tremors shake what is,
Mountains crack and forests break.
Touched by what was and what will be
All that is crumbles into dust.
And neither memory nor striving ceases.

Autumnal skies, the same in childhood,
In adulthood and in old age, I won't
Stare at you. And you, landscapes
Feeding our hearts with mild warmth,
What poison dwells in you, that seals our lips,
Makes us sit with folded arms, and the look
Of sleepy animals? Whoever finds order,
Peace, and an eternal moment in what is
Passes without trace. Do you agree then
To abolish what is, and take from movement
The eternal moment as a gleam
On the current of a black river? Yes.

Czeslaw Milosz, 1953

Contents

Acknowledgments

I wish to express my deep gratitude to Czeslaw Milosz, without whose extensive help, particularly in translating the poems not previously published in English, this book would not appear in its present form.

English translations quoted from *The Collected Poems, 1931–1987* (New York: The Ecco Press, 1988) are by Czeslaw Milosz and by Jan Darowski, Lawrence Davis, Renata Gorczynski, Robert Hass, Richard Lourie, Anthony Milosz, Leonard Nathan, Robert Pinsky, Peter Dale Scott, and Lillian Vallee. Quotes of the original Polish poems are from *Poemat o czasie zastygłym* [*Poem on Frozen Time*] (Wilno, 1933); *Nieobjęta ziemia* [*Unattainable Earth*] (Paris: Instytut Literacki, 1984); and *Wiersze* [*Poems*], vols. 1 and 2 (Kraków and Wrocław: Wydawnictwo Literackie, 1985).

I am especially grateful for the valuable comments made by the first readers of this book: Wiktor Weintraub and Stanisław Barańczak of Harvard University, and Samuel Fiszman of Indiana University.

I also wish to thank The Ford Foundation and the New York Institute for the Humanities at New York University for research grants that enabled me to complete *The Eternal Moment*.

Last, I express my gratitude to my translator, Theodosia Robertson, through whose talent and diligence the Polish text of my book could emerge in a fine English translation.

Abbreviations

Works are by Czeslaw Milosz unless otherwise noted.

CCM   *Conversations with Czeslaw Milosz,* by Ewa Czarnecka and Aleksander Fiut (San Diego: Harcourt Brace Jovanovich, 1987)

CP   *The Collected Poems, 1931–1987* (New York: The Ecco Press, 1988)

CS   *Człowiek wśród skorpionów: Studium o Stanisławie Brzozowskim* [Man Among Scorpions: A Study on Stanisław Brzozowski] (Paris: Instytut Literacki, 1962)

H   *The History of Polish Literature,* 2d ed. (Berkeley and Los Angeles: University of California Press, 1983)

K   *Kontynenty* [Continents] (Paris: Instytut Literacki, 1958)

LU   *The Land of Ulro* (New York: Farrar, Straus & Giroux, 1984)

NL   *Nobel Lecture* (New York: Farrar, Straus & Giroux, 1981)

NR   *Native Realm: A Search for Self-Definition* (Garden City, N.Y.: Doubleday, 1968)

ON   *Ogród nauk* [Garden of Sciences] (Paris: Instytut Literacki, 1979)

P   *Postwar Polish Poetry: An Anthology,* 3d ed. (Berkeley and Los Angeles: University of California Press, 1983)

PO   *Prywatne obowiązki* [Private Obligations] (Paris: Instytut Literacki, 1972)

PS   *Podróżny świata. Rozmowy z Czesławem Miłoszem. Komentarze* [Traveler of the World. Conversations with Czeslaw

Milosz. Commentaries], by Ewa Czarnecka (New York: Bicentennial Publishing, 1983)

R   *Rozmowy z Czesławem Miłoszem* [Conversations with Czeslaw Milosz], by Aleksander Fiut (Kraków: Wydawnictwo Literackie, 1981)

SN   *The Separate Notebooks* (New York: Ecco Press, 1984)

SP   *Selected Poems* (New York: Seabury Press, 1973)

UE   *Unattainable Earth* (New York: Ecco Press, 1986)

V   *Visions from San Francisco Bay* (New York: Farrar, Straus & Giroux, 1982)

WP   *The Witness of Poetry* (Cambridge, Mass.: Harvard University Press, 1983)

Introduction

For many American readers Czeslaw Milosz remains an enigmatic and paradoxical figure. He writes in Polish yet persistently emphasizes his ties with Lithuania. He is the author of *The Captive Mind*, a well-known study of communism, but has renounced political involvement. He knows and translates twentieth-century American poetry supremely well but repeatedly declares that he owes practically every line of his poetry to Polish literary tradition, recalling names unfamiliar to the inhabitants of San Francisco, Chicago, or New York. Increasingly popular, and in the words of Joseph Brodsky, "one of the greatest poets of our time, perhaps the greatest,"[1] Milosz has earned both fame and misunderstanding. He is increasingly categorized as "a poet of culture," "a poet of history," "a poet of the Holocaust"; or it is hastily concluded that "there are no direct lessons that American poets can learn from Milosz."[2] I have written this book with the intent of at least partially clearing up such confusion, revising erroneous conclusions, and bringing to light the less obvious qualities of Milosz's poetry in order to initiate a more serious discussion of his work.

In attempting to settle the question of his own origins, Milosz often jokingly remarks that he is like the Scotsman, who speaks and writes in English and was raised on English literature. This comparison is only a partial explanation. Born in 1911 on a Polish manor in Lithuania, Milosz is thus one of the last spiritual heirs of the Polish Rzeczpospolita, the old Polish Commonwealth. The Polish Commonwealth was one of the most extraordinary phenomena in European history. Inhabited by various nationalities, constituting an amalgam of many cultures, religions, and languages, it created one of the first democratic systems based on respect for the rights of the individual, freedom, and religious tolerance. That which was its moral strength, however, turned out to be its political weakness. The Polish Commonwealth was a powerful empire and controlled an enormous territory from the Baltic to the Black Sea. Between the fifteenth and seventeenth centuries it successfully warded off the incursions of its rapacious neighbors, only to fall prey to them in the eighteenth century and disappear from the map of Europe.

Attached to the historical Lithuania that had been a part of the old Polish Commonwealth, Milosz feels proud of his cultural inheritance; at the same time the fate of the Commonwealth is for him a kind of model for the growth and decline of every civilization. His imagination draws strength from this half-legendary land that, because of its distance from the major centers of Europe, preserved the relics of pagan beliefs and ancient customs. Growing up in Wilno (Vilnius), a city of churches, synagogues, and mosques, Milosz learned respect for different religions and cultures as well as an aversion to any kind of intolerance, fanaticism, or nationalism.[3] The variety of standards and the fluidity of behavior models that Milosz observed among the inhabitants of Wilno, together with a profoundly religious attitude toward nature, impel him to reflect on what man is as an individual, what constitutes his humanity, and what the limits of human freedom are when faced with the overwhelming powers of history. These questions take on a particularly tragic quality since historic Lithuania became one of the first victims of twentieth-century totalitarianism, obliterated by both Hitler and Stalin during World War II.

Milosz seeks deeper answers to his questions beneath the surface rubble of the events of our century. His poetry, an integral part of his oeuvre, is an anthropological meditation. Milosz is among those who are convinced of the unavoidable decline of our civilization as a result of its departure from its Christian roots. Thus he stands in the company of such thinkers as Berdyaev, Spengler, Ortega y Gasset, and Stanisław Ignacy Witkiewicz. He differs from them, however, in the eschatological dimension he gives to his visions of the end of the world and in the stress he places on changes in the collective imagination.

For centuries the basis of the Western vision of man and the universe has been the Christian imagination. Following Blake, Swedenborg, and the French poet Oscar Milosz, his own kinsman, Czeslaw Milosz sees the gradual erosion of this imagination in the misguided development of science after the seventeenth century. Since that time a fundamental division has opened up between the internal life of the individual and the image of man formed by scientific theory. Deprived of his central place in the universe, man has gradually come to be seen as a product of social, historical, and biological processes, alone and defenseless in an alien cosmos. This self-image has been, according to Milosz, the foundation of twentieth-century nihilism and subsequently a cradle for totalitarian doctrines. And one should not forget that Milosz has not only witnessed the impact on the modern imagination of such theories as Marxism, psychoanalysis, and existentialism but also directly experienced nazism and communism.

This situation appears in Milosz's *Visions from San Francisco Bay* and *The Land of Ulro*, but in his poetry it takes on additional meaning. There Milosz does not illustrate theological and philosophical problems; he combines them in the conventions of poetic language in an attempt to re-create a language that is both poetic and philosophical. In his poems Milosz tries to rebuild the Christian anthropocentric vision of the world, at the same time (unlike naive traditionalists) acknowledging those theories and experiences that have undermined it. This attempt explains the constant presence in his poetry of antithetical clashes, the dialectic of opposite ideas, and the ambivalence of opinions: all are called into question and reinterpreted. From this point of view, Milosz's poetry can be read as a hermeneutics of the Christian imagination, one aware of its own limitations.

Picking up this thread, I have in my own book conducted a hermeneutics of Milosz's poetic imagination. Through this method I want to sketch at least an initial outline of the fundamental problems in Milosz's poetry, grasp its inner dynamics, and indicate the degree of its complexity. I am particularly interested in the places in his poetry that are difficult to delimit but where a precise and palpable description of the world intersects with deep reflection, where the personal experiences of the writer intersect with anthropological meditation, and where the poetic meets with the philosophical and the religious. Of course, in his reflections upon human nature, European history, and Mediterranean civilization, Milosz approaches—and sometimes directly and polemically refers to—other contemporary poets, including Anglo-American ones. We need only mention Karl Shapiro, T. S. Eliot, Robinson Jeffers, or Wallace Stevens. Nevertheless, Milosz's different conception of these topics is determined by his different cultural heritage, historical experience, and literary tradition. In this study I am unable to devote as much space to these affinities as they warrant. I hope, however, that my observations will encourage substantial comparative studies. Such a comparative approach would be particularly fruitful since Milosz skillfully adapts international contemporary poetry and, distilling what is best from Polish literary tradition, especially romanticism, creates an original variant of metaphysical poetry.

The basic fabric of Milosz's poetry is a constant dialogue with the living and with those long dead, with himself and with his literary predecessors. The present study attempts to re-create that dialogue and at the same time enter into it, as a development of, and complement to, my own conversations with Milosz.[4] The point of departure for my dialogue with Milosz and his poetry has been an intriguing and mysterious statement from his poem "A Notebook: Bon by Lake Leman" ("Notatnik: Bon nad Lemanem," 1953):

> Do you agree then
> To abolish what is, and take from movement
> The eternal moment as a gleam
> On the current of the black river? Yes.
>
> Godzisz się co jest
> Niszczyć i z ruchu podjąć moment wieczny
> Jak blask na wodach czarnej rzeki? Tak.

Chapter 1, "The Traps of Mimesis," refers to a statement made by Milosz in his Nobel Prize acceptance speech. A metaphor of the poet's vocation, he says, is to fly above the earth and yet see it in great detail at the same time. This opening chapter examines how Milosz attempts to overcome the contradictions between the directness of sensual data and the distance of contemplation, the faithfulness to detail and the urge toward abstraction, the flux of things and their essence—in short, art facing the mystery and elusiveness of being.

The three subsequent chapters trace what might be called Milosz's search for the essence of human nature. This search leads the poet through such dimensions as nature, history, society, and personal relationships. The question is: Where does the core of "humanhood"— simply, what it means to be human—lie? Specifically, Chapter 2, "Love Affair with Nature," deals with such problems as dependence and independence in the face of nature, her innocence and cruelty, the contradiction between the pain of creatures and the idea of the good Creator. Here I have drawn comparisons between Milosz's poetry of nature and the Anglo-American tradition.

Chapter 3, "Facing the End of the World," describes Milosz's attempt to resolve the paradox of how man is able to exist simultaneously *in* and *beyond* history, and how history itself may be seen on one hand as a process divorced from the individual and on the other as a product of human creativity. This paradox is the focus of Milosz's concepts of historicity and eschatology.

Chapter 4, "In the 'Interhuman Church,'" refers to Polish writer Witold Gombrowicz's concept of man and demonstrates more specifically how the influence of the social community affects our view of what is irreducibly individual. Chapter 5, "In the Grip of Eros," examines the same problem from the perspective of the relationship between man and woman.

The essence and scope of these questions are embodied in a complicated network composed of the relations among the implied author, the hero, and the speaker. For Milosz, the question "What is man?" also means "Who am I?"—or the subject as a unique individual. This is the focus of Chapter 6, "The Identity Game," which discusses Milosz's originality and innovations as a poet. Drawing on the idea of the poet as seer, he creates a persona that speaks different languages, mimics other voices, and simultaneously resembles the author himself.

Within the framework of the book, the closing chapter, "Palimpsest," reverses the conceptual relationship presented in Chapter 1: instead of facing reality, art confronts its own conventions. Expressing the essence of human nature as well as the mystery of the universe, the poet is constrained by the elusiveness of these visions and the pressure of poetic convention. I show that the poet tries to overcome the latter by subtle manipulation with different voices, dialogue, and play with allusions to the classical and Christian traditions alike.

I

The Traps of Mimesis

The origin of Milosz's poetry is his enchantment with the beauty of being and with its most fundamental premise: faith in the existence of the outside world. This faith is irrespective of even the most subtle or refined philosophical speculations or magic play of fantasy. For Milosz, the world exists simply because our five senses confirm it.[1] There is, of course, no way to penetrate the mysterious essence, the core of reality, despite what philosophers may think. The world is like a garden, writes Milosz in "The World" ("Świat [poema naiwne]," 1943): "You cannot enter" ("Wejść tam nie można"), but, he adds immediately and emphatically, "you're sure it's there" ("jest na pewno"). Those who claim that "there is nothing, just a seeming, / These are the ones who don't have hope" (CP 49; "nas oko ludzi / I że nic nie ma, tylko się wydaje," "ci właśnie nie mają nadziei").

Milosz thus deliberately ignores the centuries-old debate about the existence or nonexistence of outside reality. At the same time, he separates himself from that kind of poetry which derives its inspiration from fluctuating perception, from states of madness and hallucination, or focuses its attention only on linguistic and aesthetic qualities.

In one of his essays, Milosz acknowledges:

> The reasons I have long been a proponent of understanding all art, including poetry, as mimesis are not theoretical in nature, for at work here is the experience of ceaseless pursuit of something that eludes us and remains unnamed; it is neither the harmony of the whole nor the purity of the intonation. It clearly dwells somewhere beyond language. About the rest, however, the theoretical underpinnings of art and poetry, I have many questions and few answers.[2]

Elsewhere he recalls with approval the formula of Oscar Milosz: poetry is "a passionate pursuit of the Real" (WP 25). Poetry is a "pursuit" because its essence expresses itself perhaps more by the very dynamic approach of a word to the reality than by the manipulation of the meaning of words, more by its aspiration than by its fulfillment. And this pursuit is "passionate" since, according to Milosz, the nature of any poetic act is sensual, erotic.

Milosz's poetry from the outset is marked strongly by a desire for direct contact with the visual world, for what is seen and remembered rather than interpreted, imagined, or invented. In more accurate terms, the knowledge, the fantasy, and the imagination support the eye and the memory to which Milosz has given priority. Not only are elemental experiences a supplement to intellectual operations; they are their first and most faithful stimulus. Sensualism seems then to be for Milosz both a cognitive method and the driving force of his poetry.

Milosz, in spite of his deep erudition, tries as much as possible to avoid the nuances of philosophical terminology and theoretical reasoning; he wants to think "commonsensically" and deduce his vision of the world as well as poetic theory and practice from ordinary, everyday experience. In his *Nobel Lecture* Milosz stated not by chance that he grants to reality "its naive and solemn meaning, a meaning having nothing to do with the philosophical debates of the last few centuries" (*NL* 6). His main efforts are therefore concentrated on the question of how the poetic word can penetrate being, *esse,* and how the word itself can be imbued with it. Poetic imagination constantly challenges the changeability of the world and all its phenomena. In *The Land of Ulro* (*Ziemia Ulro,* 1977) Milosz wrote, "Imagination becomes embattled with movement, on behalf of the moment, and whatever is restored to brilliance becomes, so to speak, a moment torn from the throat of motion, a testament to the durability of even the most ephemeral instant, to the trickery of the nullifying memory" (*LU* 11). Within the hallowed walls of the Swedish Academy Milosz recalled—not without some perversity—his childhood fascination with Selma Lagerlöf's *Wonderful Adventures of Nils.* He said that "a metaphor of the poet's vocation" is such that, like the hero of Lagerlöf's novel, he "flies above the earth and looks at it *from above,* but at the same time sees it in every detail" (*NL* 4).

Finally, in his Harvard lectures, Milosz stated that "the never-fulfilled desire to achieve a mimesis, to be faithful to a detail, makes for the health of poetry and gives it a chance to survive periods unpropitious to it" (*WP* 56–57). The words "to see," "movement," and "detail" are the keys to Milosz's poetic world.

The real exists independently of human consciousness and is incomparably richer, more fascinating, and more mysterious. Reality demands to be named and yet it escapes the word. An attempt to capture on paper even some tiny particular, an insignificant detail, immediately encounters both the incomprehensible complexity and the cognitive limitation and feebleness of language. Since knowledge is based on insoluble contradictions, it is no wonder that poetic mimesis must be predicated on paradox. How can direct sensory experience, transitory and impermanent, be reconciled with the distance that reflective memory grants? How can faithfulness to detail be reconciled with the natural tendency toward generalization? How can the moment be contrasted with movement, retaining both the dynamism of change and the eternal dimension of the moment, the fragility of every object and the complexity of its essence? How can something be presented simultaneously from above, from soaring heights, and yet in immediate close-up?

Beneath the contradictions of a cognitive and artistic nature lies, moreover, a serious moral dilemma, one particularly sensitive for a writer from Central Europe. Reflecting on the reaction of Polish poetry to the experience of World War II, Milosz poses the basic question: "The act of writing a poem is an act of faith; yet if the screams of the tortured are audible in the poet's room, is not his activity an offense to human suffering?" (*H* 458). From this point of view, every artistic creation becomes morally ambiguous.

Milosz expresses this dilemma most fully and most perfectly in his *Nobel Lecture:*

> Reality calls for a name, for words, but it is unbearable, and if it is touched, if it draws very close, the poet's mouth cannot even utter a complaint of Job: all art proves to be nothing compared with action. Yet to embrace reality in such a manner that it is preserved in all its old tangle of good and evil, of despair and hope, is possible only thanks to a distance, only by soaring *above* it—but this in turn seems then a moral treason.
>
> (*NL* 11–12)

Milosz's poetry can be seen as an attempt to avoid all these traps of mimesis.

SEEING AND DESCRIBING

It is no small challenge to contrast Adam Mickiewicz's motto "I see and describe" ("widzę i opisuję") with avant-garde concepts of poetry. This does not mean, of course, that Milosz recommends imitating the epic model of *Pan Tadeusz*. Milosz is fully aware that the traditional techniques of description are more than an obsolete poetics. They serve to render a vision of the world considerably different from our own and express, moreover, a dissimilar level of self-awareness and cognitive consciousness. Milosz persistently reiterates, however, that Mickiewicz's credo has not lost its relevance; at least it should be rethought. In other words, the poet must work out a method of poetic description that on one hand would be faithful to the evidence of the five senses and on the other would directly and indirectly convey the complexity of twentieth-century reflection upon cognition.

Milosz's poetry contains relatively few descriptions that have as their compositional basis either a distinctive convention or the ego of the subject. From the beginning other kinds of description dominate, ones subservient to the eye. They are based on the principle of metonymic accumulation of observed objects or scenes, or—as in the movement of a movie camera—the constant shifting between what is near and what is distant.[3] It should be added that both methods undergo changes and a gradual evolution in Milosz's poetry. This evolution is expressed by the growing, increasingly conscious clash between the desire to capture the fleeting moment and the feeling of the absence of a constant reference point that would allow separate moments of perception to be ordered. These problems appear in incipient form in Milosz's youthful "That Time" ("Pora," 1937):

Flatlands, concave like blue bowls, dense smoke. At edges fires, salvos,
    searchlights.
The sun terrifyingly sulfurous ran quickly through the fields.
Then supply columns spilled out of the current,
Cannons were leaning askew, horses in tattered girths reared.
In the suburbs. In the suburbs where locked houses stood silent,
A tank stopped.
In the crew's helmets a stinking mess of blood and sweat.
If they don't repair the engine in one hour—
So they kneel, their hands tremble with fever. Thick oil drips into the
    sand.

The poet is groping for the strong expressiveness of the image. Comparisons, epithets, metaphors, and the breathless broken flow of syntax all serve to intensify expression. Interestingly, the cameralike movement from the general and universal view to a close-up that focuses the poetic lens on one isolated particular is accompanied by a gradual removal of dark, visionary elements from the entire scene. The cannons and the startled horses in their "tattered girths" are distinct and concrete. They are almost as if actually seen. From the general chaos of defeat that initially had almost an eschatological dimension, one ordinary tank emerges at the end. The projection of states of fear upon reality is supplanted by faithfulness to the concrete. In addition, the one who observes this scene and relates it changes his attitude: cosmic, timeless distance gives way to partial identification with the protagonists. It is not at all easy to determine who pronounces these words: "If they don't repair the engine in one hour—." It might be the narrator, or it might be one of the crew in the tank.

The poem already contains all the constituent features of Milosz's type of description: shifting between the vision from above and close up, combining the abstract and the concrete, joining unrealistic elements with realistic ones in a linear order, and finally presenting phenomena through the sum of their component parts. Of course, this movement of the poetic camera does not always flow as smoothly as in this example; sometimes it moves suddenly, jumping from above to below and from below to above. This movement in Milosz's poetry has not only a quantitative meaning, as it were (thus large–small and near–far), but also a qualitative one, since it takes into consideration the various attitudes of the viewer. To continue the camera metaphor, it could be said that during the movement of the camera the poet changes its filter.

Milosz's type of description, already visible in "That Time," emphasizes a vacillation between the subject and the object. Attempts to objectify vision are set in a context marked by the presence and emotions of the viewer. Reality is not seen synthetically since this synthesis remains only an unrealized project; the "I" of the observer is divided between what his senses tell him and what memory, imagination, and feelings add. Thus a dilemma appears: either identification of the vision of the world with its creator, an illusion of fullness at the cost of violating natural law and giving up sensory evidence, or precision and detailed exactness of presentation of individual objects with the tacit agreement that it is futile to search for a unifying principle either in the subject or in the reality surrounding him. How does Milosz resolve this dilemma when he so clearly attempts to achieve an illusion of fullness and completeness in his vision of the world? What direction does the evolution of his descriptive method take?

A visionary-imaginative landscape prevails in Milosz's poetry up to 1943 ("In Fever, 1939," "W malignie, 1939"; "The Journey," "Podróż," 1942; "Land of Poetry," "W krainie poezji"). Although even there the descriptions do not lose their fantastic quality, they usually serve rather to transform concrete reality than to construct an imaginary landscape. Returning after many years to this method of assembling composite images of the world, Milosz will provide realistic motivations for it. In "Landscape" ("Widok," 1975), for example, the interpenetration of the subject with the object occurs in a dream and is a linking figure between man and nature. In simpler terms, subjective expression replaces a more objective one.

The following portion of "Outskirts" ("Przedmieście," 1943) has been cited as an example of concision:

> A broken shadow of a chimney. Thin grass.
> Farther on, the city torn into red brick.
> Brown heaps, barbed wire tangled at stations.
> Dry rib of a rusty automobile.
> A claypit glitters.
>
> (CP 66)

One would be mistaken to consider this only a genre scene from everyday life during the Occupation. Nor is it an image of random objects seen alternately close up and from far away, since the entire picture becomes, as it were, immanently interpreted. The epithets speak indirectly of lifelessness, uselessness, wreckage, and destruction. A similar chain of associations links the metaphors "the city torn into red brick" and "dry rib of a rusty automobile." The same effect is created by the motionlessness and accumulation of useless objects, the visible traces of the former presence of people. In a word, as before, the destruction of the world is described—but how differently: more reticently, more sparingly, without excessive emotional emphasis. By just his choice and description of elements Milosz achieves what would seem to be an impossible goal: the subjective and objective aspects of reality are joined in an indissoluble whole. An allusion at the end of the poem exalts the unity of the image and its symbolic value at the same time. In the next-to-last stanza of the poem Milosz uses the phrase "jałowe pole," recalling T. S. Eliot's *Waste Land,* which he had translated into Polish around 1944. This modification of Eliot's phrase speaks for itself. A prosaic "field" (*pole*) is substituted for the noble and somewhat abstract "land" (*ziemia*). Eliot's solemn, metaphysical poem is contrasted with Milosz's restrained and somehow ironic description of the scenes from everyday Polish life under the Nazi Occupation, reminiscent of Hannah Arendt's famous statement about the "banality of evil."

The filter need not necessarily be an eschatological one. It may be morally tinted. In "Songs of Adrian Zieliński" ("Pieśni Adriana Zielińskiego," 1943), the decreasing distance signifies a refusal of solidarity with the suffering and dying. The dead "lie like cramped, black ants" (CP 70; "leżą jak czarne mrówki skurczone"). Here the person of the viewer himself loses meaning: "You cannot even see yourself" (CP 69; "siebie samego nawet nie widać"). Sometimes this filter serves an aesthetic purpose, as in "To Jonathan Swift" ("Do Jonatana Swifta," 1947), where "islands shine with emerald" ("szmaragdem połyskują wyspy"). Always, however, these various shades of description go hand in hand with a concern for accuracy: the ants are "black", the ocean is "greenish" (*zielonkawy*), the shore is "rocky" (*skalisty*).

The filters change, and the range of the scale of vision changes. It is difficult even to count all the variants that appear, especially in Milosz's postwar poems. In one of them, a concert is seen with the eyes of corpses from beneath the floor ("Concert" ["Koncert", 1948]). In another, the protagonist rises up above the setting sun and from there views the world as "the mighty power of counter-fulfillment" ("How It Was," CP 203; "Jak było," 1963). In still another, the eye of the protagonist is compared with the eye of God ("*Oeconomia Divina,*" 1973, CP 235). At the same time, close-ups register not only individual objects but also their qualities, their properties. In "To Jonathan Swift," for example, the camera eye makes a foray from the ocean to the skillet.

In these examples the basic disparity between what is near and what is far, between what is general and what is particular, unique, and unknown or foreign exists only below the surface and does not constitute a problem. Quite different is "Bobo's Metamorphosis" ("Gucio zaczarowany," 1962). The first part of this poem presents the basic paradox of cognition with telegraphic brevity:

> Fields sloping down and a trumpet.
> Dusk and a bird flies low and waters flare.
> Sails unfurled to the daybreak beyond the straits.
> I was entering the interior of a lily by a bridge of brocade.
> (CP 162)

> Pochyłe pola i trąbka.
> Ten zmierzch i nisko leci ptak i błysły wody.
> Rozwinęły się żagle na brzask za cieśniną.
> Wchodziłem we wnętrze lilii mostem złotogłowiu.

These microscenes seem to be arranged quite haphazardly. With some effort we can recognize the recurring motif of water and then land. The concrete details—the fields are "sloping," the bird flies "low"—do not sufficiently offset the general character of the description. The jump from seeing from above to seeing close up is not only abrupt but also lacking in subjective motivation: we do not know if these are shots in the observation of one subject. That is rather unlikely since the subject switches from image to image, from scene to scene, and changes into an insect that enters a flower. Finally, time is also disrupted, divided into parts; it is both twilight and daybreak. The breakdown in the vision of the world is accompanied by a breakdown in the poem itself. That the lines are separate, only loosely connected with one another, already suggests a graphic notation.

In these few lines Milosz has pushed to the extreme the camera movement method of presenting the world. He has also questioned the usefulness of the other method: the creation of an image by the accumulation of individual elements. In stricter terms, in both methods he has reached limits beyond which it is difficult to go. The impenetrability of phenomena and their innumerability are not the only obstacles in achieving a complete image of reality. Equally essential are the arbitrariness of choice and the arrangement of the components. The organizing principle either cannot be grasped at all or is only suggested. The illusion of completeness cannot be more than an illusion. But without it the world is just an incomplete sum of observed objects. The observer also loses his identity: reduced to the function of noting down impressions, he fragments himself among single cognitive acts.

Recording what is impossible to describe, Milosz illustrates such attributes of human cognition as discontinuity, incompleteness, dehumanization, the intermingling within it of various points of view, as well as the influence of the manner of observation on the observed object. The resulting image of the world is flashing and dynamic, and at the same time incoherent, open, and full of dark areas.

One might say that there is nothing original in this image since it is the way the majority of twentieth-century poets present reality, particularly poets belonging to the avant-garde. Milosz's uniqueness lies in the fact that regardless of how contemporary relativism has affected and intruded on his vision of reality, it has not destroyed it entirely. Captured by his fascinated gaze or summoned up by memory, fragments of the visible world appear in his poems for a moment, only to disintegrate and disappear immediately, but without losing anything of their sensual consistency. Milosz resists the transformation of reality into a mass of undifferentiated impressions or into a collection of mirror reflections, putting his trust, despite everything, in the testimony of his five senses. This testimony is also for him a check against the deforming influence of literary conventions.

According to Milosz, in every poet, including the contemporary poet, a struggle takes place between the demands of classicism and realism:

> I affirm that, when writing, every poet is making a choice between the dictates of the poetic language and his fidelity to the real. If I cross out a word and replace it with another, because in that way the line as a whole acquires more conciseness, I follow the practice of the classics. If, however, I cross out a word because it does not convey an observed detail, I lean toward realism.

He adds: "Yet these two operations cannot be neatly separated, they are interlocked." The poet must therefore become fully conscious of the danger lurking in his falsification of the truth about the world and make a deliberate choice from among all the particulars, for—according to Milosz's second piece of advice—he "can be faithful to real things only by arranging them hierarchically" (*WP* 71). In practice, this means that the selection and arrangement of the particular details cannot be random and without some hidden design. That design must somehow point beyond itself and depict an important idea or truth directly, just as the destroyed objects in "Outskirts" form a pattern of the Apocalypse.

The word *see* takes on further meanings. For Milosz it refers not only to ordinary perception or intense imagining of past events but also to the ability to penetrate beneath the surface of phenomena in order to reach the meaning that is veiled to the uninitiated eye. It refers as much to phenomena of the contemporary world ("How It Was," *CP* 203, "Jak było," 1968; "*Oeconomia Divina*," *CP* 235, 1973), as to a prophetic power ("Letter of January 1, 1935," "List 1.1 1935"; "To Father Ch.," "Do księdza Ch.," 1934; "From the Rising of the Sun," "Gdzie wschodzi słońce i kędy zapada," 1974). As Milosz states:

> "To see" means not only to have before one's eyes. It may mean also to preserve in memory. "To see and to describe" may also mean to reconstruct in imagination. A distance achieved thanks to the mystery of time must not change events, landscapes, human figures into a tangle of shadows growing paler and paler. On the contrary, it can show them in full light, so that every fact, every date becomes expressive and persists as an eternal reminder of human depravity and human greatness. Those who are alive receive a mandate from those who are silent forever.
>
> (*NL* 21–22)

The memory of the individual man is obviously deceptive; the images it retains fade and disappear with the passage of time. It is also difficult to avoid the bias of recollection, which sometimes mythologizes past events, superimposing another scale of values on them. For this reason, beyond one's individual memory, Milosz refers to the collective memory. Collective memory, free from the defects of reminiscence—after all, its record is the entire culture—in the poet's hands takes on a vividness and emotional dynamism proper to individual memory.

When transposed into poetic language, reference to collective memory means the mingling within a poem of various dimensions of time and space and the description of scenes from the past as if they were actually happening and were a part of the author's biography. Hence, the wartime scene from 1920 is recalled twelve years later by "a citizen of the Polish Republic" ("That Time") who observes a military procession. A twentieth-century reader of Jonathan Swift seeking in the Age of Enlightenment models applicable to the era of Stalinist terror sees in his mind's eye Swift himself bent over his manuscript.

The poet, contemplating the paradoxes of cognition, takes on the identity of the hero of a book read in childhood. In a similarly modernizing way Milosz presents the ancient wedding in Sabaudia ("Treatise on Poetry," CP 109; "Traktat poetycki," 1956), the founding of Warsaw ("A Legend," CP 102; "Legenda," 1949), or Swedenborg's wanderings through hell ("On the Other Side," CP 169; "Po drugiej stronie," 1964). The descriptive technique is always similar: a frankly reporterlike faithfulness to detail, a series of carefully chosen objects, precise and at the same time general information about the time and place of the events, and the element of microaction. Viewing the world metonymically, the poet perceives and understands it metaphorically. The principle of *pars pro toto* governs Milosz's poetry, but the *totum* in question is an interpretation, a conclusion drawn from the meanings the individual parts convey as well as their arrangement and hierarchy.

In brief, an affirmation of memory seems to be a remedy for the dilemma of description. Moreover, Milosz transfers to the collective memory properties of individual memory such as the arbitrary choice of the remembered object, the fixing of attention on a particular isolated from its context, and the ability to bring the past to life, as he derives from them something more—the very foundation of his poetry. In addition, memory becomes for him something like an image of the entire culture, its model. This is all the more true as these two orders exist in an intimate symbiosis: the synchrony of culture leaves its imprint variously in the memory of the individual man, remaining in the collective memory as the potential to become present.

A POETRY OF THE CONCRETE

Poetry of the particular, it is fairly clear, is a poetry of the concrete; it is opposed to ideas and abstract concepts. This concreteness of Milosz's imagination is immediately apparent, as it is directly grounded in his sensualism. The tendency to describe concrete objects can be seen even in his early poetry. Milosz, of course, is not unique in this. A similar tendency became pronounced among both the symbolists and the imagists. After World War II the tendency acquired two further justifications: poetic models that had plunged reality into abstraction were discarded, and the preference for the concrete was combined with firsthand experience of the disintegration of the material world. This was the particular lot of poets from Central Europe, including Poland. Hence the interest in the concrete, material thing in the poetry of Tadeusz Różewicz, Zbigniew Herbert, Miron Białoszewski, and Wisława Szymborska.[4]

As a rule, Milosz describes things that are the objects of culture, or rather, of civilization. Like clothes or jewelry, they have primarily a functional character, although they may become objects of art. They are not, however, created as art objects. Statues? Yes, but they are covered with leaves in a park ("The Gates of the Arsenal," *CP* 10; "Bramy Arsenału," 1934) or stand in the sculptor's studio ("The Journey," 1942) not in a museum exhibit. Paintings? They are not abstract compositions, the object of aesthetic impressions, but rather those that are a kind of communiqué from a past world, like the works of Carpaccio, or a sensually tangible hieroglyphic of meanings, like those of Bosch. It is no accident that there are so few works of art in Milosz's poetry. Every object takes on sufficient significance simply by virtue of the fact that it bears the trace of a human hand or is rendered privileged by our gaze. Impenetrable, autonomous, set apart from other objects, the work of art is at the same time linked to other objects by an invisible thread. It continually calls to mind both its creator and its user. It refers somewhere beyond itself, beyond its own particularity.

According to Milosz's own very accurate description: "Some critics see in him [Milosz] a symbolist in reverse: in symbolism a poet proceeds from external reality towards the ineffable veiled by it, while Milosz circumvents with his symbols the essential being of things, which seems to be his main concern" (*P* 73).[5]

So it is, clearly, in all his poetry. Milosz's prewar poems illustrate, however, the manner of his genesis and his first attempts in this "detour." The poetry Milosz wrote during the Occupation up to 1943 was generally consistent with his prewar poetics. Already in 1942 one can detect perhaps another method in his treatment of objects: they are singled out from the background and connected with one another in the eye of the observer. A particularly interesting example is "Waltz" ("Walc," 1942), where the dance movement sets the entire surroundings into a seeming whirl and out of which for only a moment flashes "the glass of arms, the black of arms, the white of arms and hands" ("szkło ramion, czerń ramion, biel ramion i rąk"). Perhaps in this period Milosz realized what the basis of description was for him. To capture the peculiarity and unrepeatable quality of things, one must focus attention on one detail, feature, or property and thus halt the flow of time.

The war demonstrated not only the fragility of human life but also the transitoriness of objects. With an almost archaeological reverence, the poet examines every thing, even the most trifling, since in it may be frozen the last trace of someone's presence. "If history speaks about what was, then archaeology tells us about what has been and is. Archaeological time is embedded in things; it has injured them, but not destroyed them."[6] The poem "City" ("Miasto," 1940) speaks movingly about this:

> And the wind, when strings of wires have broke, opens a dead door
> On the knob of which remained, still not lost
> The touch of a hero who disappeared without a trace.

> I wiatr, gdy struny drutów pękły, martwe drzwi otwiera,
> Na których klamce pozostał niezmyty
> Ślad przepadłego bez wieści bohatera.

Destroyed objects testify above all to now absent people. The tautology "a dead door" forcefully accentuates the intimate link between things and their users; by means of a contradiction the poem calls back a lost life. Milosz has since then viewed objects in precisely this way. For him they are a sort of medium for the existence of individuals, cultures, and ultimately the entire world. The motif of things that retain the fading trace of people now absent recurs persistently.

Milosz's "philosophy of things" is already formed in "The World." In this respect the poem has unusual significance. Moreover, his philosophy is a voice in a prolonged discussion with the generation of young Polish poets who perished during the Nazi occupation as well as with the well-known contemporary Polish poet Zbigniew Herbert, a discussion unfortunately missing in the English translation. In these debates the most important themes of Milosz's reflection on the object are focused as in a lens. Relationships absorb his attention: the concrete—the idea; subject—object; object—name; object—another object. What is more, it seems that "The World" alone fulfills the directive that Milosz found in Schopenhauer. According to Schopenhauer, existing "as the pure subject, the clear mirror of the object," so that one "can no longer separate the perceiver from the perception," can be accomplished only if one "forgets even his individuality, his will." Contact between the object disconnected from its surroundings and the subject that frees itself from the will of power means that

that which is so known is no longer the particular thing as such; but it is the *Idea*, the eternal form, the immediate objectivity of the will at this grade; and, therefore, he who is sunk in this perception is no longer individual, for in such perception the individual has lost himself; but he is *pure*, will-less, powerless, timeless subject of knowledge.

(CP 358)

To achieve such a perception in "The World," the subjectivity of the author is transferred to the interplay of the points of view of the adult and the child; through recollection the object is freed from change, while the hierarchy of things is, on the principle of analogy, a reflection of the metaphysical order of the universe. Not accidentally was Milosz inspired by Saint Thomas Aquinas. As has been noted, the entire poem is placed in ironic parentheses. Milosz's other poems prove the fundamental otherness of the subject, the duration of perception in time, and the intangibility of the material object that cannot be avoided. In Stanisław Barańczak's words, "the veil of the senses, the veil of memory, the veil of language, and their triple imperfection" are at work.[7]

The veil of the senses appears in Milosz's poetry not as a questioning of the truth of their data but rather as an indication of their natural limitations. Thus, a view from the perspective of an insect or bird changes the scale and proportion but does not disturb the physical laws of reality. Only in the hell of Swedenborg do phenomena lose their real-life texture ("On the Other Side," CP 169).

In his precise analysis of the veil of language, Barańczak points out such qualities as the helplessness of the word facing a particular being as well as the "discrepancy between the system of names and the system of components of the world."[8] Milosz devotes extensive passages to these problems in "With Trumpets and Zithers" ("Na trąbach i na cytrze," CP 196), "From the Rising of the Sun," (CP 252), and *The Separate Notebooks*. As Barańczak shows, Milosz resists the tendency of language toward intellectualism and abstraction by extracting from each word the maximum concreteness and uniqueness. His technique relies on manipulation of vocabulary (going beyond the ethnic language, a predilection for rare and unusual expressions) as well as on synecdoches. I would add Milosz's awareness of the pressure of clichéd expressions with their weight of tradition. Culture plays an ambivalent role: it ensures continuity of tradition and guarantees its perpetuation, but as a result of its increasing, successive layers, it divides us from things in themselves.[9]

Writing about the veil of memory, Barańczak shows that Milosz is well aware of its many weak points. Memory is faulty, and time erases the freshness of first experiences and covers them with subsequent ones. "Elegy for N. N." (*CP* 239; "Elegia dla N. N.," 1962) and "Language Was Changing" ("Zmieniał się język," 1963) are primarily devoted to these experiences. In the recently published poem "How Is It Possible to Forget" ("Jak można zapomnieć," 1958), Milosz writes: "How is it possible to forget? And yet it is. / Details remain, the logic of ashes" ("Jak można zapomnieć? A jednak można zapomnieć. / Zostają szczegóły, logika popiołu"). Even here the seed of doubt is sown, but by constantly reaching back into memory, Milosz's poetry stretches its very boundaries, as in this poem. The poem is based on a paradox: the poet evokes from the past precisely what he is supposed to have forgotten. Particulars, evidently, are based on the "logic of ashes."

In "The Separate Notebooks: A Mirrored Gallery" ("Osobny zeszyt: przez galerie luster") a confession appears:

> I want to know where the house of an instant of seeing is,
> when it's liberated from the eye, in itself forever.
>
> (*CP* 353)

Milosz, therefore, wants to show not the concrete or the object, but himself or someone, the viewer, or more precisely, the act of perception as if detached from both the knower and what is known. At the same time, he is recording an elusive moment of interaction between the subject and the object.

How does Milosz show these "instants of seeing" in his poems? For the moment I will say only that one of his techniques is rendering the speaking "I" dynamic. It is both the same and not the same person who views something simultaneously in the present, the past, and sometimes the future. Milosz attempts to avoid the catch hidden in the cognitive act by making time and space relative. He shows the tension, so difficult to convey in words, between change and constancy, uniqueness and generality, through the particular in his poetry. The particular is so chosen as to suggest the totality concealed behind it. This totality is not only culture or a generally conceived reality, both of which could be said to form a model of the metaphysical order of the universe. For Milosz, the sacred sphere certainly exists, however difficult it is to approach, however hidden it may be, but material things are not its center. They inform us only vaguely about it. They are like phrases of a forgotten language known perhaps only to the "naive"—to children and simpletons. What do they really speak of—Heidegger's "being"? God?[10] Milosz avoids a straightforward answer or gives various answers out of the conviction that he stands before the mystery that no language of a particular philosophical system can express and for which every name is insufficient. More important for Milosz are the need itself and the direction in which one searches. Whereas the symbolists naively and self-confidently attempted to substitute poetry for religion, Milosz in his poems calls into question the nostalgia for the sacred that is inscribed in the evidence of culture.

MOMENTS OF PREREVELATION

Jan Błoński concludes his analysis of Milosz's poetic epiphanies thus:

> What then are these moments of revelation and manifestation? They are nothing other than what is accessible to everyone, moments of such intense sensual experience that they lead to a melding of the subject into the object. The object is that which is apparent to the senses, directly experienced. It is not the empyrean of ideas, a web of equivalents or a metaphysical structure that poetry (or art in general) allows us to reach. Poetry may be the secret, but it speaks of nothing that is mysterious; it revels in and feeds upon the world of daily experience.[11]

Despite the incisiveness and pertinence of these remarks, I fear that different things have been confused here.

First of all, Milosz speaks of at least three variations of his "feeling of the eternal" ("czucia wieczności"): the experience of a "unity in multiplicity" ("jedności w wielości"), the contemplation of the moment, and the revelations in which it seems mystery is unveiled before him.

The experiences of a "unity in multiplicity" and the contemplation of the moment concern primarily childhood and youth. Already the poem "Hymn" (1935) makes note of the sense of identification with existence:

> and we were alike:
> apples, scissors, darkness, and I
> under the same immobile
> Assyrian, Egyptian, and Roman
> moon.
>
> (CP 14)

> —a my byliśmy podobni:
> jabłka, nożyce, ciemność i ja—
> pod tym samym, nieruchomym,
> asyryjskim, egipskim i rzymskim
> księżycem.

Noteworthy is the comparison between man and things, the pointing out of their similarity as well as the halting of the passage of time through its projection into the synchrony of culture. In particular, culture constitutes here for the first time—and perhaps not completely consciously—one synonym for eternity.

A similar experience is evoked by "In Fever, 1939" and "Stanisław Ignacy Witkiewicz" (1947). In both examples Milosz takes care about the exact description of the time and place of the revelations. By contrast, in "With Trumpets and Zithers" time and space are suspended:

> Borne by an inscrutable power, one century gone, I heard, beating
>   in darkness, the heart of the dead and the living.
>
> (CP 198)
>
> Niepojęta moc mnie nosiła, jedno stulecie minęło, usłyszałem bijące
>   w ciemności serce umarłych i żywych.

The sensation extends beyond the limit of death; here subjectivity does not lose its otherness. At the same time, we see a growing distance between the poet and these revelations: after a youthful "we were alike," during the Occupation he poses the question "What's that?" and becomes someone else, to discover finally that the "power" is "inscrutable."

The intersection of the axis of time with the axis of eternity is present in another experience far more often described by Milosz: an "eternal moment" ("moment wieczny"). This experience takes on various meanings in his poetry. It can express the struggle with the destructive flow of time. In "Siena" (1937), for example, Italian culture seems to be a beautiful dream. Its fragility is emphasized by the tautology "here everything goes on but nothing passes off" ("wszystko tutaj trwa, choć nic nie mija"). It can be a synonym for a truth sought, as in "Treatise on Morals" ("Traktat moralny," 1947), or sometimes, as in "Mother's Grave" ("Grób matki," 1949), it has a moral meaning. The poet prays that he will be able to "strengthen in man" ("umocnić w człowieku") "the immovable point that to spite history divides what is fluid into good and evil" ("punkt nieruchomy, co dziejom na przekór / Na złe i dobre dzieli to co płynne"). In "Treatise on Poetry" ("Traktat poetycki," 1957) he proves that the absence of this point means that "the golden house, the word *is,* collapses / And the word *becomes* ascends to power" (*CP* 115; "Zapada się dom złoty, słowo JEST, / I STAJE SIĘ sprawuje odtąd władzę"). In these passages we can easily discern echoes of Milosz's wrestling with Hegelianism and Marxism. This complicated matter cannot be dismissed with a few generalizations. Perhaps someday a study will be written about Milosz's writing as a great debate with Hegel and Marx. I will confine myself to showing how he desires to beat the enemy at his own game.

"A Frivolous Conversation" (*CP* 135; "Rozmowa płocha," 1944) is an "instruction" concerning our experience of the eternal moment and to what it might lead. One of the interlocutors discovers in a fine-shell moment ("w pięknej muszli chwili") a pearl, a second ("perlę, sekundę"), and inside a second ("na dnie sekundy") a star ("gwiazdę"). Delving into the essence of things "when the wind of mutability ceases" ("kiedy wicher zmienności ustaje") allows one to see with delight:

> —The earth, the sky, and the sea, richly cargoed ships,
> Spring mornings full of dew and faraway princedoms.
>
> —Ziemię, niebo i morze, ładowne okręty
> Wiosny mokre od rosy i zamorskie kraje.

Thus, in order to be suspended, time and change must be transferred to spatial categories. But in Milosz's poetry space is composed of various and incongruous elements: images of natural elements, signs of human civilization, and finally nature. Movement seems potentially inherent in all and cannot be removed. Spring is a part of the cycle of seasons; "richly cargoed ships" and "faraway princedoms" naturally call to mind journeys and hence change, an attribute of time. The speaker is thus both immobile and tense with movement, whereas space is simultaneously wrenched from time and powerfully permeated with it.

Milosz recalls here Adam Mickiewicz's mystical poems, the Lausanne lyrics. This context can explain a great deal. In one of these poems, as Marian Maciejewski observes, "the preference for space as an expressive means of immortalizing a way of thinking appears in a spatial depiction of time."[12] He shows convincingly that Milosz turns to just this tradition in a few of his poems concerned with "the search for 'a homeland within himself,' perhaps an illusory homeland since it is rendered by means of elements preserved in memory."[13] In "The World" Maciejewski finds in turn the "simplicity," the "synthetic quality, totality of conception and 'finality,'" and above all the attitude of disinterested love toward all" that is characteristic of Mickiewicz's lyrics. These observations are also confirmed by the conclusion of "A Frivolous Conversation," which describes, it would seem, an experience of contemplation with a polemical echo of Mickiewicz:

> At marvels displayed in tranquil glory
> I look and do not desire for I am content.
> (CP 135)

The illumination, the existing beyond time and space, the disinterested attitude toward the world emphasized by the metaphoric use of "look," the feeling of becoming happy at last—all this is just as if taken from the vocabulary of mystic transports. Yet even an act of contemplation is called into question: the contemplative person does not lose himself in the Godhead, he does not abandon the testimony of his senses, and he takes a distant view of his moment of ecstasy. It is no surprise that the entire poem was given the ironic title "A Frivolous Conversation." In other poems Milosz no longer reduces the instant, for he knows it is impossible and accepts the paradoxical quality of its essence.

"Treatise on Poetry" brings such an admission:

> There are two dimensions. Here, the unattainable
> Truth of the essence, at the edge and border
> Of duration and nonduration. Two intersecting lines,
> Time elevated above time by time.
>
> Dwa są wymiary. Tu niedosięgalna
> Prawda istoty, tutaj, na krawędzi
> Trwania, nie-trwania. Dwie linie przecięte.
> Czas wyniesiony ponad czas przez czas.

Typically, the temporal aspect intertwines indissolubly with the essential. The depiction of the border between duration and nonduration is a declaration in favor of physical matter that is nevertheless penetrated by change. This declaration, however, cannot be expressed, since both aspects exist in every phenomenon simultaneously; separated and isolated, apart from one another, they lose their proper sense.[14] Thus, the allusion to T. S. Eliot's "Burnt Norton" is in the form of a travesty and gives the words a different meaning. What Milosz translates as "Time elevated above time and by time" is in the original "Only through time time is conquered."[15] The word "conquered" seems particularly important, since for Eliot, historical time can be "conquered, defeated" by the presence of the dimension of transcendence, the summoning up of the heavenly "rose garden."[16] Milosz, however, questions such a simple solution. He accepts the paradox that it is possible to attain the eternal moment via intuition only through its historical dimension.

Milosz's poetry speaks of yet another perception of eternity in the moment. In "The Song" (CP 8; "Pieśń," 1934) the protagonist waits for the moment when "slow movement ceases / and the real shows itself naked suddenly." "Slow River" (CP 20; "Powolna rzeka," 1936) contains a portent that "in the splendor of one moment / stand spring and the sky, the seas, the lands." Finally, in "From the Rising of the Sun" the admission is made:

> Because I wanted to earn a day of comprehension,
> Or even a single second, when those three
> Would also reveal themselves, each in his unique essence.
> (CP 292)

> Bo chciałem zapracować na dzień zrozumienia
> Czy choćby na sekundę, kiedy objawią się
> Również ci trzej w jedyności swojej.

Are these lines really about epiphany, stemming from sensual delight, intensity of feeling, and ecstasy in the particular? Surely not entirely, since the revelation comes involuntarily and carries certain conditions—for example, spiritual "rust" prevents its attainment— and a triple victory of "the false" must precede it.

As David H. Abrams has shown, the experience of a sudden manifestation, a spiritual revelation, has a long tradition in philosophy and literature.[17] The model description of this experience, the epiphany encountered by poets from romanticism to the twentieth century, is given by Saint Augustine in his *Confessions*. Augustine describes how the feeling of revelation is accompanied by an astounding clarity of the mind, which can contemplate the eternal dimension of the moment and through visible things perceive their invisible dimension. Epiphany, the source of which is God, is fleeting, short-lived, and impossible to hold onto. It foreshadows, after all, the apocalyptic vanishing of time into eternity.

Following Augustine, religious literature has through the centuries described the implosion of divine light into the darkness of consciousness. The romantics harked back to this tradition without, however, always pointing out the supernatural source of their illumination. Retaining the Augustinian term *momentum* (*der Augenblick, der Moment*), they described states of rending the veil of time and clarifying consciousness combined with feeling the spirit released from the burden of matter and transports of joy. This motif recurs in, among others, Schelling, Hölderlin, Goethe, and Blake. The true poet of the epiphany, according to Abrams, was Wordsworth. For him the flash of illumination occurs when a scene, either directly observed or recalled, loses its definite outlines and "another eye" peers into the life of the object. Sometimes an object or person evokes the revelation. As Abrams observes, Wordsworth goes to extremes and sees illuminations where in reality there are none.

The object, transparent and pointing beyond itself, is what the symbolists meant by symbol. The role of *momentum* as an independent phenomenon, separate from reality and existing exclusively in literature, may even become the compositional principle of the entire work, marking significant revelations and hastening plot development. This is the nature of Proust's "moments privilégiés," James's "acts of imagination," and Conrad's "moments of vision." In a word, by the twentieth century the eternal moment had become associated with the freshness of a direct, authentic experience and the discovery of a charismatic power in ordinary things. Such epiphanies explain or emphasize both the religious and secular contexts. T. S. Eliot in his *Four Quartets* describes moments of happiness and sudden illumination, presenting them, in accordance with Augustine, as the points of intersection of the axes of time and eternity. These moments dimly convey the mystery of the Incarnation; they depict the "fleeting passage" of the lost garden of paradise and presage its return at the end of time. James Joyce presents a different case. He translates theological terms into aesthetic ones; for him epiphany means the unexpected unveiling of another spiritual dimension in an object or person.

Augustinian inspirations are easy to find in Milosz's poems; that is not surprising, since the *Confessions* were among his favorite reading even before the war. Very likely the *Confessions* are the source of the motif of a sudden entrance of light, a blinding brightness, a radiance (*blask*) that frees one from human limitations and allows one to comprehend the moment. Though the religious origin of this revelation is not always certain, and often is only suggested, the illumination itself is placed interchangeably either in the past or in the future. The nature of this experience is ambiguous; its object is a kind of alchemical knowledge of the riddle of existence, as in "Song of a Citizen" (*CP* 58; "Pieśń obywatela," 1943). "Mittelbergheim" (1951, *CP* 107) speaks of some impassable threshold, "the moving frontier," which sometimes may be approached but is impossible to cross.

Like Wordsworth, Milosz sometimes achieves the flash of illumination in daily life. And like Wordsworth, Milosz as poet stands at the compositional center of the poem:

> I came upon it walking in the street and it seemed
> to me like a human destiny revealed.
> ("I Came upon It")

> Natrafiłem na to przechodząc ulicą i wydało mi się to jak wyjawione
> ludzkie przeznaczenie.
> ("Natrafiłem na to," 1971)

He is able to equate the dimness and intangibility of the content of this experience only with the helplessly repeated indefinite pronoun *it* and a vague simile.

In Milosz's poetry the encounter with the concrete resembles an epiphany but is qualitatively different from it. In that encounter an incomprehensible meaning is revealed to the poet. That experience, undoubtedly authentic, is granted only in the process leading up to the "moving frontier" and not in fulfillment; it remains "without a name" regardless of how it may have been defined through the ages. Perhaps objects, the feeling of unity in multiplicity, the contemplating of the moment, and the imperfect epiphany are all successive stages leading to the threshold of a perfect, eschatological epiphany. Yet Milosz treats all expressions of momentum equally since they indirectly reflect the drama of our civilization, which has forgotten its Christian source. They are for Milosz as much a content of his inner life as an expression of culture, testimonies of other people. That is why, freely employing various expressions of the eternal moment, Milosz does not identify with any of them completely.

At the same time, Milosz detaches himself from the priesthood of art and aesthetic metaphysics. The moments just before revelation are not for him, as they are for James Joyce, components in an aesthetic theory; they are a record of an existential experience. They are located somewhere between religion and art since they bear traces of their religious origin even though they have undergone a partial secularization as well. Milosz seems to be close to Eliot, although he emphasizes the vagueness or ambiguity of the message received and the inexpressibility of the experience. The concrete itself, however, permits him no insight into the unknown. The ecstasy of the particular does not bring an epiphany, just as the epiphany is not elicited by a concrete object.

TIME-SPACE

In *Visions from San Francisco Bay* Milosz declares: "My imagination is not like that of someone who lived when Thomas Aquinas's world view was reflected in Dante's symbols, though its fundamental need— to reduce everything to spatial relations—is the same" (*V* 30). This apparently clear statement contains a summary of both the drama of poetic imagination and the history of the religious imagination since the seventeenth century. At that time—something to which Milosz persistently returns in his essays written after 1960—the unity between the signifier and the signified, the symbol and its content, broke down and hierarchically ordered space collapsed. The moral and religious sense of the directions up and down and right and left lost its clarity. One might protest that the former vision was based on an anachronistic cosmology. But, as Milosz emphasizes, it allowed man to feel comfortable in the cosmos. It is difficult to build a home in a dark emptiness extending into infinity and filled with swirling galaxies. Yet one needs to rebuild a value-bearing space, keeping in mind its breakup and not descending beneath the level of contemporary knowledge about the universe. For example, a romantic affirmation of the subject as the basis for a coherent vision of the world is almost impossible, since the "I" perceives the earth as one of a multitude of fragments in space, and oneself upon it as one of a multitude of organisms subject to the law of change. Milosz adds: "What is worse, time, always strongly spatial, has increased its spatiality; it has stretched infinitely back out behind us, infinitely forward into the future toward which our faces are turned" (*V* 31). Perhaps, then, even at the cost of naiveté, we should attempt a re-creation of the universe according to the models inherited from Aquinas.

"The World" is just such an attempt. It also constitutes an ideal metric model to which earlier and later poetic solutions refer. The fundamental feature of the temporal-spatial vision outlined in the poem is that there exists a spontaneous and not predetermined correspondence between subjective and objective space, between physical and religious space. The way the narrator and the protagonists order visual reality in their imagination is in complete accord with the cosmology and philosophical-religious concepts implicit in the poem. As Jacek Łukasiewicz observes, Milosz conceives of space in two ways: "closed space (spherical, 'casket-like') and open space that is treated linearly."[18] Examples of the concept of closed spherical space are the poppy and the peony, and the homology of these concepts is best expressed in "A Parable of the Poppy" (CP 46; "Przypowieść o maku"), a mental projection of the cosmos on the principle of analogy.

In his poetry before "The World" Milosz placed his protagonists either in various expanses of space that were separate from each other or in one space located in several different axiological orders simultaneously. The absence of a point of reference means that any organization of space is possible and that none is credible, none is without some erosion, some relativity. It does not mean that subjective space plays the dominant role since it is corrected by the collective consciousness registered in the symbols of culture and in the reality we know through our senses.

"Birds" ("Ptaki," 1935) presents a particularly interesting example. Here the time-space relation changes at every turn. What is real transforms almost spontaneously into the fairy-tale, the dreamlike, the religious: "a dream's disciple" ("uczeń marzenia") "comes down on the northern lands" ("schodzi na północne kraje") to "search for live water" ("wody żywej szukać"). Of course the descent to earth—as the essay of that title ("Zejscie na ziemię," 1938) and the poem "Incarnation" ("Wcielenie") make clear—has symbolic meaning. It is connected with the motif of descent to the underworld and in particular with the recurring motif of the Fall. The religious and mythological significance of both these motifs surely does not require explanation. The protagonist of "Birds" finds himself in a garden, where he ties up a branch from a cherry tree and "slays nettles" ("morduje pokrzywy"). At the same time he is in "a chasm that does not offer tears / on broken fields, in an icy cistern" ("przepaści, która łeż nie daje, / na połamanych polach, w lodowej cysternie"). Even individual realistic elements ("white girls coming back from a bakery"; "Białe dziewczynki, które z piekarni powracały") are immediately put into a context rendering them unreal as they "hardly touched white clouds" ("ledwo tykały obłoków"). In addition, an allusion to *The Divine Comedy,*

> you, perhaps the last of the bearers of the verdict
> one of those who descend to the fiery den
>
> Ty, może już ostatni z nosicieli kary,
> z tych, którym wolno schodzić na dno gorejące

mixes by the end of the poem with a reference to biblical history, "Belshazzar's burned castles hiss" ("syczą spalone zamki króla Baltazara").

This is clearly the vocabulary of catastrophist imagery. But its grammar can hardly be defined. The rules of the spatial and temporal order barely emerge and just begin to operate before they are supplanted by other rules. Perhaps the up–down opposition seems to be the most constant. Although "up" may be additionally valued, it is not clearly depicted and is referred to more as something lost. "Down" is nothing less than a gigantic bomb crater that engulfs the entire world. It is no accident that images of the depths, abyss, ravine, and well are repeated. Dante's *Inferno* seems to have captured the imagination of the young poet.

A fragment of "Songs of Adrian Zieliński" indicates the extent to which the question of the ordering of space troubles Milosz. The protagonist complains:

> I want to bore a tunnel to the center of the earth
> So that I can see Hell.
> I want to pierce, for what it's worth,
> That blue lake of the sun's rays
> And have a look at Heaven.
>
> (CP 68–69)
>
> Chciałbym wydrążyć tunel aż do środka ziemi,
> Żeby zobaczyć Piekło.
> Chciałbym przebić jezioro słonecznych promieni,
> Żeby zobaczyć Niebo.

He laments in vain, for in the face of reality controlled by the law of brute force the opposition between good and evil loses its importance.

The crisis of morality and faith is, significantly, a crisis of the religious vision or conception of space. To recover this vision or conception, sacred space must be reconstructed.

Milosz's poetry from the war and Occupation yields a variety of temporal-spatial solutions. Up to 1943 Milosz utilizes typical devices and associates the real with the imagined or what is inspired by his own reading. In "Pastoral Song" ("Piosenka pasterska," 1942), for example, the space of arcadian myth prevails; in "A Book in the Ruins" (CP 28; "Książka z ruin," 1941) a hall in a destroyed library opens to reveal a world petrified on the pages of books; in "Flatland" ("Równina," 1941), the landscape of the Polish province Mazowsze dissolves into a vision of the earth defiled by wickedness and deprived of divine protection. Increasingly, temporal confrontations are expressed in the language of space. As "Waltz" and "Campo dei Fiori" (1943, CP 33) show, the historical imagination of the viewer becomes the center of order, since the temporal space of civilization, understood as the synchronic coexistence of generations and their deeds, acquires particular importance.

In "An Appeal" ("Wezwanie," 1954) a question is posed:

> And space, what is it like? Is it mechanical,
> Newtonian? A frozen prison?
> Or the lofty space of Einstein, the relation
> Between movement and movement?
> (CP 242–243)

> A przestrzeń jaka jest? Czy mechaniczna,
> Ta newtonowska, jak zamarzła turma
> Czy lotna przestrzeń Einsteina, relatio
> Ruchu i ruchu?

And the answer follows:

> No reason to pretend
> I know. I don't know, and if I did,
> Still my imagination is a thousand years old.
> (CP 243)

> Nie mam co udawać
> Że wiem, jeżeli nie wiem, albo wiem
> A wyobraźnię mam tysiącoletnią.

The double contradiction indicates that the most elementary concepts like space have so many meanings that they have ceased to signify anything at all. When translated into the language of competing, often mutually exclusive scientific theories, these meanings elude the imagination. Such theories are relative, for they are inevitably marked by their own historical era; but at the same time they endure. Human civilization develops because of them. The poet's imagination may freely draw on various concepts, compare them with one another, and accept or reject their anachronism. Moreover, by employing tropes poetic language may indirectly grasp those phenomena with which scientific symbols can only struggle.

This is almost Milosz's entire program. The outlines emerged in his prewar poetry, but the realization came only with his postwar work. Throughout the evolution of this spatial-temporal vision the hierarchical structure of the universe becomes exteriorized, transferred to the sphere of the imagination, which itself bears traces of an individual imagination that is historical, determined by place, time, and milieu, and of the collective imagination, which is composed of multiple symbols, myths, and images. For example, the opposition up–down or high–low can be translated into an opposition between what is on the surface and what is underneath, as in "Throughout Our Lands" ("Po ziemi naszej," *CP* 148).

It is in Milosz's postwar poetry that the horizontal configuration of the temporal-spatial dimension most often appears. It combines with the motif of traveling or wandering—not only in physical space but also in dream space, historical space, and religious space. These kinds of space are layered one on top of another. They are difficult to define because they constantly interpenetrate; they become opalescent with various meanings and arouse associations that are difficult to enumerate and classify. An increasing emotional indifference may be accounted for by geography and the course of history: childhood wandering with one's finger on a map is transformed into an imagined—possible but unfulfilled—journey into real space ("Elegy for N. N."). The impossibility of crossing the barrier between male and female is expressed by the images taken from Zeno of Elea ("Bobo's Metamorphosis"). "Album of Dreams" ("Album snów," 1959) freely associates spatial images from a psychoanalytic textbook with fairy tales for children.

Milosz's multidimensional time-space is built not only through the variety and richness of languages that serve to describe it but also through memory, both collective and individual. Wandering through memory is also a movement in different dimensions. This movement is the source of the astounding simultaneity of events and facts in Milosz's poetry:

> Till today my boat grates against the gravel
> And the reeds of the island on Lake Gaładuś rattle,
> I maneuver carefully, my right oar is cracked,
> For thirty years frightened terns circle overhead.
>
> ("How Is It Possible to Forget")

> Dotychczas moje czółno chrobocze o żwir
> I stuka trzcina wyspy na jeziorze Gaładuś,
> Manewruję ostrożnie, mam prawe wiosło pęknięte,
> Trzydzieści lat kołują spłoszone rybitwy.

Milosz frequently resorts to this device, but the dimension of memory may embrace a considerably broader horizon than an individual biography alone. In "How Is It Possible to Forget" Milosz retrieves from oblivion his own youthful summer vacations, and in "On the Road" (CP 205; "W drodze," 1967), he locates the protagonist in a dimension that is simultaneously real, dreamlike, and sacred.

"The miraculous," Milosz writes in his introduction to the essays of Stanisław Vincenz, "is the liberation of the imagination, which is always spatial." The imagination is a powerful antidote against anxiety, despair, the feeling of the absurd, those afflictions "whose true names are surely impiety and nihilism." He explains: "In the course of a day, the impious man travels many hundreds or even thousands of kilometers without observing anything that might move him. But just as for him space loses the value of the particular, so also time loses value . . . and his nihilism is the feeling of loss of a homeland, both heavenly and earthly."[19] To impiety and nihilism Milosz opposes his poetry. Precisely through the cult of the particular,[20] the miraculous, and the liberation of the imagination, Milosz seeks a return path to his spiritual homeland. In the sacral dimension, the homeland is paradise; in the historical dimension, it is Lithuania. In "From the Rising of the Sun" Milosz confesses:

> Even if I were gathering images of the earth from many countries on two continents, my imagination could cope with them only by assigning them to positions to the south, north, east, or west of the trees and hills of one district.
>
> (CP 268)

> Mimo że zbierałem obrazy ziemi w wielu krajach na dwóch kontynentach, moja wyobraźnia nie mogła z nimi sobie poradzić inaczej niż

wyznaczając im miejsce na południe, na północ, na wschód i na zachód
od drzew i pagorków jednego powiatu.

This is the hidden drama. The district Lauda no longer exists in its
ancient form; Hitler and Stalin have wiped it from the face of the map.
Its image is preserved only in the recollections of its former inhabitants. Milosz is one of them and, it should be added, one of the last.
Hence, since leaving his native region, his spatial-temporal imagination has always had two points of reference: the setting in which he
finds himself at a given time and the images of Wilno and Lithuania
that are evoked from the past.

A sign of this configuration already appears in "In My Country"
("W mojej ojczyźnie"), where "now" ("teraz") and "here" ("tu") are
supplanted by "formerly" ("dawniej") and "there" ("tam"). The
poem, as a whole devoted to the landscapes of childhood and youth, is
dated by Milosz "Warsaw, 1937." The contrast is all the more striking
since it is a Polish poet, in the capital of Poland, who writes "In my
land to which I will not return" ("W mojej ojczyźnie, do której nie
wrócę"). Milosz writes as if from the opposite shore of time, though
only a few hours' train ride separates him from Lithuania. This is all
the more true of his postwar poems, where his imagination wanders
homelessly, moving between what surrounds him in all its foreignness
and what is remembered and close to his heart.

Since this central point of reference constantly shifts and fades, it
ought to be fixed in the dimension of myth, where perhaps ultimately
the two homelands might be compared with one another. Milosz
makes that attempt in "From the Rising of the Sun." Speaking of his
native Lauda, he states:

> A certain eminent alchemist wrote of that country that it is to be found
> wherever it has been placed by the first and most important need of the
> human mind, the same need that called into being geometry and science,
> philosophy and religion, morality and art. The above-mentioned
> alchemist—he was an ally of Descartes—also wrote that the name of the
> country could be Saana or Armageddon, Patmos or Lethe, Arcadia or
> Parnassus.
>
> (CP 266)

It all sounds enigmatic and not completely comprehensible. Why
should a small Lithuanian district find itself in the company of mythi-
cal and religious conceptions of lands of happiness, suffering, and

death? How may such different conceptions be equated? And finally, to what need is Milosz referring?

An explanation is supplied by the source from which (in a somewhat parodied form) the quotation is taken. It is *Epître à Storge* by Oscar Milosz,[21] who writes:

> In truth, we do not bring either space or time into nature, but just the movement of our body and knowledge, or rather awareness and love of that movement, awareness and love which we call Thought and which is at the origin of our first and fundamental ability to situate all things, beginning with ourselves. Space and time seem to have been prepared long in advance to receive us. Yet all our anxieties come from our need to situate this very space and time.
>
> (*LU* 199)

I have deliberately quoted from *The Land of Ulro*. Milosz often repeats that the writings of his eminent relation accompany him constantly and that he owes much to Oscar Milosz. The poet stresses that in his concept of the three exclusivities of matter, time, and space united by ordinary movement, Oscar Milosz made a discovery that comes close to Einstein's theory of relativity. It is difficult to decide to what extent the metaphysical poems of Oscar Milosz inspire Czeslaw Milosz's poetry. We can assume that the author of "From the Rising of the Sun" tries to produce his own unique translation of the principles of the theory of relativity into poetic language. That would be a fair explanation of such features of time and space in his poems as discontinuity; a concealed dynamism; a diffusion of different dimensions of reality into one vanishing point; the immediacy of the entire relation of time, space, and the presented world; and finally, the intense need to locate oneself somewhere. Like Oscar Milosz, Czeslaw Milosz oversteps the bounds of physical time and space when he tries to locate Lauda:

> This space is different. Herald angels singing,
> And in the street the three kings bowing,
> And under an arcade lions kneeling
> To announce a miracle.
>
> (*CP* 266)

> Inna ta przestrzeń. Króle witają,
> Z ulic pasterze śpiewają,
> Lwy pod arkadą klękają,
> Cuda ogłaszają.

This is, then, the realm of both an earthly and a metaphysical reality, of religious rites and Nativity spectacle, of the concrete, and of bold fantasy. The spatial-temporal text, however, also comprises this vision. In this case we have a poetic stylization of a well-known Polish Christmas carol. Since the device of mythologizing the native region is set within a literary fiction, one should then treat it with a grain of salt. Unquestionably, the poet's word grants the device its validity but at the same time limits its importance because it becomes one element in literary creation. What for Oscar Milosz was a universal key to the mystery of existence for Czeslaw Milosz has value above all as a beautiful and inspiring vision that nevertheless betrays its limitations. But an important lesson stems from the writings of Oscar Milosz: the image of the world and man in both science and literature depends on how the imagination copes with the problem of the essence of human nature and how it then locates man in his surroundings.

2

Love Affair with Nature

Many years passed before Milosz decided to reveal his first and perhaps greatest love affair—a love affair that, as it turned out, largely shaped his outlook and poetic worldview. Milosz concealed its complex meaning in the cognitive adventures of Thomas in *The Issa Valley* (*Dolina Issy*, 1955) and only finally explained it in *Visions from San Francisco Bay* (*Widzenia nad zatoką San Francisco*, 1969) in the chapter entitled, significantly, "Remembrance of a Certain Love." The object of his adoration was not a woman, as would be expected, but nature, which fascinated him as a little boy with its limitless splendor of colors, forms, and shapes. As in every adventure of the heart, the enchantment with physical beauty and the need for idealization was accompanied by a strong, erotically tinged desire for possession. Milosz admits:

> But I was falling so totally in love, let us be properly suspicious, through an intermediary. What really fascinated me were the color illustrations in nature books and atlases, not the Juliet of nature, but her portrait rendered by draftsmen or photographers. I suffered no less sincerely for that, a suffering caused by the excess which could not be possessed; I was an unrequited romantic lover, until I found the way to dispel that invasion of desires, to make the desired object mine—by naming it. I made columns in thick notebooks and filled them with my pedantic categories—family, species, genus—until the names, the noun signifying the species and the adjective the genus, became one with what they signified, so that *Emberiza citrinella* did not live in thickets but in an ideal space outside of time.
>
> (*V* 19)

The end of the affair was a rude awakening:

> Suspicion, critical reflection—what had been a sheaf of colors, an undifferentiated vibration of light, instantly turns into a set of characteristics and falls under the sway of statistics. And so, even my real birds became illustrations from an anatomical atlas covered by an illusion of lovely

feathers, and the fragrance of flowers ceased to be extravagant gifts, becoming part of an impersonally calculated plan, examples of a universal law. My childhood, too, ended then. I threw my notebooks away, I demolished the paper castle where beauties had resided behind a lattice of words.

(*V* 18–19)

Perhaps the most striking feature of this confession is the motif of disillusionment, loss, expulsion from a childhood paradise. The passage to adulthood constitutes a drastic break with an intimate and pure, because unconscious, bond with nature that almost spontaneously identifies with the entire world. Consciousness destroys the illusion of self-identification and identification between an individual and all existence; it deprives the individual of cosmic coparticipation. The knowledge achieved in adulthood, in turn, challenges the testimony of the senses since in nature's beauty it discovers the trap of the law of preservation of species: fascinating in its uniqueness, the individual becomes part of a paradigm. In this way the basic split arises in Milosz's poetry between his strong attachment to the beauty of the visual world and his feeling unable to grasp it, between his enchantment with nature's colorful spectacle and his refusal to accept the brutality of the laws that govern it, between the changeability of phenomena, subject to time and space, and language that can comprehend these phenomena only at the cost of schematizing them. Thus initiation is—not for Milosz alone—a drama of knowing and naming that can be reduced to revealing the opposition between consciousness and existence and between language and object.

The demon who visits the poet scorns in particular his attachment to life and the feeling of the extraordinariness of *esse* and his desire for meaning, order, and harmony in the universe. The demon alternately suggests images of existence as senseless vegetation and the temptation to consider human fate as only the mathematical chance of impersonal processes. Milosz testifies in *The Land of Ulro:*

When my guardian angel (who resides in an internalized external space) is triumphant, the earth looks precious to me and I live in ecstasy; I am perfectly at ease because I am surrounded by a divine protection, my health is good, I feel within me the rush of a mighty rhythm, my dreams are of magically rich landscapes, and I forget about death, because whether it comes in a month or five years it will be done as it was decreed, not by the God of the philosophers but by the God of Abra-

ham, Isaac, and Jacob. When the devil triumphs, I am appalled when I look at trees in bloom as they blindly repeat every spring what has been willed by the law of natural selection; the sea evokes in me a battleground of monstrous, antediluvian crustaceans, I am oppressed by the randomness and absurdity of my individual existence, and I feel excluded from the world's rhythm, cast up from it, a piece of detritus, and then the terror; my life is over, I won't get another, only death now.
(*LU* 246)

The dialectic of these contradictory views marks Milosz's whole oeuvre, including his poetry. Through his poems Milosz directly and indirectly presents the drama of his childhood initiation, seeing in it the drama of our whole civilization. Thus he not only expresses in various ways the realization of the sudden disintegration of a coherent vision of the world followed by the feeling of disinheritance but also attempts to oppose these experiences and to understand better the origins, forms, and consequences of that disintegration.

TAMING THE OTHER

Milosz's prewar poetry, at first socially engaged and later tracing the landscape of the world's cosmic destruction, makes few references to childhood initiations. But already, though not entirely clear, the fundamental differentness of man from nature appears in outline. A fascination with even the ordinary forms of existence (the source of his carefully detailed descriptions in an effort to render the atmosphere, sounds, and tones of events) tinges the bitter thought of the changeableness and transitoriness of phenomena; the ecstasy evoked by nature's beauty is cut short by the awareness of the external world as completely impenetrable and foreign to man; the fact that nature endures unloved makes the realization of the accidental quality of human life all the more acute. These oppositions do not have here such dramatic expression as they do in Milosz's wartime and postwar poetry. Nature not only enchants but also threatens. It is, however, comprehended and tamed, even domesticated. It can be the countryside of Lithuania or the northern Poland well known to Milosz.

In Milosz's early poems nature successfully maintains its autonomy and impenetrability in even the most hallucinatory surroundings without permitting itself to be completely interiorized. But the image of nature may at times lose its sensual tangibility. That occurs especially when the description turns into a sign that refers beyond itself. When writing a line like "Large hawks fly over a pure land" ("Wielkie jastrzębie lecą nad krainą czystą"; "Letter of January 1, 1935"), Milosz reduces the image-creating power of expression to the minimum, for the connotations are more important than the literal meanings. Like a riddle or not entirely comprehensible omen, the line expresses the premonition of a holocaust. The phrase *pure land* entails an entire series of associations connected, we may assume, with both childhood and an imagined biblical paradise that is also the native landscape. Threat hangs over the most valued and cherished regions. It has, in addition, as much a historical character—fear of the coming war easily can be seen here—as a metaphysical one; as much a personal—it is a farewell to the years of childhood—as a supra-individual one. In "One More Poem on Country" ("Jeszcze wiersz o ojczyźnie," 1931) the native land is openly equated with the Garden of Eden, and a hawk becomes a symbol of a good God.

The tendency to identify nature with God has a long and distinguished tradition as well as a solid philosophical foundation in European literature. Limiting ourselves to only nineteenth-century poetry, which saw both the rise and fall of the modern concept of nature, we should remember that the basis for this conception, as Joseph Warren Beach shows,[1] is a peculiar synthesis of elements taken as much from contemporary science as from religion. In this synthesis poets attempted in various ways to harmonize knowledge about the constant, unchangeable, and universal laws with faith in Providence, who watches over the world. From it emerged an image of nature disposed toward man and at the same time itself a complete harmony, fulfilling its own goals. In a word, "providentialism" combines with teleology. Beach further observes that a dangerous contraband is smuggled in by such an image of nature, which in essence is antireligious. By maintaining the *possibility* of substituting scientific ideas for religious concepts (albeit scientific ideas simplified and adapted to literary needs), this image of nature paved the way for the invasion of positivistic thought. Positivism, denying any irrational elements of the cosmos, dug the grave for the poetry of nature.

How does Milosz's poetry appear against the background of that tradition? Skipping a bit ahead, I will say that its relation to nature is ambivalent, again ranging between contradictions. On the one hand, it remains faithful to his naturalist interests, and on the other hand, it asks whether poetry should completely shed all remnants of religious imagery. Here Milosz refers not to Christianity, but to Gnosticism, especially Manichaeanism, from which he derives the idea of the pain of all creation negating the existence of a benevolent God.

NATURA DEVORANS, NATURA DEVORATA

The Occupation years are critical, for during that time Milosz attempts to break with all forms of the animist tradition. In "Songs of Adrian Zieliński" the desire that

> If only the poorest of devils, Hell's bellhop,
> Showed his horns from under the primrose leaf,
> If only the angel in Heaven who chops wood
> By beating his little wings waved down from a cloud.
> (CP 69)

> Żeby choć najuboższy z diabłów, sługa sług,
> Pokazał rogi spod liścia pierwiosnka.
> Żeby choć anioł, który w niebie rąbie drwa,
> Bijąc małym skrzydełkiem na obłokach został!

is opposed by the knowledge that

> Without end or beginning, Nature breeds
> Nothing, except this: there is life, there is death.
> (CP 69)

> Bez początku ni końca pleni się przyroda.
> I nic prócz tego, że życie, że śmierć.

A reflection on the total indifference of nature to the projections of human desires and expectations opposes the understandable need to give nature a more accessible and familiar appearance by filling it with comically inept, and yet consolingly expressive, folk-religious imagination. Nature's infinity is oppressive, and man may really see in nature only the elementary law of life and death. Nature is not subject to evaluation according to our moral categories. Only a benevolent smile separates us "from the bloody but innocent horrors of nature" ("od okrucieństw natury, krwawych a niewinnych"; "The Journey," 1942). The paradox is perhaps best expressed by the helplessness of both ethics and language (which sets up a system of moral principles by the naming of values) in the face of phenomena that escape all understanding and judgment.

The Occupation, with all its brutality and directness, was a reminder that men suffer and die just like other creatures. There is apparently nothing revelatory in this truth, but Milosz's originality lies in his presentation of it. No Polish poet ever so radically equated the destruction of human beings, races, and nations with the death of fish, insects, crabs, and reptiles:

> A stone from the depths that has witnessed the seas drying up
> and a million white fish leaping in agony,
> I, poor man, see a multitude of white-bellied nations
> without freedom. I see the crab feeding on their flesh.
>   ("Song of a Citizen," *CP* 58)
>
> Kamień z dna, który widział wysychanie mórz
> I milion białych ryb skaczących w męczarni—
> Ja, biedny człowiek, widzę mrowie białych obnażonych ludów
> Bez wolności. Kraba widzę, który ich ciałem się karmi.

In "Songs of Adrian Zieliński" the dead "lie like cramped, black ants" ("leżą, jak czarne mrówki skurczone"); in "Reflections" ("Odbicia," 1942) "an ant trodden upon" ("mrówka zdeptana") is compared to a "razed city" ("miasto zburzone"), and a "dead field mouse" ("mysz polna martwa") to a "defeated tribe" ("plemię pobite").

Such comparisons challenged a literature then accustomed to a noble, martyrological tone. Polish war poetry either lamented the innocent victims or called for revenge, invoking hackneyed romantic stereotypes. Milosz does not seek justification for those who have perished, nor does he judge their moral attitudes; the corpses of the coward and the hero, the base and the virtuous, the collaborator and the resistance fighter, in no way differ. What is more, he denies to those who have died any human qualities and reduces them to the level of the lowest animal organisms. He does so not only to remind us that man constitutes an indissoluble part of nature and must submit to those laws that bind all creatures regardless of their level of development. Nor does Milosz simply want to demonstrate that wartime conditions, stripping the collective of the façade of culture, good manners, or legal safeguards—all that separates the human element from the animal and allows the collective to function normally—place it face to face with naked existence. Perhaps the essential point of this comparison is the discovery of the nihilistic implication contained in the ideology of fascism, which turned the laws of nature into regulations for social life. More precisely, in its political and social aims fascism utilized, among others, a vulgarized version of scientific theories, especially Darwinism. The universality and unpredictability of death, the struggle for existence determined by strength and the ability to survive, the interchangeability of individual specimens with a species, and the annihilation without trace of whole groups are all commonly accepted axioms in the biological sciences. But their application to human relations calls the entire humanist tradition into question.

Milosz referred indirectly to this problem in his *Witness of Poetry* (1983). In the course of his reflections on the situation of the contemporary poet, he notes that the discovery of the animal origins of man was no less a shock than the Copernican revolution because it called into question the individuality and uniqueness of human existence and indirectly invested death with new significance. Scientific discoveries, turned into commonly accepted truth, gradually penetrate the mass consciousness and imperceptibly alter concepts and moral attitudes. Milosz further speculates whether the introduction of the law of numbers into our thought about man created a positive climate for the birth of racial theories, becoming one of the indirect preconditions for genocide.

When faced with such experiences, both the value system based on liberal models and the literary language that transmits those values turn out to be powerless. The accusation that the Nazis violated fundamental ethical principles is hollow so long as it employs notions completely foreign or indifferent to nazism. Of course, those principles, even so drastically violated, do not lose their importance and reality. There is no way, after all, to defend them with the trappings of moralistic rhetoric, with a feeling of wounded personal dignity on the part of the innocent observer. This world can be described only from inside by accepting, but not agreeing to, its brutal laws. An inhuman reality demands a nonhuman descriptive language.

Only with the perspective of time do the originality and novelty of Milosz's reflection and artistic invention in the context of both Polish and Anglo-American literature become visible. Writing on the twentieth century, Robert Langbaum observes that it most readily immerses itself in exotic landscapes and focuses on primitive forms of life that arise as if from the loam of matter.[2] In the poetry of Marianne Moore,

D. H. Lawrence, Ted Hughes, and Theodore Roethke descriptions of rats, snakes, and fish serve as an exploration of a sphere that is difficult to grasp, where the unconscious world becomes transformed into the conscious world. According to Langbaum, one reason for the decline of traditional nature poetry was, in addition to Darwin's discovery, the introduction of the notion of the unconscious, which shifted human intelligence to a borderline between animate and inanimate life. The revelation of the biological roots of thought processes, of an entire field of impulses uncontrolled by consciousness, not only removed man from his privileged place in nature but also unexpectedly made him a relative of creatures on the lowest rung of the evolutionary ladder.

Milosz is concerned with the unique limitation of human nature, and he returns to this idea on numerous occasions. When he explores it for the first time, it is in a manner entirely different from that of the above-mentioned poets. Their fascination with the world of reptiles and amphibians assumes the unquestioned superiority of man, who looks on fauna with mixed feelings of amazement and fear, curiosity and revulsion, all the while secure in his sense of separateness. In none of the poems cited by Langbaum are human beings equated with animals. Nature ceases to be an idyllic picture; its hidden brutality is exposed, to be sure, but it is seen as if through clear glass. Milosz breaks that glass. Denying superiority to his human heroes, he endows them with the realization that the invaders annihilate nations with an indifferent dullness like that with which a crab eats a fish. The vanquished are only food for the victors; they are denied a human face and are reduced to only the reflexes of suffering. Degradation overwhelms both sides.

In Anglo-American poetry the shift of interest from landscape to animals was dictated by the attraction of psychoanalysis. In Milosz's poetry, however, psychoanalytic theory had rather faint reverberations. Milosz himself realizes just how fragile the barrier between the human and animal worlds is through his own participation in the horror of twentieth-century history.

The problem outlined here undergoes its greatest condensation in the poem "A Poor Christian Looks at the Ghetto" (*CP* 64; "Biedny chrześcijanin patrzy na getto," 1943). Describing the Jewish uprising against the Nazis in 1943, Milosz shows the process of the complete annihilation of the world. The poem is striking in the detail and almost scientific objectivity of its description. Images such as "bees build around" ("pszczoły obudowują"), "ants build around" ("mrówki obudowują"), "red liver" ("czerwona wątroba"), "honeycomb of lungs" ("plaster płuc"), "red trace" ("czerwony ślad"), "black bone" ("czarna kość"), "white bone" ("biała kość"), and "the place left by my body" ("miejsce po moim ciele") mingle with images of material destruction whose dimensions can be expressed only in an enumeration:

> It has begun: the breaking of glass, wood, copper, nickel, silver, foam
> Of gypsum, iron sheets, violin strings, trumpets, leaves, balls, crystals.
>
> (CP 64)
>
> Rozpoczyna się tłuczenie szkła, drzewa, miedzi, niklu, srebra, pian
> Gipsowych, blach, strun, trąbek, liści, kul, kryształów.

The destructive force of nature reveals itself in what is most brutal and degrading—in the insects greedily consuming the human body. But man ceases to exist not only as a biological organism: broken down into individual organs, he turns into shapeless meat. Decomposition of the material body is accompanied by the destruction of particular objects (violin strings, trumpets, leaves, balls) as well as the stuff from which they are made (glass, wood, copper, nickel, silver). In the flames of the ghetto all matter is destroyed and dispersed; the Apocalypse is fulfilled. And yet here the images of physical decay are not proof of the vanity of human life in the face of the gates of eternity, as they are in medieval or baroque literature. Nor does personal innocence exonerate anyone. Judgment is given to a "guardian mole" ("strażnik kret"), who has "swollen eyelids, like a Patriarch" ("powieka obrzmiała jak u patriarchy"), and it falls without equivocation:

> What will I tell him, I a Jew of the New Testament,
> Waiting two thousand years for the second coming of Jesus?
> My broken body will deliver me to his sight
> And he will count me among the helpers of death:
> The uncircumcised.
>
> (CP 65)
>
> Cóż powiem mu, ja Żyd Nowego Testamentu,
> Czekający od dwóch tysięcy lat na powrót Jezusa?
> Moje rozbite ciało wyda mnie jego spojrzeniu
> I policzy mnie między pomocników śmierci:
> Nieobrzezanych.

The extermination of the Jews indicts every Christian, regardless of whether he was actually involved in the crime or was only its passive witness. No one is without blame; everyone is both victim and executioner. Indeed, whether by a gesture of affirmation or negation all Europeans confirm their ties to Mediterranean culture, the basis of which is a system of moral values, concepts, and customs of the Judeo-Christian religion. The discarding of that heritage would reduce humanity to a swarm of savage insects.

Only this context makes apparent the extent of idealization and sublimation that the surrounding reality undergoes in "The World," written in the same year as "A Poor Christian Looks at the Ghetto" and the cycle it belongs to, "Voices of Poor People" ("Głosy biednych ludzi," 1943). In a *de profundis* of the greatest torment, shame, and despair, Milosz's imagination turns toward the land of his childhood years, where home guaranteed safety, the imponderables were sacred, and nature, robed in all its gleaming colors, was a blessing to man.

GARDEN OF EDEN OR TORTURE CHAMBER?

In "Treatise on Poetry" ("Traktat poetycki," 1957) the next scene in the childhood drama of initiation opens with a deliberate dissonance:

> The garden of nature opens.
> The grass on the threshold greens.
> The almond tree is blooming.
>
> Ogród natury otwiera się.
> Trawa na progu zielenieje.
> Migdałowe drzewo zakwita.

So answers the dull silence of nature. Only human fantasy, affected by the crushing indifference of nature, once populated it with human creations. Nature, meanwhile, is not a garden but a torture chamber, where

> With a brown drop at its mouth
> A grasshopper impaled on a thorn is sweating
> Unaware either of torture or law.
>
> Brunatną kroplą poci się u pyska
> Na gwóźdź tarniny wbity konik polny,
> Ani tortury świadomy, ni prawa.

Man, that "Socrates of snails" ("Sokrates ślimaków"), that "principal phantom" ("upior naczelny"), that "musician of pears" ("muzykant gruszek"),³ can do nothing in the face of an eternity filled with pain. Philosophy, art, and law are his only paltry defense. He ought, then, the poet advises, to overcome his pride and pay tribute to the overwhelming power of nature, to walk "behind a coffin of foresters / Whom a mountain devil, an ibex, threw down" ("za trumną leśniczych / Których obalił górski diabeł, kozioł") or look at the "cemetery of harpooners" ("cmentarz harpunników") to be reminded of his own physical weakness. Though enigmatic and unattainable, nature does not lose its magnetic power. Observing a beaver, the speaker in the poem says:

> I am not, I won't be nonmaterial.
> Such an unfleshy glance is not for me.
>
> Niematerialny nie jestem, nie będę.
> Tak niecielesne nie dla mnie spojrzenie.

One year later Witold Gombrowicz wrote in his *Diary* (*Dziennik*): "How to act in the face of nature? I walk along a path overgrown with pampas grass and feel that I am an alien in all this nature, I in my human skin am foreign. Disturbingly other; a different creation." And further, "Man is unnatural, antinatural."⁴

Gombrowicz seeks contact with nature by means of his fascination with inferiority. Yet he admits: "And yet a glacial boredom, almost a torpor seizes me when I want to compare my existence with these creatures and I attempt to grant them the full right to exist."⁵ Gombrowicz protects himself with his superiority; his humanity, his "church," is "interhuman" and does not include animals. Milosz, however, demolishes the seemingly impassable wall and reverses the antinomy: the gaze of the animal literally annihilates man since it makes him realize that human superiority is superficial and relative; it is a superiority for and among people, confirmed by the entire development of civilization. Beyond the radius examined and assimilated by culture there extends a dark and totally inaccessible sphere confronting its language, and its categories, including time, are helpless. The problem, says the speaker in the poem, is not only how the beaver sees him but also in what system of signs that seeing can be expressed. As always when confronted with the inexpressible, language has recourse to contradiction and paradox; it borders on gibberish.

How can this observation be reconciled with the elementary knowledge that man belongs to the genus of subhuman apes? The speaker observes:

> My common smell, my animal smell
> Shimmers rainbowlike, hums, will scare the beaver.
>
> Mój odór wspólny, mój odór zwierzęcy,
> Mieni się tęczą, huczy, bobra spłoszy.

Paradoxically, what would seem to be common also divides us; the animal side of human nature prevents us from entering the world of animals, from breaking the magic circle of differentness, because in the animal world ruled by its own laws people are either a neutral fragment of the landscape or a potential threat or prey. The speaker then relies on his imagination, which enables him to follow the underwater travels of the beaver:

> How the four-fingered paws work there,
> How the hair shakes itself free in a wet tunnel.
>
> Jak tam pracują czwórpalczaste łapy,
> Jak się otrząsa włos w mokrym tunelu.

And a new paradox arises:

> It does not know time and does not know death.
> It is subordinate to me, for I know I will die.
>
> On nie zna czasu i nie wie o śmierci.
> Mnie jest poddany, bo ja wiem że umrę.

Man is guaranteed dominance by the very knowledge that brings him acute pain: that all reality is transitory and that death is inevitable.

There is a point, however, on which Gombrowicz and Milosz do agree. I have in mind their exceptional sensitivity to the pain of all creatures. Gombrowicz states that "pain is pain, wherever it occurs, equally terrifying in man or in a fly; an experience has taken shape in us of pure suffering, our hell has become universal."[6] Milosz would certainly agree with that opinion. But, interestingly, he pushes the line of thought further, drawing crucial conclusions from it. Since the grass-hopper suffers "unaware either of torture or law," perhaps the feeling of pain is limited to more highly developed organisms and is really only imputed to nature as a result of our own experience. In *Visions from San Francisco Bay* Milosz writes:

> However, I do suspect that in humanizing pain—i.e., applying man's pain to everything alive—an error is committed: different from the earlier belief that animals were just living machines, but not a much better error nevertheless. Perhaps those creatures without consciousness bear no suffering in our sense of the word, and besides, there is very little chance that we will ever succeed in reproducing the sensations of nervous systems less developed than ours: a wasp cut in two with a knife, or rather, the part of it separated from the thorax, will continue to sip honey; a beetle who has just lost a leg will continue scurrying down a path with undiminished energy.
>
> (V 24)

Then he adds: "My would-be compassion conceals my fear for myself: for I know that at any moment I can be exposed to an ordeal like that of a moth burning in a candle flame, and not only that, I know with certainty that a more or less excruciating death agony awaits me." In conclusion, he states: "One way or the other, I bear the stamp of civilization, and if I guard against using standards which are too human, the alien Other besieges me all the more and I can derive no law for myself from its laws" (V 25). In poetry, however, contrary to the consolation of rational reasoning, Milosz remains on the side of the suffering creatures. The image of their undeserved pain returns in "Three Talks on Civilization" ("Trzy rozmowy o cywilizacji," 1963) and "From the Rising of the Sun."

I think that the poet Milosz, captivated by nature's beauty and constantly celebrating its charms, trembles before it more than does the novelist and playwright Gombrowicz. Milosz is not assured of protection either by his works, which spring more from endless struggles with the world than from attempts to reinterpret it in a concept taken a priori from a system of ideas, or even less by his own ego, subverted by memory of the finiteness of the human being.

In stressing the parallel between Gombrowicz and Milosz I am developing the observations of Konstanty A. Jeleński, who first wisely pointed out the fundamental similarities and differences in the atti-

tudes of the two writers. He connected them with the "two philosophical currents, one ancient (yet very up to date) and the other new:
gnosticism and ahumanism." Jeleński says that ahumanism stems from
the conviction that "man is neither the 'king of creation' nor the center
of the universe, and so every variety of 'humanism' is impossible today." Hence his conclusion: "Milosz, a writer-humanist, is the greatest
contemporary poet of ahumanism (which is not to be confused with
antihumanism)."[7] This formulation of Milosz's position seems a bit
extreme. In carefully sounding the thin wall that divides the human
from the nonhuman, Milosz never questions man's right to a central
place in the universe. Of course he shows the disintegration of the
anthropocentric vision of reality, but he does so to draw attention to
the unchanged significance of that vision. In his derision of human
claims it is not difficult to hear, in addition to a sense of loss, a tone of
hope and faith that one day "the king of creation"—in some transformed vision of the world—will be returned to his proper place.
Instead of calling Milosz a poet of ahumanism, it would be preferable
to present him as one who explores the terrain between humanism,
ahumanism, and antihumanism.

I should add that unjustified suffering creates a basic dilemma that
is as much moral as religious. The presence of pain in nature inclined
the Gnostics of the past to abandon the idea of a good God and to put
an evil demiurge in his place. According to Milosz, that problem is still
present:

> Yet never was the position of those who defend the idea of a hidden
> harmony more difficult, never was Manichaean ferocity more aggressive
> than when the nineteenth century observed that the suffering of living
> matter is the mainspring of its Movement and that the individual crea-
> ture is sacrificed in the name of a splendid and enormous transforma-
> tion without purpose or goal.
>
> (V 23–24)

The same idea, in a more compact form, appears in the "Treatise on
Poetry."

How, then, can man defend himself? One cannot give in to naive
illusions or simply accept the senselessness of one's own existence.
Perhaps, Milosz suggests, without giving up the cruel knowledge that
quickly dispatches comfortable delusions, one might seek refuge in
what is most deeply rooted and authentic—the living and wise child-

hood vision—and seek the known in the unknown, ordering the world as formerly, by naming it. Milosz's hero observes that a big owl seen in an American forest is "my acquaintance / unchanged by time or space, / the same *Bubo* I found in a book by Linnaeus" ("mój znajomy, / Nieodmieniony przez epokę, przestrzeń, / *Bubo* ten sam z dzieła Linneusza"). Biological erudition and a knowledge from boyhood of Latin terms expanded to include new species of animals and plants come to the aid of ordinary observation. Metaphorically presenting his vision of the American continent, Milosz uses the English names for rodents, birds, and snakes. One passage opens, "America has for me the fur of a raccoon" ("Ameryka ma dla mnie sierść racoona"). Milosz suggests that, tamed in this way, nature promises to be a safe refuge, and he adds that historical knowledge, literature, or cultural tradition will then be superfluous:

> The river Delaware does not say anything
> Of King Zygmunt August's court.
> We do not need "The Dismissal of the Greek Envoys."
>
> O dworze króla Zygmunta Augusta
> Nic nam nie mówi rzeka Delaware.
> "Odprawy posłów greckich" nie potrzeba.

This illusion soon evaporates. Our image of nature inevitably shapes both painting and literary works; practically every detail immediately becomes overgrown with various associations. That is why a "rose, sexual symbol / or symbol of superterrestrial beauty and love" ("róża, symbol seksualny, / Albo miłości, piękności nadziemskiej") inspires the imagination to embark on a fantastic journey to the center of the flower. Likewise, writing an ode to October, Milosz is unable to free himself from different recollections. His description of the seasons involves scenes from the American revolutionary war, and the figure of Tadeusz Kościuszko emerges fighting at West Point, along with a hazy vision of a camp of Polish insurgents probably from the January Uprising of 1863. The conclusion to be drawn is that man cannot extricate himself from the unchanged circle of tradition; but precisely that tradition preserves him from returning to the state of primitive savagery. Our home in nature is made from another material than nature itself; it stands on fragile foundations, but we simply do not have any other home.

EPISTEMOLOGICAL VARIATIONS

In the poetry of Czeslaw Milosz the "Treatise on Poetry" opens two important avenues of reflection, one concerning the process of knowing and the other concerning the relation of the sign to the object. As before, however, the poems do not illustrate intellectual arguments but present a repeated situation or an ordinary event, the deeper sense of which is revealed only through our reading them with increasing discernment, our placing them in various contexts.

In Milosz's poetic world birds occupy a privileged place. It is not surprising, then, that poetic epistemological variations begin with "Magpiety," ("Sroczość," 1958), a poem transparent on its surface but so dense in meaning that its interpretation here must be limited to the simplest commentary. The protagonist recalls:

> The same and not quite the same, I walked through oak forests
> Amazed that my Muse, Mnemosyne,
> Has in no way diminished my amazement.
>
> (CP 120)

> Ten sam i nie ten sam szedłem przez las dębowy
> Dziwiąc się, że muza moja, Mnemozyne,
> Nic nie ujęła mojemu zdziwieniu.

The thoughts of both individual and collective memory accompany the conscious sense of one's own nonidentity, the source of which, it may be guessed, is the variety of perceptions of oneself at different times of life. Memory, momentarily abrogated, does not inhibit the attitude of spontaneous amazement at the world; and this amazement, as is well known, was recognized by Plato as the beginning of philosophy. It could also be said that this amazement is contradicted since knowledge of another source of philosophy, despair, is passed over in silence. In any case, emotion, anchored in observation, requires intellectual verification:

> A magpie was screeching and I said: Magpiety?
> What is magpiety? I shall never achieve
> A magpie heart, a hairy nostril over the beak, a flight
> That always renews just when coming down,
> And so I shall never comprehend magpiety.
> If however magpiety does not exist
> My nature does not exist either.
> Who would have guessed that, centuries later,
> I would invent the question of universals?
>
> (CP 120)

Skrzeczała sroka i mówiłem: sroczość,
Czymże jest sroczość? Do sroczego serca,
Do włochatego nozdrza nad dziobem i lotu
Który odnawia się kiedy obniża
Nigdy nie sięgnę a więc jej nie poznam.
Jeżeli jednak sroczość nie istnieje
To nie istnieje i moja natura.
Kto by pomyślał, że tak, po stuleciach,
Wynajdę spór o uniwersalia.

At the heart of the medieval debate about universals was the question of whether general concepts, concepts of qualities and relations, match real objects. Grossly simplified, this centuries-old debate divided philosophers into adherents of either conceptual realists, who granted autonomous existence to ideas, or nominalists, who maintained that the contents of abstract knowledge have their counterparts only in individual objects. It is hard to say which side the poet is on, given the deliberate semantic imprecision of his words. With a distinguished Polish philosopher, Tadeusz Kotarbiński, one might ask if by magpiety Milosz means "the content of a general name," "a general term understood as a sound (or as a graphic sign) connected with meaning an immanent image, always linked associatively with a general name," or "an intentional object denoted by a general name."[8]

On the basis of one example I wish to show the complexity and abstruseness concealed beneath simple formulations in Milosz's poetry. It would be pointless to call him to account with the precision of a philosophical argument; after all, Milosz is writing not philosophical treatises but literary works. He is not illustrating previously accepted theses but directing the course of his readers' associations, which can certainly go far beyond those associations referred to here. Even my analysis passes over a matter important in questions of philosophical statements, namely, to which assumption Milosz is addressing his "I said."

In brief, "Magpiety" is—after "The World"—an interesting example of how poetic language may express philosophical problems without losing its autonomy and uniqueness. The word *achieve* surely does not belong to the vocabulary arguing for universals, yet how accurately it conveys the meaning intended by the poet. It expresses more the aspiration, the effort to grasp the object, than an operation carried out. Moreover, in line with Milosz's sensualist outlook, it emphasizes the implicit limitations of sight and touch since ordinarily the word is applied to those senses. The careful choice of extraordinarily concrete terms, almost palpable and at the same time able to bear the framework of intellectual digressions, the vividness of detailed description ("hairy nostril"), and the philosophical allusion contained in the terms *magpiety* and *question of universals* promote the intensification and expansion of meaning that the poem may carry. That is why the conclusion ("If however magpiety does not exist / My nature does not exist either") can be understood in two ways—epistemologically and ethically. If I question the existence of universal concepts, I will not be able to describe myself as well as differentiate myself from others. In other words, my humanity blends into the surroundings. But a moral postulate also emerges here, as Jacek Trznadel has written. The humanist outlook demands recognition—contrary to the temptations of historical relativism—that "something like human nature exists, given to us in culture and phenomenological intuition. That human nature despite historical change continues to signify regard for man and respect for his nontransferrable laws, not yielding to pliable and sophistic lies."[9]

Milosz does not take a clear position in the debate on universals. He sharpens the perplexities inherent in it but leaves its resolution open. His attitude toward that debate is marked by distance and humor. No doubt Milosz is closer to the realist option, but that does not mean that he denigrates the counterarguments. In this connection, it is significant that toward the end of the poem he writes, "I would invent," not "I would remind" or "I would repeat." For him, real meaning is above all based in personal experience, interiorized and not extracted from a theory. Mnemosyne is the hidden patron of Milosz's cognitive efforts; she reminds him of the nature of the medieval debate and the conceptual framework that it employed. In other words, without this philosophical knowledge held in reserve, Milosz would not be able to penetrate the deeper meaning of his own experiences, and the reader tracing his footsteps would not grasp the poet's hidden intent.[10]

The problem of the role of language in the cognitive process is examined already in "Ode to a Bird" (*CP* 124; "Oda do ptaka," 1948). Here from another angle Milosz approaches the borderline dividing the human world from the animal without overlooking the mysterious links that unite man with nature. The conclusion implied in this poem can be summarized as follows: the phenomena of nature I encounter daily, especially birds, says the author of the ode, continually amaze me. But how can this amazement be communicated? The most simple description runs into extraordinary difficulties. The bird claws alone carry varied associations. Their metaphoric approximation may refer most simply to the names of human extremities ("feathery palms"; "dłonie pierzaste"); it may call to mind the reptilian origin of birds ("gray lizard legs"; "skoki z szarego jaszczura"); it may even indicate the technological application of the operations performed by the body ("cybernetic gloves"; "cybernetyczne rękawice").

But do not these attempts grasp the different attributes of the phenomenon rather than its essence? Their vague intuition may at best be expressed in negative terms: the bird is "unconscious" ("nieświadomy"), "incommensurate" ("niewspólmierny"), "beyond will, without will" ("poza wolą, bez woli"). All these categories are means of understanding and judging reality and ourselves, whereas nature remains an area absolutely void of signification, indifferent to our attitude toward it and effectively resisting all our attempts to humanize it. It is difficult to forget that the link between the word and the object is completely arbitrary. There are so many words for *bird* in different languages. Even an investigation of its origins is of little help: neither the Old Church Slavonic *pta,* nor the Greek *pteron,* nor the Gothic *fvgls,* nor the English *brd* can define the winged creature unequivocally. This plethora of words for one phenomenon is visible proof of the inadequacy of language when confronted with something beyond language. The bird soars "beyond name, without name" ("poza nazwą, bez nazwy"), illustrating "what divides me from things I name every day" ("co mnie dzieli / Od rzeczy, którym co dzień nadaję imiona"). But in meditating on the process of giving meaning, the poet may realize the otherness of his "I" from the surrounding world and perceive the gap between the sign and the object. Even though an invisible veil divides him from other phenomena, he cannot cease renewing his efforts to name. Acceptance of the defeat of speech would be tantamount to silence and being lost in ignorance. The lines "my vertical figure / Though it extends itself upward to the zenith" ("moja postać pionowa / Choć przedłuża siebie do zenitu") are less an amusing claim than an essential condition of his humanity. Nor can we make light of the basic difference between the living world and the dead world, between fauna and flora. Our relation to a bird is different from that to a tree. Milosz says:

> But your half-opened beak is with me always.
> Its inside is so fleshy and amorous
> That a shiver makes my hair stand up
> In kinship with your ecstasy.
>
> (*CP* 125)

> Ale dziób twój półotwarty zawsze ze mną.
> Jego wnętrze tak cielesne i miłosne,
> Że na karku włos mi jeży drżenie
> Pokrewieństwa i twojej ekstazy.

Through our corporeality we are a part of nature and hear nature's commands, the most important of which is to procreate. In amorous ritual the human and animal worlds are united.

BEYOND THE "CHILDISH EARTH OF ILLUSION"

After the "Treatise on Poetry" Milosz opposes the adapted, somewhat domesticated image of nature in America to another image of nature that is oppressive in its inhuman otherness. Of course his move from the East Coast to the West Coast in 1961 strongly influenced this change. However, this fact does not call into question the inner dynamic of his poetry, the tendency to use contradictions and think in terms of oppositions. Of the many California landscapes that appear in his poems, an interesting example is included in *The Separate Notebooks*, a vision of California through the eyes of an exile:

> I did not choose California. It was given to me.
> What can the wet north say to this scorched emptiness?
> Grayish clay, dried-up creek beds,
> Hills the color of straw, and the rocks assembled
> Like Jurassic reptiles: for me this is
> The spirit of the place.
> And the fog from the ocean creeping over it all,
> Incubating the green in the arroyos
> And the prickly oak and the thistles.
>
> (*CP* 349–350)

> Nie wybierałem Kalifornii. Była mi dana.
> Skąd miezkańcowi północy do sprażonej pustki?

Szara glina, suche łożyska potoków,
Pagórki koloru słomy i gromady skał
Jak jurajskich jaszczurów: tym jest dla mnie
Dusza tych okolic.
I mgła wpełzająca na to z oceanu,
Która zalęga zieleń w kotlinach,
I dąb kolczasty, i osty.

This description is concise, clear, and condensed. It is built as much on personal observation as on previous knowledge; it contains both the ordinary "hills the color of straw" and the scientific "Jurassic reptiles." Arranged without clear indication of point of view, the geological material and the desolation and contour of the land are in essence a concretization of the metaphor *parched wasteland*. Moreover, just as metonymy clarifies metaphor, material elements become equivalents of the rather anachronistic "spirit of the place." This spirit does not appear accidentally and is not the essence of the landscape alone. Later the significant opposition appears:

Where is it written that we deserve the earth for a bride,
That we plunge in her deep, clear waters
And swim, carried by generous currents?

(CP 350)

Gdzie powiedziane, że należy się nam ziemia-oblubienica,
Abyśmy zanurzyli się w jej rzekach głębokich i czystych,
I płynęli, żyznymi prądami niesieni?

Not only does the romantic exile take refuge from his alien surroundings in the memory of his native land; "the Earth for a bride" also circuitously evokes the image of the biblical paradise. The dryness, emptiness, and deadness of the California landscape take on additional meaning, becoming signs of an earthly hell, perhaps the Land of Ulro.

The fullest overview of the problems, images, and motifs in Milosz's nature poetry is "Diary of a Naturalist" ("Pamiętnik naturalisty"), one part of the long poem "From the Rising of the Sun" (CP 255). Once again Milosz returns to his boyhood love affair with nature, unveiling its consequences to an even greater degree than in *Visions from San Francisco Bay*. "Diary" contains a series of autobiographical elements, such as the name of a high-school teacher, Stefan Bagiński, who taught Milosz biology and botany, and the titles of Milosz's youthful naturalist readings. But the hero of the poem should not be identified simply with Milosz; there is a distance between them. The story is about the disillusionment experienced by the hero in his encounter with nature, as a result of which the naturalist, despite his real interest in the biological sciences, did not decide to become a professional biologist.

The beginning of "Diary" suggests that nature is like a safe home; there the "oak our father" ("dąb nasz ojciec") and "sister birch" ("siostra brzoza") lead us "to meet / The living water" ("szliśmy na spotkanie / Wody żywej"). But the vision of childish paradise is contradicted by the reflection that animals, without souls, are doomed to eternal oblivion. Moreover, because of man's civilizing activities, nature has undergone a humiliating degradation, losing its noble majesty. A bear in a national park begs from the tourists; a cougar appears only to confirm the accuracy of statistical estimates of its numbers. The farewell to the fairy-tale dignity of nature is therefore final, all the more so since the recollection of the moment when the hero's "childish dream was denied" ("dziecinne marzenie zostało zaprzeczone") remains in his memory like a thorn. Such dreams spun at a school desk, allowing the hero to escape boring lessons and enter the world of nature, are opposed by the subsequent knowledge that aside from the illusions fostered by Eros, there is only "nakedness, nothing more, a cloudless picture of Motion" ("nagość, nic więcej, bezobłoczny wizerunek Ruchu"). Hence the question for which all of Milosz's poetry seeks an answer:

> " . . . Should we then trust
> The alchemy of blood, marry forever the childish earth of illusion?
> Or bear a naked light without color, without speech,
> That demands nothing from us and calls us nowhere?"
>
> (CP 257)

> " . . . Więc krwi alchemiom zawierzyć,
> Dziecinną ziemię ułudy poślubiać na zawsze?
> Czy znosić gołe światło bez barw i bez mowy
> Które niczego nie chce, do nikąd nie wzywa?"

The "childish earth of illusion" has a broad sense, implied in those artistic, philosophical, and religious conceptions that, presuming the presence of God and a metaphysical order in existence, or at least accepting that such an order is reasonable, make man a legitimate inhabitant of the universe and give meaning to his life. It also includes, obviously, the image of the nature-garden. But that image cannot be reconciled with the realization that the destruction of all its forms is final, that a colorful curtain hides a spectacle of torment and death. This recurrent motif in Milosz's work appears here with redoubled force and brutality:

> Sucking, munching, digesting,
> Growing, and being annihilated. A callous mother.
> If the wax in our ears could melt, a moth on pine needles,
> A beetle half-eaten by a bird, a wounded lizard
> Would all lie at the center of the expanding circles
> Of their vibrating agony.
>
> (CP 260)

> Ssanie, mlaskanie, trawienie,
> Rośnięcie i nicestwienie. Matka obojętna.
> Gdyby stopić wosk w uszach, motyl na igliwiu,
> Żuk napoczęty przez ptaka, zraniona jeszczurka
> Leżałyby pośrodku koncentrycznych kół
> Wibrującej swojej agonii.

Contrary to intellectual understanding, Milosz's imagination stubbornly wanders along a horizon of pain for which there is no rational explanation. Gombrowicz wrote in his *Diary* that even if he did believe in God, the Catholic attitude toward nature would be unacceptable to him: "Human pain has meaning for the Catholic—it undergoes redemption. But a horse? A worm? They are forgotten. That suffering is denied righteousness—there is only the naked fact of despair, gaping with utter finality."[11] Absence of metaphysical sanction for the suffering of animals then becomes an argument used to deny the existence of God. Here Gombrowicz, like Dostoevsky—who held the absolute responsible for the tear of a suffering, innocent child—follows in the footsteps of the Manichaeans. Similarly, Milosz notes that "when our descendants seek to define our times, they will probably make use of the term 'neo-Manichaeanism' to describe our characteristic resentment of evil Matter to which we desperately oppose value, but value no longer flowing from a divine source and now exclusively human" (V 24).

Therefore, at its deepest level Milosz's childhood drama of initiation is a debate over the existence and role of values—a meaning apparent only in its final act. It is not only a religious debate but also an axiological one. The dialogue between nature and the human body, consciousness, and language, and the whole effort to know nature that is a part of self-knowledge become possible only when the imponderables support it. Naturally, this is in contradiction to the "naked light" of contemporary scientific arguments, of science that is so terrifying in its knowledge of an all-encompassing and all-annihilating movement. None of the choices can be good: one errs in the naiveté of a self-delusion; the other presumes a silent acquiescence to the senselessness of human existence. The poetic, and hence childlike and religious, side of Milosz's imagination instinctively seeks the "childish earth of illusion," while another side, rational and infected with the poisons of twentieth-century science, history, and philosophy, scornfully mocks the first. The dilemma remains unresolved, but it stimulates the poet's imagination.

What was the origin of Milosz's views about the relation between man and nature? The answer is simple, but the entire problem requires deeper study. Milosz admits:

> My pessimistic vision of the world was formed early in life, around the age of fifteen; and if I am sensitive to the Schopenhauerian impulse in Gombrowicz and the Moderns, it is because as a boy I was initiated into Nature's reckless indifference by Nusbaum-Hilarowicz's book on Darwin and natural selection. Nor was my early fascination with the Manichaean heresy merely incidental.
>
> (*LU* 37)

Milosz's childhood initiation into the cruelty of nature was deepened through carefully chosen books. But none of the ready answers satisfied him. Although the Manichaean vision of nature as contaminated by evil because of the Fall is close to Milosz, its placing of blame for the evil on the Creator seems naive to him and opposes his attachment to earthly beauty. In Schopenhauer Milosz was intrigued by the idea of sensitization to pain, the concept of *natura devorans, natura devorata*, and an extreme determinism, although he rejected the metaphysical implications of those ideas as well as the cult of art as an ultimate resolution. Darwinism seems to be an effective antidote against any kind of spiritualism. Perhaps for this reason the discovery of Simone Weil was such a revelation for Milosz, for she elevated to the level of the foundation of existence those very contradictions over which he agonized. She did not suggest any simplistic solutions.

Repeating with approval Weil's formula, "la distance infinie qui sépare le nécessaire et le bien," Milosz adds: "Weil, well-versed in mathematics and physics, verges on the 'scientific worldview.' As used by her, the word 'necessity' ('*le nécessaire*') refers to the entire universe, the earth and the history of man as a system of causes and effects subject to mathematical determinism (whose variant is contingency)" (*LU* 256). Nature is beyond good and evil. Did then the Creator leave the world to its own fate? Is this "another version of that indifferent God, the Clockmaker of the eighteenth-century Deists? No: Weil's God is tragic, loving, the dying God on the cross. The words spoken by Christ before his death, 'Lord, why hast Thou forsaken me,' were, for her, the most powerful affirmation of Christianity, and of humanity, which occupies the lowest of all levels, above the innocence of Nature but bound by her laws, longing for the good 'not of this world' " (*LU* 257).

Milosz did not find in Simone Weil an effective remedy for his sorrow since he adds that she "was much too Neoplatonic and Manichaean and intellectual for my coarse Eastern European skin" (*LU* 164). Milosz calls himself an "ecstatic pessimist" (*LU* 163), explaining that he "was too enthralled by the earth to see in it a reflection of pure, unattainable Good, as Simone Weil did" (*LU* 163).

For a better understanding of the core of Milosz's philosophy as well as its main source, one more parallel must be drawn, the parallel between his own worldview and the worldview of modernist and postmodernist writers. Milosz, fully aware of this inheritance, intensifies the fundamental antinomy inherent in this worldview, pushes it to the extreme, and draws his own conclusions from it. In these efforts he is not alone, as he explains:

> The most outstanding twentieth-century Polish writers represent the typical Modernist co-existence of positivist premises with a rebellion against these very premises, compelling us to use Witkiewicz's term, "the Metaphysical Feeling of the Strangeness of Existence." . . . This is the case of Witkiewicz with his hopeless system of Particular Existences, monads that do not communicate with one another. Finally, an ontological fear lies at the very foundations of Gombrowicz's thought, a fear of a vastness arbitrarily ordered by consciousness.
>
> (*PO* 130)

It is easy to add Milosz himself to this list, as a witness of the decay of Christian civilization and the explorer of the essence and the boundaries of Christian imagination. His rebellion is directed not only against the mechanistic and deterministic conception of nature but also against history—even as, paradoxically, he remains faithful to these conceptions.

3

Facing the End of the World

Although for Milosz nature is both "indifferent" and at the same time "mother," history is denied a human face in his poetry. Viewed from the standpoint of its destructive results, history takes on the identity of a blind force—a mighty gale, a deluge, a cosmic conflagration, a rushing stream, or a rocky avalanche. Without scruple, it destroys individuals and whole nations, states, and civilizations. Utterly objectified and depersonalized, history is astounding in its bloody absurdity. In Milosz's "Treatise on Poetry" the poetic personification of the Hegelian "Spirit of History" is reminiscent of the cruel goddess Kali: "His face is huge like ten moons, / On his neck a chain of still-dripping heads" ("Twarz jego wielka jak dziesięć księżyców, / Na szyi łańcuch z nieobeschłych głów"). One could say that in Milosz's poetry biological determinism is transformed into historical fatalism.

In addition to his interest in the biological sciences as a former "naturalist," Milosz's own historical experiences were influential. In his early childhood Milosz was an eyewitness to World War I. Then traveling with his father through Russia (as he relates in *Native Realm*), he saw with his own eyes the outbreak of the Russian revolution. Those experiences can be heard in his poetry as an echo of stifled horror. Scenes from the 1920 Russo-Polish war remain vivid, first appearing in "A Poem on Frozen Time" ("Poemat o czasie zastygłym," 1933) and returning many years later in "The Separate Notebooks: Pages Concerning the Years of Independence" ("Osobny zeszyt: kartki dotyczące lat niepodległości, 1977–1979). In his adulthood Milosz witnessed the birth and gradual expansion of twentieth-century totalitarianism and the bestiality of World War II. Milosz's own biography therefore encompassed those events and sociopolitical phenomena of this century that provide sufficient arguments for a pessimistic appraisal of the direction of world history, regardless of the desires and expectations of individuals.

The conviction that history either obeys unfathomable laws or is ruled by blind chance, which appeared already in vague presentiments in his prewar poetry, intensifies during the Occupation. After the war, especially in "Treatise on Poetry," it emerges as a frontal attack on philosophy that, in Milosz's words, suffers from the "Hegelian temptation." Milosz seems to hold that what passes for an inexorable logic of historical processes progressing through ever more perfect stages is really only an intellectual hypostasis. It is a theory, not an attribute of reality itself. For Milosz, ascribing features of consciousness and friendly intentions toward man is an indirect anthropomorphization of the mathematical necessity that controls all life. Is not the Spirit of History, asks Milosz, one of the embodiments of the Spirit of Earth? Civilizations and nations rise and fall like biological species. By dehumanizing history, Milosz seems to be—consciously or unconsciously— a continuer of the modernists who derided the positivists' faith in a beneficent self-controlled progress. In any case, Milosz raises the same question: either the meaning of human events is external to them, something difficult to accept, or history is the domain of cruel chance.[1]

Milosz's own experience, however, had convinced him that utopian expectations, when projected on historical reality, could have dangerous consequences because the law of historical development, when abstracted and transformed into a political dogma, can under certain conditions become a justification for totalitarianism. In addition to "Treatise on Morals" and "Child of Europe," Milosz devoted *The Captive Mind* and *The Seizure of Power* to the depersonalizing role of communism, the "new faith." He traced a subtle analysis of the human personality affected with a unique variety of schizophrenia: under the pressure of various external forces, it separates the public sphere from the private, publicly expressed opinions from those secretly espoused. Milosz's testimony is all the more important since he too experienced this schizophrenia.

"Mid-Twentieth-Century Portrait" (*CP* 90; "Portret z połowy XX wieku," 1945) is a powerful depiction of this kind of schizophrenia. Milosz shows that it was the result not only of fear and political opportunism but also of the war experience, which demonstrated the instability of all standards and the fragility of ethical principles under the pressure of limitless terror. The conviction that with just a change in the circumstances man can be totally transformed was an additional argument for those who thought they had the key to history. The subject of Milosz's "Portrait," "hidden behind his smile of brotherly regard" ("ukryty za uśmiechem braterstwa") and saying " 'Democracy' with a wink" ("wymawiający słowo demokracja ze zmrużeniem oka") thinks that all the noble slogans and ideals are of pragmatic value only. He "recommends dances and garden parties to defuse public anger" ("dancingi i zabawy w ogrodach jako sposób na publiczne gniewy"). He "shouts 'Culture!' and 'Art!' but means circus games really" ("wołający Kultura i Sztuka, a myślący o igrzyskach w cyrku"). Everything has lost meaning for him; he is infected with decay and deluded by appearances. He seeks refuge in the conviction that he is the possessor of knowledge not available to others, knowledge that allows him to look with disdain on "processions leaving burned-out churches" ("procesję wychodzącą z robitego kościoła"). Discarding metaphysical consolation as a naive daydream, he nevertheless experiences a gnawing feeling of emptiness and absurdity; he discovers his own dependence on those biological laws he would like to control and on that history he would reshape into a new form. Beneath the acuity of his vision lie fear and stifled longings:

> Mumbles in sleep or anaesthesia: "God, oh God!"
> Compares himself to a Roman in whom the Mithras cult has mixed
>   with the cult of Jesus.
>
> (CP 90)
>
> We śnie albo w narkozie mamroczący: Boże, Boże.
> Porównuje siebie do Rzymianina w którym kult Mitry zmieszał się
>   z kultem Jezusa.

Paralyzed by mutually exclusive contradictions, the subject of the portrait suffers a duality of models, standards, and systems: "Keeping one hand on Marx's writings, he reads the Bible in private" ("Rękę oparł na pismach Marksa, ale w domu czyta Ewangelię"). In short, he is an inhabitant of two eras simultaneously, an adherent of two opposed worldviews.

The poem is not only a satiric description of the mind-set of the postwar intelligentsia. In Milosz's poetry even Piłsudski is affected by history and divided within himself. Naturally, Piłsudski's worldview is fundamentally different from that of the subject of "Mid-Twentieth-Century Portrait"; it is based on antinomies that follow a different course. Still, they can be expressed through an analogous opposition between knowledge and powerlessness.

In a word, the overwhelming pressure of history is felt both by those at the top and by those on the bottom, by the rulers and ruled. Neither cynical manipulators nor noble leaders can avoid the judgment of history. This fatalism also stems from reflection on Polish history and its tragic repetitiveness and inertia, which pain Milosz acutely. In the poem "Buried in Their Forefathers" ("W praojcach swoich pogrze-bani"), Milosz sets forth Polish history from the Kościuszko insurrec-tion of 1794, through the January Uprising of 1863, to the interwar years and World War II as a rhythmic series of heroic and bloody, but also futile, outbursts of freedom followed by inevitable defeats.

CATASTROPHISM AND NOTHING ELSE?

Several clarifications should be made at this point. Milosz does not deal with history *en bloc*. It appears in his poetry in two clusters. First is its incidental variability, best seen in individual political acts and sudden outbreaks of social or armed conflict. Second is its crys-tallization in the same forms over and over again, despite the confused external appearances. The first form of history appears primarily in "A Poem on Frozen Time"—not surprisingly, considering the nature of the poem, which shifts from poetic reportage to outright journalism in verse when it refers to actual political events. One can find the same approach to history in Milosz's wartime poems, particularly those describing the Warsaw ghetto uprising ("Campo dei Fiori" and "A Poor Christian Looks at the Ghetto"). Finally it returns many years later in *The Separate Notebooks* in his reminiscences of the Russo-Polish War of 1920. Significantly, Polish history, rather than the events of world politics, preoccupies Milosz.

Since his prewar days a second image of historical time has mat-tered to Milosz, one created by the constant repetition of the same situations, gestures, and behavior, regardless of costume or era. The tendency to generalize and ascribe a universal meaning to ordinary events means that in the poet's words historical time instantly crys-tallizes into cultural ornament, falls into familiar patterns, and begins to resonate with various literary associations. The flight from Warsaw in flames recalls the scene of Adam and Eve's expulsion from Eden, Lot's escape from Sodom and Gomorrah, and the rescue of Aeneas ("Flight," *CP* 75; "Ucieczka," 1945). A group of prisoners in a Nazi work camp recalls a procession of slaves in antiquity ("River";

"Rzeka," 1940); a vision of Giordano Bruno burned at the stake is superimposed on the conflagration of the ghetto ("Campo dei Fiori"); politicians debating in Washington

> write down, with a wink,
> a Holy Alliance in a script of deception
> or a pact between Athens and Lacedaemon.
>   ("Central Park," 1948)

> wypisują z okiem przymrużonem
> Święte Przymierze inkaustem obłudy
> czy Ateńczyków pakt z Lacedemonem.

Kazimierz Wyka offers a fine explanation: "This poetry is in one sense the most 'occasional,' the most sensitive to the changeable emotional and mental aspects of time, and at the same time it most emphatically and consistently sublimates them to fate, to the content of phenomena, to the sense of history."[2] But on what can morality be based if we must eliminate values from both history and nature while admitting that man cannot exist outside history? How can we reconcile the dynamics of historical laws with our need to imbue them with sense and timeless significance? In Milosz's work it would seem that he attempts to resolve these fundamental contradictions through his unique understanding of historicity and eschatology.

History, conceived as a mindless process or an insane whirlwind, is contradicted by the memory of an ever-present inheritance of generations and the daily increase of basic humanitarian values. In *The Land of Ulro* Milosz writes: "That society and civilization endure, I would contend, is due to those minute particles of virtue residing in specific individuals, who affect the whole through a complex process whereby each particle, or grain, is multiplied by others" (*LU* 229). He had expressed a similar thought earlier, in a more profound form, in "Treatise on Poetry":

> Yes, to make into one
> The hairiness of a beaver and the smell of the rushes
> And the wrinkles of a hand resting on a pitcher
> Out of which wine dribbles. Why exclaim
> That historicity destroys our substance
> If it truly is given to us,
> That Muse of our gray-haired father, Herodotus,
> As an arm and an instrument?

Tak, połączyć w jedno
Kosmatość bobra i zapach sitowia
I zmarszczki dłoni leżącej na dzbanie
Z którego ścieka wino. Czemuż wołać
Że historyczność niszczy nam substancję,
Jeżeli ona właśnie jest nam dana,
Muza siwego ojca, Herodota,
Jako broń i instrument?

Jan Błoński once observed that "by 'historicity' [Milosz] means neither real events nor laws that history obeys. Rather [he means] the material of human experience, embedded in the codes of human interaction, in culture as most broadly conceived."[3]

Milosz's poetic anthropology is thus based on the conviction that in the case of both history and nature we should not look to the laws they exhibit—they will only appall us with their inhuman necessity. Rather, we should focus our attention on what is transitory and vanishing, signs of existence all the more valuable. Then man will find support in the beauty of each marvel of nature, despite his awareness of the deceptive illusion of its splendor, and in the momentary passage of historical time, which spontaneously and without compulsion, like a banquet, unites the ancient human collective, becoming its defense against constant change and death. "To make into one" the cultural and the natural, the human and the animal, as well as the particular and the universal, the changing and the constant, means to accept the paradoxical quality of human nature and the unattainability of a synthesis. One may approximate such a synthesis, noticing at every moment the reflection of eternity and seeing in the "minute particles of virtue" a sum of values hard to imagine as the basis of all culture. The road to reality seems to lead through the particular rather than through hasty generalization. We can better grasp the substance of things through their tangible attributes—hairiness, smell, wrinkles— than with the aid of abstract ideas. Historicity will only become a successful defense against the reification of the human person who faces the alienating laws of nature and history, as well as an instrument strengthening the power of the imponderables, when man within himself can harmonize duration with movement, the individual with the social. Accordingly, we should amend Jan Błoński's observation: historicity is perhaps not so much the substance of human experience as the internalization of its process of creation and growth.

The constant increase of the sum of fundamental values is significant in not only the earthly dimension but also the metaphysical, for it brings us closer to the state of existence that will be attained when human history ends. History seems to be transformed into eschatology. I say "seems to be" because we may only guess at the relation between historicity and eschatology, since it has never been defined by Milosz. In any case, in resolving the debate over the existence of values in life, Milosz defines them as existing both in the "momentariness" that allows us to give meaning to individual existence and in eternity, which, from the perspective of the ultimate goal of the world, enables us to evaluate the laws governing history. The continual interpenetration of the dimensions of historical time and sacral time is extraordinarily important for Milosz and should be borne in mind when discussing his links with catastrophism.

Notably this problem appears in one form in Milosz's poetry and in another form in his essays. Taking stock of his attitude before the war, Milosz admits: "As a young man I was struck by the magnitude of what was occurring in my century, a magnitude equaling, perhaps even surpassing the decline and fall of antiquity" (*LU* 5).

This conviction has not weakened over the years. In Milosz's view the annihilation of our civilization signals the fact that it has now turned against its Christian roots. Further on in *The Land of Ulro* he praises the significance of the "little particles of virtue": "In European civilization these grains were nurtured on an ontological soil. By the law of retardation . . . the influence of religion has proved far more durable than religion itself; it has sustained customs and institutions in the face of universal or nearly universal secularization" (*LU* 229). That is why the watch words of freedom, equality, and brotherhood have survived. But the law of retardation does not halt the inexorable process of erosion that causes a value system, denied metaphysical sanction, to hang suspended in midair and lose its justification. The conclusion is: "No one of sound mind, who has lived long in a country of the West, can have any illusions as to the utter failure of secular humanism, a failure sponsored by the very successes of that same humanism" (*LU* 229).

In accord with Oscar Milosz, whose own diagnosis was confirmed by Milosz's subsequent reading of Swedenborg and Blake, Milosz sees the origin of the coming catastrophe in the mechanistic approach to science that dates from Newton and the accompanying excessive cult of technical progress. Scientific thought totally dissociated from faith and imagination, the intellect cocksure of its ability to control nature and functioning in an axiological vacuum since even the notion of truth is relative—these are the reasons for the present danger. Similar views have been expressed in Erich Heller's studies on modern literature, *The Disinherited Mind*, and Milosz paraphrases Heller: the dethroning of God and the deification of science, which, paradoxically, through its achievements made earth no longer the center of the universe and denied man his privileged position in the animal kingdom, give birth to "the 'disinherited mind' in the ontological sense, . . . a mind torn between the certainty of man's insignificance in the immensity of a hostile universe, and an urge, born of wounded pride, to endow man with preeminence" (*LU* 95).

Milosz, however, seems not to have lost hope. On one hand, in the final chapter of *The Land of Ulro* he speaks about a future "renewed civilization" based perhaps on a new conception of science, harmonizing intellect with faith and drawing religious implications from the discoveries of physics. The Harvard lectures, on the other hand, close with a lecture entitled, significantly, "On Hope," in which Milosz speculates about a world society that draws its strength and inspiration from the cultural past of all humanity.

Milosz's futuristic prognoses should not be taken too seriously. It is easy to see that he himself enunciates them with a certain distance. They are more intriguing as a projection into humanity's future of his own convictions and ideas, suppositions and intuitions, fears and hopes. What is curious in this regard is that Milosz the poet does not share the optimism of Milosz the essayist. Beginning in the prewar period, his poems prophesy the imminent destruction of the human species. The sole exception is "Spring 1932" ("Wiosna 1932"):

> Cities in the sun, in the green, will grow,
> The earth will become the happiest planet.

> Miasta w słońcu zieleni będą rosły,
> Ziemia stanie się najszczęśliwszą planetą.

This youthful illusion is scornfully denied many years later by an image of the world imperium, the totalitarian state, something like a new incarnation of "Diocletian's Rome" ("Rzym Dioklecjana," 1977–78), where man, denied freedom and dignity, "gathered bitter bread" ("zbierał gorzki chleb"). Mankind will be reduced to the level of its animal beginnings:

They traced their origin to the dinosaur
And took their deftness from the lemur's paw.
Above the cities of the thinking lichen,
Flights of pterodactyls proclaimed the law.
                    ("The Wormwood Star," CP 381)

Od dinozaura swój ród wywodzili.
Zręczność lemurów z grot skalnych przynieśli
I nad miastami lot pterodaktyli
Ogłaszał prawo dla myślącej pleśni.
                    ("Gwiazda piołun," 1982)

The obliteration of the line between the human and the animal, so important for Milosz, is accomplished here by an image that refers both to primitive forms of life in remote geological epochs and to signs of civilization. The "thinking lichen" is an ironic echo of the "snails of Socrates" and at the same time an indication of the progressive reduction of human nature.

But other visions lend Milosz's poetry its tone. From the 1936 poem "Assizes" ("Roki"):

All now is over, all is forgotten,
only the smoke on the earth, dead clouds
and above the ashy rivers some smoldering
wings and the poisoned sun recedes
and damnation's daybreak steps out of the seas.

Wszystko minione, wszystko zapomniane,
tylko na ziemi dym, umarłe chmury,
i nad rzekami z popiołu tlejące
skrzydła i cofa się zatrute słońce,
a potępienia brzask wychodzi z mórz.

to "From the Rising of the Sun":

And if the city, there below, was consumed by fire,
Together with the cities of all the continents,
I would not say with my mouth of ashes that it was unjust.
                    (CP 313)

A gdyby miasto, tam w dole, zgorzało
I zgorzały miasta wszystkich kontynentów
Nie powiedziałbym, ustami popiołu, że niesprawiedliwie.

the end of the human race is associated with the annihilation of the whole world. In the former poem the prophecy of destruction led critics to consider Milosz part of the catastrophist trend.

The problem is that catastrophism has come to be an imprecise and rather extensive term. On one hand, it is defined historically as a trend in Polish poetry in the 1930s, referring particularly to the Żagary group of poets, a trend that returned in the poetry of the Occupation years by young poets like Krzysztof Kamil Baczyński, Tadeusz Borowski, and Tadeusz Gajcy. On the other hand, the term includes the belief that European civilization is in a state of crisis, a conviction that was shared by various thinkers since the end of the nineteenth century and culminated in the works of Spengler, Ortega y Gasset, and, in Poland, Marian Zdziechowski and Stanisław Ignacy Witkiewicz (Witkacy). A further complication is that catastrophism, clearly a historiosophic diagnosis, is also a term used in poetics. It would be helpful, therefore, to refine this term, limiting it to those characteristics that seem integral to the catastrophist world view.

Studies in the 1970s of the writings of Stanisław Ignacy Witkiewicz agree that catastrophism is a conviction voicing the inevitable annihilation of the highest values, those essential to a given cultural system and elitist in character.[4] This definition gives rise to many questions: Whence will this annihilation come? What is the nature of the process that leads to it? What will the world look like after the catastrophe? The answers have varied depending on the philosophical school that formulated them. Generally, catastrophism is a historiosophic diagnosis, postulated for contemporary times, that inevitably leads to a pessimistic conclusion. It presumes the existence of two mutually incompatible value systems, one of which (that affirmed by the catastrophist) will certainly be destroyed, as well as a cyclical concept of historical time: one civilization gives way to another, the dying civilization fertilizing the new one. Catastrophism defends lost causes and identifies with values whose destruction seems certain. It is a tragic outlook. It can be considered an expression of conservative opinions because it reacts with fear at any change in the status quo, turns away from the present disillusioned, and eagerly becomes absorbed in the past, where ideals are to be found.

As is well known, Stanisław Ignacy Witkiewicz opposed individual values to social ones. On one side (the side he chose) he placed metaphysical experience, which became the basis first of religion, art, and philosophy, then of beauty, freedom, intellect, and absolute truth. On the other side (the side he rejected) he placed general happiness, as expressed through the satisfaction of basic needs: safety, justice, equality, and ethics. Axiological dualism also colors his interpretation of history and becomes the premise on which he constructs a utopian model of society whose positive version is projected into the past, its negative version to come in the future after the destruction of contemporary civilization. He divided the entire history of mankind into four basic states: positive utopia, its gradual degeneration, catastrophe, and negative utopia. This mythic framework can be "understood as an attempt at intellectual mastery, a kind of positive response to the experience of alienation and the disintegration of traditional cultural values."[5]

In light of the above remarks it is difficult to classify Milosz as a catastrophist. Although he transfers the laws of nature to history, his thinking focuses on only one part of the evolutionary chain for a model: the declining phase. In other words, the life of an individual or species becomes the matrix of events locked in the rhythm of all existence, moving from peak to decay to annihilation. At this point the entire process ends and is not repeated because—and this is essential— it occurs in both a historical and a metaphysical dimension. Milosz prophesies the inevitable destruction of humanity, not just one civilization. He speaks of the destruction of the universe, not of one sociopolitical order.

Milosz's poetry of the 1930s has been mistakenly understood as a harbinger of World War II. Of course, Milosz did not construct his vision in isolation from his surroundings and from contemporary imagination. He perceived, as I have mentioned, the negative outcome of the economic crisis and the threat of fascism, sharing his own generation's vague premonition of a coming catastrophe and the tense atmosphere of the years leading up to September 1939. To a large degree his views were also probably influenced by the geopolitical situation of Poland at that time. Aleksander Wat compares the outlook of his own generation to that of Milosz:

> The catastrophism of [Milosz's] generation coincided with Stalinism on one side and Hitlerism on the other. You were caught in that scissors, especially in Poland. You too had a feeling, perhaps a deeper one, that an era had ended, that the world had ended, that civilization was impossible, but at the same time you were caught between two enormously powerful, dynamic monsters. . . . My generation, that is, people like myself had the same feeling of catastrophism. But we didn't have those monsters in front of us; just the reverse, we had a chasm in front of us,

ruins, *à la longue* cheerful ruins . . . because here, precisely, something new could be built.[6]

Milosz himself adds: "The 'Russian experience,' here understood in the broadest sense to include not only the Revolution but its portents and consequences as expressed in the literature, also played a role" (*LU* 271).

A fear of the consequences of the both fascinating and alarming Russian revolution was perhaps the major factor in the catastrophists' worldview, and thus their poetry should be understood as a coded message primarily about that fear. It is not accidental that in their poetry an image of new hordes of Genghis Khan or some imminent destruction from the East appears. In any case, the ambiguous fascination with the Russian revolution did not incline Milosz (as it did some of his fellow writers in Żagary) to picture a social utopia that would be realized at the cost of bloody class upheaval. One may say that the metaphysical in Milosz comes to the aid of Milosz the historiosopher and moralist. Catastrophism is transformed into eschatology.

POETIC ESCHATOLOGY

As J. Hering demonstrates, eschatology is a "complex of convictions that express religious hope about the coming of a world considered to be ideal; at the same time, this world will be preceded by a Judgment (this, however, presumes the destruction of present reality or the power to which it has been subject)."[7] Among the numerous common conceptions about the end of the world, the Judeo-Christian has a special place, for it breaks with the cyclic concept of time: "The Universe that will reappear after the catastrophe will be the same Universe created by God at the beginning of time, but it will be purified, reborn, and renewed in its original glory. This earthly Paradise will never again be destroyed and will have no end."[8] But before that happens, the world will be given over to the Antichrist, who will destroy all moral, social, political, and religious order. Wars, plagues, and natural disasters will accompany his reign (see Matthew 24:7). In short, according to the Christian eschatology to which Milosz refers, the history of man and the world can be formulated as follows: Paradise—Fall—Apocalypse—the return of Paradise. The parallelism between this cycle and the catastrophist cycle described above is striking. Nevertheless, an essential difference emerges: in contrast to catastrophism, eschatology projects the positive utopia into the future; hence it has a different, consolatory function.

Milosz speaks least about the lost Paradise. Its existence, or rather absence, is expressed in nostalgia for a wholeness, a happy and spontaneous acceptance, an "at-homeness" in the universe, a state of innocent ignorance. The second phase appears in a negative assessment of the present, paralyzed by moral crime and a feeling of the senselessness of existence. Even in a journalistic work like "A Poem on Frozen Time," hunger, poverty, suffering, and exploitation seem isolated from reality, their socioeconomic causes unclear. They become, above all, a manifestation of timeless evil.

The best evidence of the decay of our era is the horror of World War II. God, even if he exists, is silent in the face of the enormity of the crime and leaves the world to its own processes, as in "Flatland" ("Równina," 1941):

> Neither a pillar of revelation, nor the bush of Moses
> will shoot up at the edge of the horizon.

> Ni słup objawień, ani krzak Mojzesza
> Na widnokręgu krańcach nie wystrzeli.

The judgments of fate are fulfilled in the world, deserted by God and given over to the demonic powers dormant in man. The *sacrum* is only a faint memory of another heaven and earth described by the prophets.

In a similar fashion, years later in "How It Was" (CP 203) Milosz describes a holiness degraded and reduced to a dismal caricature. The narrator says, "I saw absence; the mighty power of counter-fulfillment; the penalty of a promise lost forever" ("Widziałem nieobecność; mocarstwo przeciw-spełnienia; karę utraconej na zawsze obietnicy"). The penalty appears in contemporary reality, which, indifferent to religion, has become second-rate and one-dimensional. Ancient protective spirits hide themselves. God the Father no longer walks about the earth and Christ averts his eyes "when passing by a neon cross flat as a movie screen showing a striptease" ("mijając krzyż neonowy, płaski jak ekran striptease") since along with the imagination, sacral art has undergone degradation and decay. People have abandoned hope in redemption and take refuge from the enigma of existence in magic or a narcotic daze:

> And those who longed for the Kingdom took refuge like
> me in the mountains to become the last heirs of a
> dishonored myth.
>
> (CP 204)

> A którzy tęsknili do Królestwa, jak ja dziczeli
> w górach, potomkowie zhańbionego mitu.

Milosz does not believe that the disappearance of religious sensibility stems solely from growing indifference to the sacred and the spread of an *unreflective* atheism fed by the droppings of contemporary science. (It should be noted that he does not disregard atheism itself: "A true atheist, I believe, is a rare bird" [LU 252].) It also stems from the mistaken tactics of the Catholic church, particularly in America in the 1960s, as he maintains in *The Land of Ulro:*

> Theologians, Catholics included, casting themselves as clowns, gleefully proclaimed that Christianity, hitherto in opposition to the world, was now both in and of the world. Meanwhile, their audience, beholders of a spectacle more pathetic than funny, took this to mean that Christians wished to be the "same as others," that is, to give up their Christianity.

The greatest danger, in fact, was that "the power before which they prostrated themselves was an anti-Christian mentality urged upon the masses by science" (LU 248–249). Milosz expressed this view in abbreviated and ironic form in "From the Rising of the Sun" when writing about a religious service:

> Where the liturgy consisted of discussion
> Under the guidance of a priest in Easter vestment
> On whether we should believe in life after death,
> Which the president then put to the vote.
>
> (CP 299–300)

> Którego liturgia polegała na dyskusji
> Pod przewodnictwem księdza w wielkanocnej szacie
> O tym, czy da się wierzyć w życie po śmierci,
> Co rozstrzygano przez głosowanie.

In this case, as in the previous ones, Milosz does not debate the sociocultural and sociopolitical origin of the situation he describes: it is sufficient to register the symptoms without going into the causes.

Thus, evil takes on a universal significance, as if the earth really had been given over to the power of the Antichrist.

It is not surprising, then, that the portent of the Apocalypse—the third phase of history—recurs obsessively, taking various forms. Milosz first turns to the Book of Revelation for images of the destroyed world order. Of many examples from his prewar poetry, the following is perhaps the most typical:

> As if the years have passed and crosses started blooming,
> a transformed fire of the four heavens surges
>
> ("Birds")

> Jakby minęły lata i zakwitły krzyże,
> kłębi się przemieniony ogień czworga nieb
> ("Ptaki")

Here already we can discern the basic characteristics of Milosz's apocalyptic vision. He draws on the ancient biblical model but also modifies and recreates it in an original way. Above all, however, he detects and imitates such features of biblical poetics as the supernatural qualities of objects (blooming crosses), the change of the substance of elements (transformed fire), the symbolism of numbers (four heavens), and the superficiality of causal relationships (the blooming of the cross is in no way connected with the appearance of fire). All these aspects of his vision undergo such an immense condensation that the epic narration of the scriptural apocalypse becomes almost an epigram in Milosz's poetic art. In any case, his techniques combine to recreate the two fundamental rules of the poetic text of the scriptural apocalypse: it is hermetic, and it is symbolic. The poetry takes on the nobility of a sacral message accessible only to the chosen few.

Milosz's vision of the end of human history has nevertheless undergone an evolution. "A Song on the End of the World" ("Piosenka o końcu świata"), written in 1943 during the same dark years of the Occupation, opens with the words:

> On the day the world ends
> A bee circles a clover,
> A fisherman mends a glimmering net.
> Happy porpoises jump in the sea,
> By the rainspout young sparrows are playing
> And the snake is gold-skinned as it should always be.
>
> (CP 56)

W dzień końca świata
Pszczoła krąży nad kwiatem nasturcji,
Rybak naprawia błyszczącą sieć.
Skaczą w morzu wesołe delfiny,
Młode wróble czepiają się rynny
I wąż ma złotą skórę, jak powinien mieć.

Apparently, then, nothing essential has changed. Minute events follow their own course; human activity is joined to the eternal rhythm of natural change. All, regardless of its meaning, occurs in a kind simultaneity. Existence endures despite change.

After the war "A Song on the End of the World" was understood as a "recovery from the times of catastrophism, an ironic afterword to *Three Winters.*"[9] I would propose yet another interpretation: the end of the world occurs without interruption, for it is always possible, always potentially present in the sacral dimension of human existence. The possibility of both the Fall and redemption continually pierces through the density of existence. As Rudolf Bultmann reminds us, the paradox of being a Christian lies in the fact that by an act of faith man is able to rise above historical time while still remaining in it. "Every moment can become an eschatological moment and in Christianity that possibility is realized."[10] As it turns out, however, few know this. Milosz's old man, "who would be a prophet / Yet is not a prophet, for he's much too busy" (CP 56; "który byłby prorokiem, / Ale nie jest prorokiem bo ma inne zajęcie") stubbornly repeats: "There will be no other end of the world."

Many years later Milosz added a kind of personal commentary to this poem:

For we lived under the Judgment, unaware.
Which Judgment began in the year one thousand seven hundred fifty-seven,
Though not for certain, perhaps in some other year.
It shall come to completion in the sixth millennium, or next Tuesday.
("From the Rising of the Sun," CP 313)

Bo żyliśmy pod Sądem, nic nie wiedząc o tym.
Który to Sąd zaczął się w roku tysiąc siedemset pięćdziesiątym siódmym,
Choć nie na pewno, może w którymś innym.
Dopełni się w szóstym millenium albo w następny wtorek.

The date 1757 is deliberately chosen. Swedenborg gave it as the year of the Last Judgment, closing the fourth and inaugurating the fifth church in the history of mankind. Interpreting the apocalypse in an entirely allegorical way, Swedenborg (as Milosz explains in *The Land of Ulro*) maintained that "the Judgment took place in the other world; neither Earth nor mankind would come to an end, because the higher world could exist without mankind as little as mankind could exist without the higher world" (*LU* 150–151).

Milosz seems to contest this interpretation, noting that the actual date is not important—in the history of Christianity various dates have been used. What matters is the crossing of an invisible barrier into an inner experience and complete belief in being called to judgment. But our age considers this either a myth that may elicit interest but is hardly worth taking seriously or an element of literary tradition. Since the sense of sacral time is today in decline, the Apocalypse has become totally incomprehensible. Eluding rational categories and contrary to historical experience, it fades from the field of contemporary imagination. As in "A Song on the End of the World," people do not believe in it. In a rather baffling way the Last Judgment has not so much a moral meaning as an ontological one. More than a just assessment of human actions, it signifies a change in all reality.

"*Oeconomia Divina*" demonstrates this point with its indirect question about the meaning of eschatology. Posing the problem paradoxically, one might say that the poem tells of the end of the world, which is happening precisely because it is not supposed to occur. The poem is incredibly dense; practically each phrase requires extensive commentary. Hence I will touch on only its most important aspects.

"*Oeconomia Divina*" presumes a situation in which the Divine Householder has turned away from human beings, "allowing them to act whatever way they wished, / leaving to them conclusions, saying nothing" ("pozwoliwszy im działać jak tylko zapragną, / Im zostawiając wnioski i nie mówiąc nic"). He denies them judgment. Milosz shows that in such circumstances the world loses its reason for being, both in its material form and, what is more painful, in its ontological dimension:

> Out of trees, field stones, even lemons on the table,
> materiality escaped and their spectrum
> proved to be a void, a haze on a film.
>
> (*CP* 235)

Z drzew, polnych kamieni, nawet cytryn na stole
Uciekła materialność i widmo ich
Okazywało się pustką, dymem na kliszy.

Reality exists only in an apparent way; it does not permit deeper knowledge or imitation. As a result, the categories ordering human knowledge lose their meaning: "Everywhere was nowhere and nowhere, everywhere" ("Wszędzie było nigdzie i nigdzie, wszędzie"). Paradox seems best suited to this unreal reality, for even language turns out to be powerless before such an experience. Art also loses its meaning, as does all human symbolic activity. "The hand was not able to trace the palm sign, the river sign, or the sign of ibis" ("Ręka nie mogła nakreślić znaku palmy, znaku rzeki, ni znaku ibisa") since no signification matched them. Milosz's symbols here are deliberately chosen. The palm is the classical emblem of fertility and victory; the river, an ambivalent symbol, signifies either abundance or the irreversible flow of time and, hence, loss and oblivion; finally, the ibis was the Egyptian god of wisdom.[11] Life-giving strength ebbs away from art, too, since the archetypes preserved in the collective unconscious lack transcendental models. This weakening rules out any possibility of communication. As a result, the "mortality of the language" ("śmiertelność mowy") is proclaimed. In addition, a "complaint was forbidden as it complained to itself" ("zabroniona była skarga, bo skarżyła się samej sobie")—ethics without metaphysical sanction ceases to bind. Without a merciful Father to whose divine justice one might appeal,

> People, afflicted with an incomprehensible distress,
> were throwing off their clothes on the piazzas so that nakedness might
>   call for judgment.
> But in vain they were longing after horror, pity, and anger.
>
> (CP 235)
>
> Ludzie, dotknięci niezrozumiałą udręką,
> Zrzucali suknie na placach żeby sądu wzywała ich nagość.
> Ale na próżno tęsknili do grozy, litości i gniewu.

They longed in vain because they did not believe in the Apocalypse, which, as in a syllogism, destroying the earthly order, returns it or rather confirms its meaning through negation. Milosz would say that this always occurs when our conception of the world does not include God, the ultimate guarantor of its meaning and the only unshakable value. Without him reality loses its own existential coherence and disintegrates into nothingness—literally and metaphorically, visually and intangibly. The lines "airfields larger than tribal dominions / suddenly ran short of their essence and disintegrated" ("Lotniskom rozleglejszym niż plemienne państwa / Nagle zabrakło zasady i rozpadły się") are both a description of the real destruction of material objects and a symbolic representation of ontology, one might say, contradicted.

The meaning of Milosz's poetic Apocalypse should be explained precisely in this way, that is, ambivalently. In the language of symbols, it foresees the end of human history prefigured by the death of each individual man, at the same time as it allows the repetition of all its phases in man's own religious experience, expressed in the constant dialectic of Fall and redemption. The Apocalypse is thus located simultaneously in a mysterious future and in the present; it is acted out in a cosmic theater but constantly repeated in the soul of each Christian. It is difficult to say which of these two explanations, present at the beginning of Christian thought, is closer to Milosz. The apocalyptic vision, however, is gradually and ever more clearly internalized; it is transformed from a prophecy into an existential postulate. The possibility that it was a postulate from the beginning with Milosz cannot be ruled out, but his prewar poetry does not reveal this two-dimensionality.

It is possible that God may turn away from man when man forgets him. At least that is the way God acts in *"Oeconomia Divina"*: "the God of thunders and of rocky heights, / the Lord of hosts, Kyrios Sabaoth" ("Bóg skalnych wyżyn i gromów, / Pan Zastępów, Kyrios Sabaoth") is the God of the Old Testament, who is closer to Milosz than the Great Clockmaker or the Guardian of Laws. Undoubtedly, Milosz is connected in many ways to that line of Christian philosophy which from Ecclesiastes and Job through Pascal and Kierkegaard leads to existentialism. With good reason Milosz repeats the words of Simone Weil, "Contradiction is the instrument of transcendence" (*LU* 257), and then comments that "man must conceive of God as retiring, absent, yet sustain a belief in Providence" (*LU* 257). Almost an echo of this maxim is Milosz's statement, "And the holy had its abode only in denial" ("From the Rising of the Sun," *CP* 265; "I tylko w zaprzeczeniu dom swój miała świętość"). A longtime reader of Lev Shestov would perhaps agree with Milosz when he warns against the identification (in accordance with Platonic and Stoic traditions) of God with the good. Shestov says, "We must seek that which is *above* pity, *above* good. We must seek God."[12] The problem of evil is one of the major questions in Milosz's poetry. Still, he does not enter into a dialogue with the tradition of theodicy.[13]

APOKATASTASIS: FULFILLMENT OF FORMS

In *The Land of Ulro* Milosz says that had he lived in the early centuries of Christianity, "a certain sensibility, a certain cast of mind would have attracted me to the Gnostics rather than to the Christians" (*LU* 264). It is no surprise, then, that in his conceptions of a recovered paradise (the final phase in the history of the individual and mankind), Milosz refers to views that were mistrusted and that evoked numerous reservations on the part of the Catholic church. Derived from an interpretation of references in the Acts of the Apostles that speak of "the time of universal restoration which God spoke of long ago through his holy prophets" (Acts 3:21), the concept of *apokatastasis* promises a return of the entire universe to its ideal state, snatched from the jaws of change and death. With its roots in Gnosticism and Platonism,[14] the theory has not lost its relevance throughout the centuries and reappears, for example, in the writings of Saint Gregory of Nyssa, Origen, Blake, Soloviev, and Berdyaev.[15] It acquires various interpretations—ontological, moralistic, existential.[16] Milosz describes his understanding of the concept when, acknowledging his belief in *apokatastasis*, he observes:

> That word promises reverse movement,
> Not the one that was set in *katastasis*,
>
> . . . .
> For me, therefore, everything has a double existence.
> Both in time and when time shall be no more.
> <div style="text-align:right">(<i>CP</i> 310)</div>
>
> Słowo to przyobiecuje ruch odwrotny,
> Nie ten co zastygł w *katastasis*,
>
> . . . .
> Każda rzecz ma więc dla mnie podwójne trwanie.
> I w czasie i kiedy czasu już nie będzie.

Milosz emphasizes that existence is simultaneously changing and constant, mortal and immortal. Because this two-dimensionality is attached to every phenomenon of life, even the most minute, Milosz does not want to accept a diminishing of it even in the sacral aspect. Instead he favors the divine transformation of all. The description of the Last Judgment cited earlier in "From the Rising of the Sun" goes on to read:

> The demiurge's workshop will suddenly be stilled. Unimaginable
>   silence.
> And the form of every single grain will be restored in glory.
>
> (CP 314)
>
> Nagle umilknie warsztat demiurga. Nie do wyobrażenia cisza.
> I forma pojedyńczego ziarna wróci w chwale.

Different sources coincide in these few phrases. First the Gnostic, since a demiurge is mentioned who, instead of God, weaves the fabric of existence. Next, a Blakean inspiration appears: Milosz repeats that Blake believed that " 'whatever can be Created can be Annihilated; Forms cannot' " (CP 313). The halting of time and the opening of a timeless sphere calls to mind Berdyaev. He differentiated between historical time and "existential" time, that is, metahistorical time that cannot be measured physically and extends beyond the end of history.[17] More important, Milosz's affinities with Russian religious thought at the turn of the century are not accidental. That thought drew much from the tradition of Orthodoxy, which made belief in *apokatastasis,* the conviction that all nature, including Satan, will be redeemed, one of its basic doctrines. Perhaps that is why—considering his early contact with the Orthodox church and his later reading of Russian religious philosophers— precisely this belief strongly impressed Milosz's imagination. It is tempting to say that Milosz the essayist would like to be rationalistic, clear, optimistic—in a word, Western—while Milosz the poet remains in his deepest soul mystical, dark, pessimistic—Eastern. In fact, it is more a case of Milosz playing in two keys in his work, taking advantage of his borderland heritage.

A metaphysical, rather than historical, perspective in evaluating change in human history; a monistic, rather than dualistic, system of values; a linear, rather than cyclical, conception of time; and finally a future, rather than past, projection of a positive utopia—in these contrasts the uniqueness of Milosz's position compared to that of the catastrophists clearly emerges. Of course, it is difficult to deny the similarity between catastrophism and eschatology. They have the same source: resistance to, and negation of, the world as it appears in both the prophecy of its destruction and the search for compensation in utopian creations. But what is analogous should not immediately cancel out what divides these two positions.

Milosz turned to Christian eschatology to give meaning to historical changes, to find the sacral dimension in the present, and, indirectly, to return to poetry the range that it has lost. For it is poetry that expresses our premonition of, and hope for, redemption.

THE DEFENSE OF THE IMAGINATION

Such an explanation is only partially true, for it leaves aside an entire series of thorny problems. We could respond to Milosz's eschatology by acknowledging it only as an artistic creation of the imagination, an element of literary fiction. But that response would be inadequate since Milosz attaches such significance to these problems. He clearly says that a "non-eschatological poetry" is impossible because it would contradict the nature of our civilization, "shaped as it is by the Bible and, for that reason, eschatological to the core" (*WP* 37). What then explains the divergence we have noted between Milosz's essays and his poetry? Moreover, what is his attitude toward *apokatastasis*? Does he really believe that it will come to pass, or does he simply put this belief in the mouths of his characters? Finally, why the references to such diverse thinkers as Blake, Swedenborg, and Oscar Milosz? What links them?

I will begin with these last questions. A common trait in the writings of those thinkers is the revolt against science deriving from the tradition of Newton and Locke, their diagnosis of the "disinherited intellect," and their search for remedies for it. Not without reason does Milosz consider himself part of their tradition. He constantly emphasizes the decisive role of the twentieth century and the ruining of beliefs and conceptualizations that has resulted from the scientific revolution. In *The Land of Ulro* Milosz says:

> In the literature of the mid- and late twentieth century, no one would presume to challenge the laws of physics, biology, psychology, sociology, and so on; they are flatly taken for granted. But if as a result of continual reduction man was no longer king but some subspecies of anthropoidal ape; if he was stripped of Eden, of Heaven and Hell, of good and evil, now defined as the product of social determinants, then was he not ripe

for the ultimate reduction, for his metamorphosis into a planetary society of two-legged insects?

(*LU* 157)

The reduction of man, the atrophy of religious symbolism, ethical relativism, and the destruction of a hierarchical and value-carrying spatial vision—these are the conditions whose gradual rise was noted by Blake, Swedenborg, and Oscar Milosz, a rise they endeavored to oppose through the invention of their own mystical constructs. Although he follows in their footsteps, Milosz does not negate the achievements of contemporary science, for he is aware that it alone may find an effective remedy for the disinherited intellect. Mysticism is also foreign to Milosz, as is apparent in the humor and objectivity with which he describes the ideas of Blake, Swedenborg, and Oscar Milosz in *The Land of Ulro*. Although that book may be termed an encomium to the wisdom of madness, Milosz seems to contend that only at the limit of psychological equilibrium and common sense can we glimpse what normally eludes us.[18]

The primary object of the writings of these three thinkers was, Milosz argues, "a major defense of Christianity, and it was addressed to atheists and Deists as much as to the theologians" (*LU* 141). Pascal, clearly foreseeing the tendency of the European mind, already laid out the direction for this defense, which cuts across particular denominational and sectarian lines. He restored the meaning of an anthropocentric formulation asserting the "anti-naturalness of that unique phenomenon called consciousness" (*LU* 142). Despite all their differences, Blake, Swedenborg, and Oscar Milosz also have anthropocentric conceptions, as does Czeslaw Milosz, who follows them and openly admits:

> Only now do I discern the thread joining the various phases of, and influences on, my mind's progress: Catholicism, Stanisław Brzozowski, Oscar Milosz, Hegelianism (in the person of my friend Tadeusz Juliusz Kroński), Swedenborg, Simone Weil, Shestov, Blake. That thread is my anthropocentrism and my bias against Nature. The succession of influences forms a pattern that begins with my interest in Manichaeanism, first stirred by my readings in Church history, and ends with my course on Manichaeanism at Berkeley.

(*LU* 159–160)

This crucial admission explains why Milosz so stubbornly investigates the realm where the human jousts with the animal and where the mind carries on a discussion with nature. This deepest tradition is surely also the nucleus of his reflection on history and eschatology. In this context anthropocentrism means nothing other than the hope, maintained despite so many doubts, that man is the true center and goal of the universe because he may gain ultimate victory over the laws of nature. Only in this dimension does the dilemma between freedom and necessity disappear and is the fundamental debate over values positively resolved.

Describing the history of the European religious mind since the seventeenth century, Milosz in essence presents the fate of the religious imagination in its struggle with the scientific worldview. Thus the nonpoet Swedenborg evokes the following recognition from Milosz: "Swedenborg's importance lies not in his theology so much as in his effort to decode the Bible, to build a 'verbal space,' as Osip Mandelstam once said of Dante. Though non-poetic in style, Swedenborg's work, no less than *The Divine Comedy,* is a vast honeycomb built by the bees of the imagination and obeying a certain imperative" (*LU* 151–152).

A study of the Bible is so important because it brings us close to the secret of speech that with overpowering force calls on the treasury of archetypes and ancient symbols embedded in the collective imagination. In the Scriptures there is a unity between sign and meaning, between symbol and the content it conceals, that was later destroyed. The Scriptures remind us of the weight of a hierarchical spatial pattern in the imagination. Although a direct return to biblical cosmology is impossible, a return to its anthropocentric basis seems still attainable by means of a new language that must be created to support a transformed vision of the world. Milosz points out that all three thinkers understood this necessity: Swedenborg, creating his "internal space"; Blake, as the creator of an original grammar of symbols; and Oscar Milosz, who ascribed metaphysical meaning to the theory of relativity. Each of them relied on various sources in addition to the Bible, turning to Gnosticism, Manichaeanism, the Cabala, and alchemy.

In Dante's *Divine Comedy* Milosz finds and applauds an inner necessity that weaves different classical, Christian, historical, and political motifs into a clear design located in an imaginative physical space. In *The Divine Comedy* actual persons and fictional creations appear on an equal footing, but that in no way detracts from the seriousness and passion of the religious argument. Milosz shows that

"Dante's *Inferno* suggests, finally, that we really do not know what it is to believe or 'not to believe' in someone or something, that the human mind eludes facile division into 'the real' and 'the imaginary,' 'the literal' and 'the figurative' " (*LU* 130–131). Thus the opposition of physical space to symbolic space loses its prior basis. At best, it can be treated as a convention, not only because it constitutes a part of literary fiction; more important, this ambivalence reflects a major characteristic of the human imagination. The question of whether Milosz believes that the *apokatastasis* will actually occur also seems irrelevant. Like Blake, he would no doubt answer that it is real because it has been imagined.

Perhaps, then, Milosz's eschatology belongs to his own personal religious convictions, on one hand, and is a kind of mythic creation, on the other. Embracing both religious belief and literature, it is marked by a unique obliqueness, incompleteness, and ontological vagueness. It maintains the tradition of the sacral origins of signs and symbols it uses; but at the same time this sacred quality is weakened in comparison with literary fiction. Yet even that explanation is not completely satisfactory. Did not other mythic creations from different sources than those used by Milosz produce their own visionaries? Milosz himself thinks that "Blake was, if it's possible to say it this way, an anthropological poet because he filled the entire universe with his *human* myth" (*CS* 33; italics added). If Swedenborg and Oscar Milosz seem to do the same, what, in Czeslaw Milosz's view, distinguishes them?

Without doubt, Swedenborg and Oscar Milosz believed in the seriousness of their missions and in their message as a revelation addressed—over the heads of their contemporaries—to future generations. They acted in the tradition of the romantics. Milosz questions the status of the contemporary prophet through the very prophecy he utters and the speech by which he expresses it. For Milosz, the writings of mystic visionaries are primarily intriguing documents of the adventures of the imagination, a source of anthropological reflection and poetic inspiration. They tell of hope in a final salvation after ultimate destruction, and they show once again the futile effort to penetrate the very real but inexpressible realm of the transcendental. Probably more important, however, is that these thinkers, enriching and developing Christian eschatology, find a refuge from the feeling of meaninglessness and disinheritance. Herein lies the profound concealed meaning of their writings, a message that not everyone is able to understand. Since the metaphysical basis of values that appear in history is not visible or accessible, the major value becomes our very striving for them, the nostalgia for values. Blinded by the cruelty and absurdity of history, just the possibility of giving history some eternal sense seems to justify our striving.

The discrepancy between the convictions that Milosz expresses in his poetry and those expressed in his prose is perhaps not as crucial as it seemed at the outset of this discussion. In his youth Milosz foresaw world catastrophe as inevitable; in his later years he now speaks of it as possible or probable. The conditional mood has replaced the indicative, and in "From the Rising of the Sun" the catastrophic-eschatological theme is hardly present. Milosz may have exhausted it, or it may have lost meaning for him. Drawing extensively on the writings of the three mystics Blake, Swedenborg, and Oscar Milosz, referring to the Bible, the Cabala, alchemy, and twentieth-century physics, finding unexpected possibilities in the obsolete law of ordinary analogy and in the multilayered concrete, Milosz's poetry perhaps is a sign and intimation of another kind of language, which one day will express a more human vision of the universe. A defense of the Christian imagination with a particular emphasis on its anthropocentric foundation, this language would be not only a remedy for historiosophical pessimism but also a way to hasten the coming of that happier day for mankind. Or, at least, it would point in that direction.

4

In the "Interhuman Church"

If man represents merely a fleeting moment in the face of nature, history, and eternity, should he not seek security in those near to him, who, like him, are lonely and condemned? This ancient question seems to take on particular relevance and intensity in contemporary philosophical reflection, especially in its antinaturalistic orientation, to which Milosz, like Gombrowicz, has many links.[1]

In the worldview of Gombrowicz, however, a dilemma emerges in this regard, which Milosz formulates as follows: "If we have nothing but ourselves, human beings, nothing other than our acutely isolated species, then out of interaction with one another let us try to bring to life some goodness or even divinity. Nevertheless, what is human is a joke, and in any case theatrical, subject to the rules of acting."[2] In other words, Gombrowicz's "interhuman church" is an institution both worthy of respect, since it heroically rejects the otherness of nature that is everywhere around it, and suspect and untrustworthy, since it arises from sometimes egotistical motives, whisperings of the unconscious, and caprices of human nature. The basis of this "church" is not a collection of commonly held moral principles but the rapacious desire to dominate, which camouflages itself in various, often noble, forms. In addition, the manner of its realization is determined in advance by a system of behavior considered essential by society, which always deforms the individual. In this quadrille of appearances, good and evil are lost, and that purely human "divinity" wears the jester's cap.

Although Milosz basically accepts and shares Gombrowicz's antinaturalistic attitude, he has hit on the flaw in Gombrowicz's views. He points out that the implications contained in the concept of the "interhuman church" are dangerous, even disastrous. The concept clearly subverts the independence of the individual and the timeless significance of moral laws which that individual transmits. Milosz points out that "for centuries civilization has sustained itself through a belief in the uniqueness of the individual human soul as the source of our decisions; through the belief that the soul's good or evil intention would tip the scale on the Day of Judgment" (*LU* 42). In this perspective it is truly difficult to defend Gombrowicz's point of view because the uniqueness and particularity of persons is, according to him, lost in the process of interaction, and the decisions made by individuals are not accountable to an ethical code. In a word, Gombrowicz is only a step away from relativism and nihilism. Hence Milosz concludes: "Alas, Gombrowicz's 'interhuman church' seems an illustration of the theory of those behaviorists who proclaim the model society to be one of absolute slavery—a state that can be achieved when human animals, those statistical units making up the genus Homo, become so trained as to look upon slavery as freedom perfected" (*LU* 43).

Gombrowicz himself would certainly resent such a description, maintaining that he constantly struggles for nothing but freedom of choice, the free and spontaneous gesture with which man shakes off ossified forms and reveals their deepest essence—immaturity, inferiority, youth, and authenticity. Still, this sphere of freedom is accessible only to the writer and not to the characters created by him.

I have devoted some attention to this debate because it concerns problems that continually disturb Milosz and constitute an extremely important component of his poetic anthropology. Perhaps only a dialogue with so formidable an adversary as Gombrowicz allowed Milosz to conceptualize and clarify his own distinct position. It is not difficult to show that the countless forms that the individual's entanglements with the collective take—entanglements summed up especially in the conflict between freedom and necessity, between norms imposed on him and those considered his own, between social or national obligations and the desire for independence, between art and ethics—all are the object of Milosz's careful attention. But Milosz differs considerably from Gombrowicz both in the way he presents those conflicts and in the solutions he proposes.

THE INDIVIDUAL WITHIN THE FAMILY
AND SOCIAL MILIEU

For a picture of the relationships in Milosz's "interhuman church" one should begin with a description of his attitude toward those who are closest. Milosz himself says that this issue conceals the main source of the differences between himself and Gombrowicz: "If it hadn't been for our similar fates . . . no one would have even thought to compare Gombrowicz and me. If the comparison is to be made, the key lies in our different attitudes to our background—our family home, parents, relatives, and so on." (*CCM* 285). Appreciating the significance of this admission, Jerzy Jarzębski notes that Milosz

> throughout his entire life has, as it were, rebuilt his family home that was lost so early, and this reconstruction may have either a literal dimension (as in "The World" or *The Issa Valley*) or a metaphoric dimension, where the idea of family absorbs entire cultural heritages common to many nations (note, for example, the symbolic title *Native Realm*). It is the reverse with Gombrowicz: the family emerges as an insatiable demon in the face of which the hero initially loses; he is unable to avoid taking on the stereotypical role that family existence thrusts on him. Almost all Gombrowicz's works tell of the destruction of the family, of its deliberate dismantling.[3]

This comparison, though undoubtedly accurate in its basic outline, requires one more element to be complete. Gombrowicz's gesture, as Jarzębski demonstrates in his book, is not confined to revolt and negation. It also contains the promise, continually coming to ruin and then recaptured, of basing interhuman relationships on authenticity and freedom. Similarly, Milosz not only rebuilds his home but also in the course of this reconstruction again and again destroys or contradicts its existence. In other words, he searches for it and longs for it but does not completely believe in the possibility of its return. As Jarzębski puts it, "For him, the family is the center of world order."[4] But it is precisely this image of family that is lacking in his poems. "The World" is an exception, but it is a consciously idealized vision, a shape of reality—and thus also of home—as it *should* be, presented, moreover, with a question mark. Not by chance do scenes of children leaving home recur in his other poems, as well as the impossibility of transmitting one's parental experiences or the fragility of the family circle in the face of the enemy.

Even in the autobiographical "Lessons" (*CP* 121; "Nauki," 1957) the home is surrounded with mines laid by various threatening forces:

> Since that moment when in a house with low eaves
> A doctor from the town cut the navel-string
> And pears dotted with white mildew
> Reposed in their nests of luxuriant weeds,
> I have been in the hands of humans. They could have strangled

My first scream, squeezed with a giant hand
The defenseless throat that aroused their tenderness.

From them I received the names of plants and birds,
I lived in their country that was not too barren,
Not too cultivated, with a field, a meadow,
And water in a boat moored behind a shed.

Their lessons met, it is true, with a barrier
Deep in myself and my will was dark,
Not very compliant with their intents or mine.
Others, whom I did not know or knew only by name
Were pacing in me and I, terrified,
Heard, in myself, locked creaky rooms
That one should not peep into through a keyhole.
They did not mean much to me—Kazimir, Hrehory
Or Emilia or Margareta.
But I had to reenact all by myself
Every flaw and sin of theirs. This humiliated me.
So that I wanted to shout: you are to blame
For my not being what I want and being what I am.

Sunlight would fall in my book upon Original Sin.
And more than once, when noon was humming in the grass
I would imagine the two of them, with my guilt,
Trampling a wasp beneath the apple tree in Eden.

Od tamtej chwili, kiedy w domu o niskich okapach
Doktór z miasteczka przeciął pępowinę
A pleniły się w sadach szczawie i lebiody,
Gniazda dla kropkowanych białą pleśnią gruszek,
Byłem już w rękach ludzi. Mogli przecie zdławić
Mój krzyk pierwszy, nacisnąć swoją wielką dłonią
Gardło bezbronne, budzące ich czułość.
Od nich przejąłem nazwy ptaków i owoców,
W ich kraju zamieszkałem, nie zanadto dzikim,
Nie zanadto uprawnym, z łąką, ornym polem
I wodą na dnie czółna w gąszczu za stolarnią.

Ich nauki znalazły co prawda granicę
We mnie samym, a wola moja była ciemna,
Mało posłuszna moim albo ich zamiarom.
Inni, których nie znałem, czy tylko z imienia,
Stąpali we mnie i ja, przerażony,
Słyszałem w sobie skrzypiące pokoje
Dokąd się nie zagląda przez dziurkę od klucza.
Nic nie znaczyli dla mnie Kaźmierz ni Hrehory
Ani Emilia ani Margareta.

Ale każdą ich skazę i każde kalectwo
Musiałem sam powtórzyć. To mnie poniżało.
Że gotów byłbym krzyczeć: Wy, odpowiedzialni,
Przez was nie mogę zostać kim chcę, tylko sobą.

Słonce padało w książce na grzech pierworodny.
I nieraz, kiedy huczy w trawach popołudnie,
Wyobrażałem sobie dwoje, z moją winą,
Jak depczą osę pod rajską jablonią.

The narrator says that from birth he was "in the hands of humans" who shaped his habits, value system, customs, and speech. He then adds: "They could have strangled / My first scream, squeezed with a giant hand / The defenseless throat." The danger does not arise only from the possibility of death (here the exteriorization of the feeling of danger is, considering the given surroundings, emphatic). The pressure of the past remains equally important. The narrator goes on to argue that man pays a high price for his bond with the entire human family. One inherits both ancient values and past errors, the faults and crimes of those to whom one owes everything. This inheritance is not only genetic but, more important, cultural. One must cope with the difficult heritage of the physical and intellectual defects of one's forebears, even those distant and unknown (signaled in the poem by archaic forms for the names of relatives), as well as undertake for oneself a dialogue with the individual and collective historical past. This dialogue inclines one to reconsider both the achievements of tradition and one's personal choices. What does it matter if those choices are to a great degree limited and freedom of self-realization is hampered by the very presence of that heritage in relation to which one must somehow define oneself? One cannot, therefore, be whom one wants, shaping one's own "I" by a totally unencumbered act of will, even though it is necessary to be oneself—that is, determined by birthplace, social origins, cultural allegiance, and language. It may be true, Milosz says, that we are not entirely homeless since besides our own personal home we have the home of an entire culture; but this home does not completely belong to us, and some of its rooms are haunted.

The family seat is usually associated both with a safe haven and with stability, continuity, attachment to a particular place. We would search in vain for those elements in Milosz's poetry. Instead, like a persistent refrain, the motif of independence and rootlessness returns.

Apart from his subsequent fate as a wandering émigré, this motif may have its source in his early childhood experiences connected, as he describes in *Native Realm,* with continual traveling, a constant change of place and surroundings. For someone who writes that "home was often a covered wagon, sometimes an army railroad car with a samovar on the floor, which used to tip over when the train started up suddenly" (*NR* 41), it is not easy to include stability in the concept of home. One might say that those experiences were impressed on Milosz's consciousness in the form of a paradigm of his own existential situation. The result is statements like, "Such a lack of stability, the unconscious feeling that everything is temporary, cannot but affect, it seems to me, our mature judgments" and (*NR* 41). Other reflections in later chapters show how this lack of stability entered the paradigm of Milosz's own situation.

In his poem "Toast," which can serve as a kind of prolegomenon to *The Issa Valley* and *Native Realm,* Milosz hypothesizes that just as his childhood travels shaped his awareness of his personal existential situation as a model, so his relation to his classmates became a kind of protomodel for his attitude toward all groups. This attitude consists of an aversion to the herd instinct and imitation of commonly accepted models, a defense of the independence of his own opinions, and a proud individualism coupled with an awareness of separation from the group and an experience of isolation and otherness. To the reluctance of his classmates to accept what was new, then exemplified by the art of Picasso, the young Milosz opposes serious interest in poetry and contemporary art. To their seeming maturity, permeated with conformity and unreflective repetition of ready-made schemas, he opposes his own searching—even at the cost of confusion and error, all the more inevitable because he had been out on his own from early youth. Finally, to their attachment to gentry traditions that went hand in hand with nationalism he opposes an aversion to the country estate and to idolatrous worship of the Polish nation and its historical past. At work beneath all these manifestations is a compensatory mechanism he openly reveals, though not without some self-irony. The feeling of being rejected probably inclined him to seek out allies all his life among those who, like himself, were outsiders. This model helps us interpret Milosz's school and university friendships, his participation in the Żagary group of poets, and his attraction toward the political orientation represented by Dwight Macdonald. This same model also helps explain his recognition of an intellectual debt to Oscar Milosz, Simone Weil, and Lev Shestov.

THE INDIVIDUAL WITHIN THE NATION

Milosz, whose poems belong without a doubt to the canon of Polish national poetry, openly admits that he is "allergic to 'Polishness' " (*PO* 82). He asks himself whether "one can be faithful to Polish literature, love it, serve it, and at the same time exhibit an almost national indifference" (*PO* 81). Milosz also castigates Poles no less than did the Polish romantic poets, Wyspiański, or Witkiewicz—certainly not an indication of indifference. The role of national bard is unpleasant for Milosz, yet he does not cease to warn, teach, or prophesy. He grumbles about literature in the service of the national cause but writes a poem entitled "To Lech Wałęsa" ("Do Lecha Wałęsa," 1982).

Leading into the very heart of this extraordinarily complex problem of Milosz and Polishness is the poet's own terse statement: "I was not born in Poland, I was not raised in Poland, I do not live in Poland, but I write in Polish" (*PO* 80). In other words, although his birthplace, his models developed in childhood and youth, and his emigration all distance him from Poland, Polish culture, together with its entire complement of myths, stereotypes, and symbols assimilated through the language he speaks have powerfully and permanently shaped his sensibility. I note these basic facts here to illustrate that Milosz belongs to an era that was already dying out in the first decades of the twentieth century. He can be considered one of the last citizens of the old Polish Commonwealth. He grew up in a milieu for which the atmosphere of the nineteenth century and the traditions of the Grand Duchy of Lithuania were still very much alive. A multicultural situation was commonplace, and Milosz acquired a strong aversion to all varieties of chauvinism and nationalism, especially since these tendencies in Europe as well as Poland sometimes appeared in the 1930s in brutal forms. In the Wilno area the proximity of Lithuanian, Jewish, and Belorussian elements denied Polish culture preeminence, inclined Milosz to evaluate it in the context of other cultures, and influenced his unique linguistic sensitivity. Milosz encountered a somewhat similar situation, but on a larger scale, when he emigrated—on the one hand, the pressure of a foreign environment, and on the other, the obstinate cultivation of Polish poetry, pervaded by the fear of being forced into inferiority, into being second-rate. Taken together, these factors foster a constant tension in him between love and hate, attachment and aversion, compassion and indifference.

When accused of Lithuanian snobbism, Milosz responds that for him Lithuania is a "metaphor for 'coming from the outside,' for some otherness and distance that allows otherness" (*PO* 81).[5] This distance illustrates above all that a culture once rich and universal has, as a result of unfavorable historical circumstances, undergone a gradual contraction and degradation, revolving obsessively around the same ideas. As proof, literature becomes dominated by the "martyrial-messianic reflex" (*PO* 86), an inferiority complex seeking compensation in showing off the national martyrdom, a "claim neither comprehensible nor attractive" (*PO* 86). The sources of these attitudes go deeper than are ordinarily thought and extend, as Milosz perceptively observes, beyond romanticism: "The whole of Polish culture—a basically gentry, bucolic, and social culture—effectively endeavored to avoid the existence of cruelty. Thus it was a particular shock when it had to encounter cruelty in its political forms coming from the outside (the Russians and the Germans)" (*PO* 89). The conflict between remaining faithful to national tradition and achieving a universality becomes even more acute for anyone writing in Polish.

The constant struggle with Polishness has yet another, by no means trivial, aspect for Milosz. He admits that

> all my books testify to my conflict with the national ethos, which even for me remains something mysterious, painful, and to this day inexplicable. And deep down I am still not certain but that this quarrel was not a rationalization of my conflict with the human community at large, that my aversion mixed with sympathetic attachment was not always leavened with a sense of guilt. For surely the ideal to which I have always aspired, then as now, is membership in a human community, of the sort where communion with others comes of a shared set of values and an emotional closeness.
>
> (*LU* 259–260)

Here, too, just as with his relation to his social milieu, a dialectic of opposing tendencies appears: a need for participation is opposed by a drive toward separateness; involvement, by a nostalgia for total freedom; acceptance, by distance. One tendency is supported by a simple, heartfelt solidarity, the other by a fear of loss of the individual "I."

Milosz seems to ask whether that fear is not a mask for egoism and a form of unwarranted haughtiness. In addition, moral qualms relentlessly accompany his indecision: an "aversion mixed with sympathetic attachment" is connected with "a sense of guilt."

We may look to Milosz's poetry for some kind of clear and faithful record of those struggles. His prewar poems basically pass over the problem of nationalism. Moreover, his attention is not so much directed toward manifestations of nationalism as toward economic exploitation, poverty, and social injustice. But a consciousness of isolation and a fear of dissolving into the mass stands in the way of his revolutionary zeal. His "A Poem on Frozen Time" is a particularly interesting document of his inner struggles as a young man. The hero of the poem is seemingly immobilized by mutually neutralizing contradictions. Combined with terror at the absurdity of existence, social protest leads him to accept revolutionary slogans that promise a fundamental rebuilding of the world. But enthusiasm is quickly mired down in revulsion and unbelief. A sense of complicity accompanies the hero's expressions of condemnation, while political pragmatism is undermined by his awareness that the laws of history are implacable and by a fear of the bloody price to be paid for upheaval. The hero persistently desires to drown out his inner dilemma with the rhythm of the joyous march into the future, but he senses his own uniqueness and secretly despises others.

Distance from the collective clearly increases in Milosz's poetry written immediately after the war, in the form of a national appraisal that in its harsh relentlessness is equal to that of the romantics. Milosz's formula in "On a Certain Book" ("Na pewną książkę," 1943–1944) sounds almost like an echo of the romantic poets:

> Miserable are good-tempered nations that take but half a step in their
>   thought
> Yet know no limits in spilling their own blood.

> Nieszczęsne narody łagodne, które w myślach stawiają pół kroku,
> A za to granic nie znają w szafowaniu krwią.

Lines like the following from "A Nation" ("Naród," 1945) could have been penned by Juliusz Słowacki—a twentieth-century version of his definition of the Polish national character as "an angelic soul in a coarse skull":

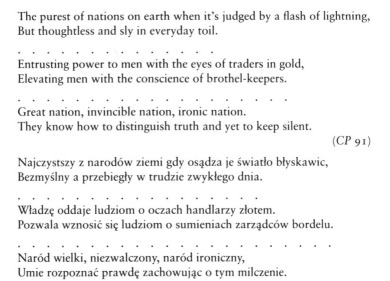

The purest of nations on earth when it's judged by a flash of lightning,
But thoughtless and sly in everyday toil.

. . . .

Entrusting power to men with the eyes of traders in gold,
Elevating men with the conscience of brothel-keepers.

. . . .

Great nation, invincible nation, ironic nation.
They know how to distinguish truth and yet to keep silent.

(CP 91)

Najczystszy z narodów ziemi gdy osądza je światło błyskawic,
Bezmyślny a przebiegły w trudzie zwykłego dnia.

. . . .

Władzę oddaje ludziom o oczach handlarzy złotem.
Pozwala wznosić się ludziom o sumieniach zarządców bordelu.

. . . .

Naród wielki, niezwalczony, naród ironiczny,
Umie rozpoznać prawdę zachowując o tym milczenie.

Once again the description of national characteristics is constructed on
oppositions: capability of heroic outburst exists alongside ordinary
foolishness; faith in a metaphysical world order does not interfere with
a lack of compassion for the weak; honor and love of the law go hand
in hand with a low level of political sophistication. It is difficult to
determine precisely where the angelic quality and the coarseness lie
since the former social and class structures were destroyed after World
War II. That is why Mickiewicz's ghost now visits the world of the
subculture, the world of the people who "camp on the marketplaces"
and "deal in old door handles stolen from ruins." The date and place
of the poem's composition—Kraków, 1945—are clearly important,
and we should not overlook the almost journalistic recording of phenomena observed by Milosz at the time. Still, the poem is at its most
powerful in generalization signaled by the use of synecdoche (*totum
pro partes*). In this connection, we should note the perceptivity with
which Milosz recorded the first effects of the revolutionary upheaval:
the total declassing and pauperizing of society (partly as a result of the
war) is accompanied by a fluidity of all norms and a faltering of the
criteria needed for value judgments. What was positive quickly turns
into its opposite: cunning enables one to survive, certainly, but it also
teaches ruthlessness; the spilling of blood was unavoidable, but the

public slaughter is really a futile offering; everyone knows that jokes and irony fend off despair, but they are also a convenient alibi for passivity.

The clear irony in the text directed as much against the subject as against the object indicates conflicting attachments. This reading is confirmed by the lone hero who appears at the end, the "man of that nation" ("mężczyzna tego narodu") who "repeats words of hope, always, till now, in vain" ("powtarza słowa nadziei zawsze dotychczas daremne"). It is hard to say whether the "man of that nation" is a mask for the author: since the "he" inevitably fades, we must be cautious of simplistic identification.

In different ways, then, Milosz tries to express the hard-to-grasp instability of his national feelings that constantly oscillate between two poles, the ambivalence of his attitudes, and the dialectic of points of view that are contradictory in their relation to society. Thus in "Treatise on Morals" scoffing is the counterpoint to solicitous moralizing—scoffing at Polish provincialism, at narrow patriotism as manifested in the mindless cult of military tradition, at attachment to the crude idyll of the ancient Slavs, at pride in the "Sarmatian animus," and at cheap sentimentalism.

Milosz's *Separate Notebooks* also reveal his tendency to locate his struggle with Polishness in twentieth-century spatial time while simultaneously reaching back into the past. Now the speaker is no longer just a Pole but also a Slav, not a citizen of the land between the Oder and Vistula rivers but an inhabitant of East Central Europe:

> In the shadow of the Empire, in Old Slavonic long-johns,
> You better learn to like your shame because it will stay with you.
> It won't go away even if you change your country and your name.
> The dolorous shame of failure. Shame of the muttony heart.
> Of fawning eagerness. Of clever pretending.
>
> (CP 362–363)

> W cieniu imperium, z kurami, w gaciach prasłowiańskich,
> Naucz się lubić swój wstyd, bo zawsze będzie przy tobie,
> I nie odstąpi ciebie, choćbyś zmienił kraj i nazwisko.
> Twój wstyd niewydarzenia. Miękkiej sercowiny.
> Skwapliwej uniżonosci. Zmyślnego udania.
>
> (SN 50)

Over centuries empires came and went on these territories of East Central Europe. Even today the inhabitants of these lands labor under their implacable shadow. But other expressions allow us to discern familiar outlines in this description even though the name of the country is never given: the allusion to a temporary existence that cannot put down deeper roots since it is burdened with historical memory of the fragility and impermanence of all objects and emotional ties ("You sit in a shabby house, putting things off until spring. / No flowers in the garden—they would be trampled anyway"; "W bylejakim siedzisz domu, aby do wiosny. / Kwiatów nie ma w ogrodzie, bo i tak stratują"); the allusion to the primitivism and low level of development of civilization, apparent even in the kitchen ("You eat lazy pancakes, the soupy dessert called 'Nothing-served-cold' "; "Pierogi jesz leniwe, zupę nic na zimno"); and the awareness of humiliation and hatred toward outsiders. Milosz seems to say that although history has not spared this land painful experiences, historical fatalism can also be sealed by passive acceptance of the status quo. He rebukes those who quietly accepted their situation. Milosz suggests that it is difficult to imagine, however, a change in the geopolitical situation that perpetuates these attitudes, and there is no way to erase the resentment that wounds individual and collective memory.

Irony becomes an expression of both the impossibility of reconciling these contradictions and helpless dissent, but it does not resolve the dilemma. In *The Separate Notebooks* the ironic "you" hits home all the more painfully because it is addressed as much to Milosz's fellow countrymen as to the subject himself. To use an old-fashioned expression, the dialogue centers around the poet's soul. In his attempt at self-reflection and bitter self-education he states, "Learn to love your shame."

Consequently, Milosz remains a constant "critical patriot." According to Stanisław Barańczak, "[Milosz's] vision of national questions does justice to both the dark and light sides of our history and of our collective character by emphasizing the profound contradictions created by the pressure of historical catastrophes."[6] It should be added that these contradictions are a part of the personality of the poet, who is constantly grappling with the Pole residing in himself. Here lies probably the most sensitive nerve connecting Milosz with the collective. At the same time the pressure of romantic tradition intensifies the burden of an accursed inheritance of national myths combined with recent historical experience. Milosz confesses, "I revolted against romanticism at times, but when Mickiewicz, Słowacki, and Norwid are read when one is very young, there is no remedy—they remain" (*PO* 83). Milosz's debate with the nation and with Polishness will be unavoidably and permanently woven into historical and literary contexts. Deeply private and most painfully experienced, it echoes a tone well-known in Polish literature. But he reveals and intensifies the basic contradiction in the romantic consciousness of which Mickiewicz was not aware when he wrote in Polish the words "Lithuania, my homeland." One of the last citizens of the old Polish Commonwealth has presented and analyzed the uniqueness of his national-cultural status.

THE INDIVIDUAL WITHIN HUMANKIND

Milosz's relation to humanity is also marked by the dialectic between involvement and isolation. The lines here are fluid and blurred because at times, as I have indicated, when speaking about his own generation or nation, Milosz also has in mind the human community in general. The opposite is true as well: when he describes the collective, it may signify the generation or the nation. However, the clear posing of the problem of the individual versus the species *Homo sapiens* or all men who now live on earth constitutes a separate subject in Milosz's poetry.

Reiterating declarations of solidarity with all humanity is perhaps an expression of the émigré poet's search for some community in which he would feel less isolated, his own generation having scattered throughout the world and links with his homeland having become tenuous. The universal conception of Milosz's poetry is as important as the autobiographical basis of the poems—always crucial but not fully explanatory—particularly since here too it takes up established romantic models and reinterprets them in an original way. The basic difference, obviously, is that Milosz's hero wants to identify himself with humankind, not with his own nation. This desire considerably expands and multiplies the possibilities of the hero. He can secure strong support in his struggles with a neutral and enduring nature. He can cross barriers of both time and space, such as the barrier between life and death:

Borne by an inscrutable power, one century gone, I heard, beating
in darkness, the heart of the dead and the living.
("With Trumpets and Zithers," CP 198)

Niepojęta moc mnie nosiła, jedno stulecie minęło, usłyszałem bijące
w ciemności serce umarłych i żywych.

He may learn humility:

I was getting rid of my faith so as not to be better than men and
women who are certain only of their unknowing.
("With Trumpets and Zithers," CP 202)

Pozbywałem się wiary żeby nie być lepszym od mężczyn i kobiet
pewnych tylko swojej niewiedzy.

The poems "On the Shore" ("Na brzegu," 1967) and "Anybody"
("Ktokolwiek," 1961) also illustrate the dangers hidden in identification with humankind. On the beach the narrator says:

The insufficient essence was weakening, neither I nor she nor he,
neither a man nor a woman, only nakedness, nothing is mine,
everything is ours.
("On the Shore")

Słabła istność niedostateczna, ani ja, ona, on, ani mężczyzna, kobieta,
nagość tylko, nic nie moje, nasze.

Subject to the law of large numbers, one naked body loses it separateness and becomes like all others; the human mass obliterates distinctions or even cancels out distinctions and differences. Not only does
the individual disappear in the human mass, but the gender difference
ceases to have any significance. "Physiological humanity clinging to
itself resembles a sort of coral reef," wrote Milosz in *Visions from San
Francisco Bay* (101). It is difficult to defend the individual when,
submerged in an anonymous crowd, the individual loses specificity.
Maintaining faith in the immortal soul, the sign of the unique and
unrepeatable *individuum*, is impossible if it is only an element in an
innumerable collective. It would be easy, Milosz says in "Anybody," to
believe in the uniqueness of the human person, in his or her "royal
crown" ("królewska korona"), if the physical similarity of all people
"wherever they are" ("gdziekolwiek są") did not shock the imagina-

tion "in one piercing flash" ("w jednym przebijającym błysku") and if, stripped of intimacy and uniqueness, they did not hear indivisible life throbbing individually ("nie słyszeli jak pulsuje podzielne niepodzielne życie"):

> And if not, instead of me, naked before the mirror, touching every spot
> on a common body,
> every one, she, he were staring, caught between the province "is" and
> the province "is not".
>
> ("Anybody")

> I gdyby nago przed lustrem, dotykając każdej części powszechnego
> ciała,
> Nie patrzył zamiast mnie ktokolwiek, ona, on między prowincją jest i
> prowincją nie jest.

Here again Gombrowicz comes to mind. Like Milosz, he is sensitive to the human element, and he perceptively observed that "up until now, man has never taken on the problem of his own numbers. These numbers have not yet fully penetrated his mind. . . . Adam's lonely self-awareness is alive in us. Our philosophy is the philosophy of Adam. Our art is Adam's art." Our morality, too, is Adam's. How, asks Gombrowicz, can I be compassionate toward my sick servant, address her as "O one and only Eve," when I am overcome with an "Olympian indifference, stemming from the interchangeability of one woman with another?" Gombrowicz finds it impossible to comprehend the pain of all humanity; instead pain produces the opposite reaction, evoking exasperating statements such as "suffering in such quantities bores me" and "pity in such numbers amuses me." Not only is it a question here of the well-known and often described phenomenon of our contemporary dulling of ethical sensitivity, primarily the result of our acceptance of genocide. Nor is it a question of the natural limitations of the human psyche, which can comprehend with real and authentic feeling the suffering of only a single man or a small group of people but is lost when confronted with the suffering of millions. Nor, as Gombrowicz emphatically states, is it a question of the need for greater concern with the human element in the masses: "It is not enough for me that Homer or Zola will extol and describe the masses, or that Marx will analyze them; I would like something to appear in their own voice so that it could be said that one person was one of thousands and another person one of millions. I would like to see them penetrated by the concept of number to their very root."[7] In other words, the introduction and gradual interiorization of the numerical factor in humanist reflection forces us to verify the traditional idea of human nature.

Since the birth of Western culture the foundation of our idea of human nature has been an obvious fact that is now increasingly losing significance—the sovereignty of the individual, with his own world of imagination, thoughts, and feelings. Some Adam, someone unrepeatable, unique, and set apart by name, addresses some equally unique Eve. The root of this concept of human nature lies in religion: a child of God cannot be anonymous, a vague someone, a number in some general reckoning. On the contrary, raised above other beings, marked with the charisma of immortality, and endowed with the love of the Creator, he is the center of the universe. Traditionally the numerical factor bore a completely different meaning since throughout centuries all humanity was a collection of equal persons, each destined for salvation. This foundation was inherited and long maintained by philosophy and art, which measured their own development by the achievements of individuals. Morality too, although undergoing a gradual laicization, had been placed before the tribunal of the sovereign "I" until the time when the death of man was proclaimed.

Transferring this argument to the realm of ontology Milosz shows that the twentieth-century Everyman becomes, simply, No One. He points out that thought about the individual in numerical categories deprives the individual of his ontic essence and thrusts him into a realm of vague obliquity between existence and nonexistence. In both the poems cited, the sign of interchangeability of the *individuum* is the serial enumeration of personal pronouns, which, set alongside one another in a relation of equality, mutually cancel one another out. In "Anybody" the fluidity of the substance of human nature matches the vagueness of the subject, simultaneously individual and collective, concrete (he touches his body in front of the mirror) and abstract (the body is common). This corporeality is extremely important here and imparts a painful tangibility to an abstract problem. Whereas Gombrowicz approached this question through an analysis of the "interhuman" acted out in the emotional sphere, Milosz explains it through observation of the material, biological side of human nature.

The denial of a name and the objectification of the individual is also expressed in the language of the body: "A naked heel stepped across his forehead and no one knows whose look deprived his face of its name" ("Goła pięta przestąpiła jego czoło i wzrok nie wiadomo czyj odebrał twarzy imię"). If we recall the significance that the bestowal of a name has had in even the most primitive cults and religions, the disturbing import of this line becomes clearer. In addition, however, both "Anybody" and "On the Shore" contain positive meanings. They argue that the new, so painfully conscious, sense of the unity of the human species on a planetary scale enables us to control our increasing awareness of our huge numbers and inclines us to defend the dignity of the individual person, a defense all the more essential since the importance of the individual is more threatened. The use of the conditional mood in "Anybody" expresses nostalgia for what has been lost, the half-magical, half-religious (hence the royal crown and the "incantations of fairies at a cradle," "inkantacje wróżek nad kołyską"), and consequently naive anthropocentric vision of the universe, as well as an awareness of its incompatibility with contemporary knowledge of man and the need to return to such a vision in a new form.

In summary, how—aside from all these drawbacks—can one anchor oneself in a community? How can one affirm one's own self as subject and avoid being reified by others? According to Milosz, the solution is ritual, and he emphasizes its role particularly in his poetry of the 1970s and 1980s. When in "From the Rising of the Sun" Milosz writes, "And now we are joined in a ritual" ("A teraz jesteśmy złączeni w obrzędzie"), he doubtless has in mind all those who throughout the centuries are united in their attachment to the Lauda district, who exist in mythic space, in a reality free of the flow of time.

Milosz returns to a similar theme in "Consciousness" ("Świadomość"), tracing a journey to the sources (surely his own) of personality. Here he unveils his earliest recollected, most elementary, and not yet fully conscious encounter with the sacred:

> Evening devotions of the household in May,
> Litanies to the Maiden,
> Mother of the Creator.
>
> (CP 421)

> Majowe dla domowników i czeladzi,
> Litanie do Panny Możnej,
> Matki Stworzyciela.

Here is participation in ritual in which the religious is harmoniously entwined with the familial and the social. When recalled many years later, such attempts to approach the incomprehensible may be humorous in their awkward helplessness. However, the "regimental brasses / On which the moustachioed ones blew for the Elevation" ("trąby, w które wąsaci dmą na podniesienie") and the "musket volleys on Easter Saturday night" ("palba muszkietów na Rezurekcję w nocy") are not only relics of archaic Lithuanian culture but also events that nurtured in Milosz the conviction for the rest of his life that adoration of the Godhead fulfilled a series of essential functions. "If man is a Homo ritualis, then ritual, which takes us into the realm of the sacred, is not a value to be easily dismissed" (*LU* 261). Building a bridge to transcendence, ritual is as much an expression of human helplessness before the mystery of existence as a testimony to a power stronger than time. Ritual frees man from historical conditions without isolating him from the flow of history, since one of the basic characteristics of ritual is the search for a metaphysical sanction of existence. It allows man to avoid the trap of the egotistical "I" by creating the possibility of seeing others as sovereign individuals. At the same time ritual transcends national and generational division and guards against the anonymity of the crowd.

At this point Milosz's thought becomes similar to Gombrowicz's. Gombrowicz also based his reflections on ritual, but with a fundamental difference. For him, ritual appeared only momentarily when even just two persons encountered one another; their behavior and speech created a ritual of compulsion and mutual deformation that disintegrated immediately upon their separation. Some of the rules of this ritual are transmitted by culture, constituting an unbearable burden for the individual who is fighting for his independence. God, to whose presence they appeal, is only an "interhuman" God, a misshapen caricature. Gombrowicz sighs:

> Oh, were I finally able, I myself, to run away—escape the Idea—live forever in this other church created out of people! Were I able to force myself to recognize *such a divinity*—and worry no longer about the absolute and only feel for myself, not high, just barely a meter above my head, such a play of creative forces arising out of us like an attainable Olympus itself—and to worship that. And yet! Never was I able to humble myself—and always between the interhuman God and myself something grotesque arose instead of a prayer.[8]

Milosz would surely never accept such a divinity because the existence of God (even if constantly undermined) constitutes for him a certainty that returns meaning and order to existence. Even when most perplexed, he is not deserted by the faith "that a shining point exists where all lines intersect" and the conviction that when it is negated, "things as well as aspirations [will] turn to dust" (*NR* 87). To grossly simplify the difference between the two writers, we may say that while Gombrowicz does not believe, he longs for faith, whereas Milosz, although he doubts, never ceases to believe.

If Gombrowicz claims a concept of God through the dimension of human interaction, Milosz does so through the dimension of history. Thus, ritual is not a momentary phantasmagoria for him but one of the most important forms of perpetuating culture, enabling it to survive through different human gestures, costumes, and words. Ritual creates an intermediate sphere between our animal nature and our immortal human essence, and it centers symbolic and sign-making activity around itself, making dialogue with the historical past possible. It concentrates everything that emanates from man and at the same time surpasses him. It even purifies sexuality, absorbing it and placing it on a pedestal:

> And erotic: they guess under the fabric
> Dark triangles of hair, are attentive to convexities in silk.
> ("Consciousness," *CP* 423)

> Erotyczni, zagadujący pod tkaniną ciemne trójkąty uwłosień,
> Uważni na wypukłości w płótnie i jedwabiu.

Ultimately ritual is so important to man because

> Faithful to the ritual because it differs so much from their natures,
> And soars above them, above the warmth of mucous membrane,
> On the incomprehensible borderline between mind and flesh.
> (*CP* 423)

> Tylko dlatego wierni obrzędowi, że jest tak różny od nich
> I unosi się nad nimi, nad ich ciepłem śluzowej błony,
> Na niepojętej granicy umysłu i ciała.

5

In the Grip of Eros

Love relations are commonly considered the realm in which human beings express their uniqueness most completely, exposing themselves to countless dangers in the process. In love relationships the psychomachy, or battle between the souls, of two persons reaches its greatest proportions. Here, in this most restricted of "interhuman" spheres, are waged the most passionate struggles between the tendency to meld oneself with others and the wish to preserve one's sovereignty at all costs, between willing submission and restrained desire for domination and total control over another human being, between altruism and egoism. In short, the antinomies typical of relations between the individual and the collective converge, intensifying and becoming all the more painful because they involve the most private and secret regions of the human personality, regions ordinarily inaccessible to those around us.

Love can also focus and arrange the elements of human nature—the animal, the historical, the cultural, and the metaphysical—into various constellations. From the shape of these constellations as recorded in literature, particularly the love lyric, we can decipher the beliefs of a given epoch concerning man, his value system, and his place in the world—beliefs that usually are only dimly reflected or incompletely expressed in other art forms. Consequently, in attempting to understand the eroticism of Milosz's poetry, it would be well to grasp it at its very core, without excessive delving into literary parallels that might obscure its distinctive character.

Unashamedly in the grip of Eros, Milosz's poetic oeuvre contains a substantial group of poems in which the lyric "you" is a woman. Love, however, is not their subject. Dialogue with the feminine interlocutor, whether recalled from the past or taken from the speaker's present surroundings, is always a pretext to debate matters of life and death, in time and space, and discuss historical events or existential, aesthetic, moral, and philosophical problems.

Milosz's poetry outlines the dualistic vision of Eros, woman, and love that is continually present in literature, inherited from ancient myths, and, in a modified form, accepted by Christianity. Milosz, however, rejects the idealistic conception of love and gives priority to the sensual, dark, and instinctual side of love. He wants to extol the beauty of woman, but it is a corporeal beauty that arouses a trembling desire:

> If only I could describe the courtesans of Venice
> As in a loggia they teased a peacock with a twig,
> And out of brocade, the pearls of their belt,
> Set free heavy breasts and the reddish weal
> Where the buttoned dress marked the belly . . .
> ("No More," *CP* 123)

> Gdybym ja mógł weneckie kurtyzany
> Opisać, jak w podwórzu witką drażnią pawia,
> I z tkaniny jedwabnej, z perłowej przepaski
> Wyłuskać ociężałe piersi, czerwonawą
> Pręgę na brzuchu od zapięcia sukni . . .
> ("Nie więcej," 1957)

Desire inescapably objectifies and depersonalizes: the characters of the courtesans disintegrate into random fragments, eluding recognition and concealing their essence. A projection of secret desires, a play of an imagination tossed about by desire, is substituted for real people. A new synthesis is reconstructed by halting time, by simultaneously describing its constituent moments. Thus the courtesans appear both dressed and undressed in the poem; the parts of their bodies get mixed up with pieces of their clothing. Both the fragmentariness of the vision and the appearance on an equal basis of costume and human anatomy increase the reification of the women. What they really look like is hard to make out. The most we can say is who or what they are for the one who observes them. Only his vision of them establishes their transitory existence.

UNDER THE SIGN OF INSATIABILITY

In this context it is not surprising that eroticism in Milosz's work is expressed primarily as the feeling of a lack, a tormenting incompleteness and insatiability. This tone makes itself felt even in his early works. In "Daina" (1934) physical union is the sinful temptation to withdraw from the questions of the world. But the act of love brings no consolation. On the contrary, a momentary intoxication is followed by an unpleasant return to reality. Transports of sensual enchantment end in painful collapse. Love is associated more with suffering than with delight.

Milosz's wartime poems in principle avoid the theme of the erotic, but there too the feminine figure is either an object of aesthetic admiration, of enchantment with the beauty of youth ("The Journey," 1942; "Morning," "Ranek") or an object of desire ("Outskirts," "Songs of Adrian Zieliński"). This is also true of his poetry written after the war. Although the somber tone of eroticism does not change, slight shifts occur in its significance:

> Had I overturned the table what would we have accomplished.
> That act, a non-act, always no more than potential
> Like the attempt to penetrate water, wood, minerals.
> ("Bobo's Metamorphosis," CP 166)

> Gdybym przewrócił stół, co byśmy spełnili.
> Ten akt, nie-akt, bo zawsze potencjalny
> Jak zamiar wejścia w drzewo, w wodę, w minerały.
> ("Gucio zaczarowany," 1962)

In the poems of his youth Milosz depicted the craving for erotic fulfillment as if he were following the handbook of Father Prefect—as a yawning chasm between the luminous land of religious experiences and the dark compulsion and burden of sexual drives. The inevitability of defeat embraced both submission to sensual temptation and the improper, because earthly, object of maximalistic desires. That is why a feeling of guilt shadowed his descriptions of the joys of love. In his mature years Milosz is more intrigued by the existence of an impenetrable wall that grows up between two people in the moment of greatest intimacy. The sexual act becomes a synonym for an attempt (condemned to failure from the beginning) to attain complete union with another person, and through this other person to regain the natural, unconscious link with the universe. In both cases the barrier cannot be crossed, just as a defeat of the resistance of organic and inorganic material, the penetration of "water, wood, minerals," is beyond human capability. Hence insatiability gives way to resignation and a feeling of futility. Significantly, the hero of "Bobo's Metamorphosis" experiences his defeat *before* he decides to take up the game of love.

The essence and expression of the sexual drive also constitute an intriguing problem for Milosz. The transport of desire both unites and divides; it promises the attainment of delight while simultaneously destroying us, since it is anonymous yet omnipresent throughout the history of humanity. Eros is a capricious and inexorable ruler, arising from mysterious biological impulses and functioning beyond rational explanations; always perceptible and displaying its power, it eludes unambiguous definition. One of Milosz's poems seems to identify Eros with libido:

> A coelentera, all pulsating flesh, animal-flower,
> All fire, made up of falling bodies joined by the black pin of sex.
> It breathes in the center of a galaxy, drawing to itself star after star.
> ("With Trumpets and Zithers" CP 202)

> Jamochłonne, z różowego pulsującego mięsa, kwiatozwierzę,
> Z ogni i spadania ciał spiętych po parze czarną szpilką sexu,
> Oddycha w centrum galaktyki przyciągając gwiazdę za gwiazdą.

Such a vision surely could not have arisen without the twentieth-century cult of sex. Yet it is difficult to consider Milosz an adherent of Freud, although Freudian theory can easily be found in his poetry. Milosz's poetic "pansexualism" has a different character than Freud's and is, above all, associated with nature. It is a vision on a cosmic scale, freely combining botanical, animal, and human motifs. Milosz is less troubled by the hidden pressure of the subconscious than by the awareness that the rites of love uniting all of creation may be a deception on the part of a nature faithful to its own procreative purposes. Eros serves the Spirit of Earth for whom

> The trills of a nightingale and our inspiration
> Are merely his prodigal lure,
> So that the law of the species may be fulfilled.
> ("Treatise on Poetry")

> Trele słowika i nasz natchnienie
> Są tylko jego rozrzutną przynętą,
> Żeby spełniło się prawo gatunku.

True, this mysterious impulse returns us to our animal origins; but at the same time inspiration is born, sensitivity to beauty, longing for ideals. Hence it is difficult to identify Eros with the impulse itself in all its brutality.

In one sense Milosz is undoubtedly close to the traditional under-standing of Eros found, for example, in Plato's *Dialogues,* where it simultaneously means an attraction stimulated by what is physically beautiful, an intoxicating madness sent by the gods, an impulse to philosophical reflection on the world and existence, and a power en-abling one to ascend to the vision of what is divine and beautiful. In another sense Milosz's sometimes brutal sexuality and emphasis on the biological origins of Eros distances him from the classical under-standing. For Milosz, it is an ambivalent power—the light and the dark; the creative and the destructive; death and delight; the sensual and the spiritual; the sexual and the aesthetic forge an indissoluble bond in Eros. Consequently, his poetry suffers from an internal contra-diction: in heeding Eros, one achieves beauty only at the price of submersion in sin, evil, and the pride of the grasping ego.

What controls Milosz's Eros? These lines clearly describe its power:

> I was running, as the silks rustled, through room after room without stopping, for I believed in the existence of a last door.
> But the shape of lips and an apple and a flower pinned to a dress were all that one was permitted to know and take away.
> ("City Without a Name," *CP* 191)

> Przez pokoje z szelestem jedwabi, jeden, drugi, dziesiąty, biegłem nie zatrzymany, bo wierzyłem w ostatnie drzwi.
> Ale wykrój ust i jabłko, i kwiat przypięty do sukni było wszystkim, co poznać i wziąć było dano.
> ("Miasto bez imienia," 1968; *SN* 174, 176)

Such signs have been chosen with extraordinary care, and the met-onymic side of Milosz's imagination triumphs here. What is single and individual is constantly supplanted by what is collective and general: the shape of the lips, signifying sensual indulgence, is noted instead of the whole face; an apple appears, a reminder of original sin as well as a sign of nature; instead of a tree, a flower is pinned to the dress—an expression of fashion, a symbol of culture's adaptation of the natural, used instead of the total person. A part regularly stands for the whole. Such lines display a lack of fullness, although a drive toward complete-ness persists:

And one runs and sails through archipelagoes in the hope of finding a
place of immutable possession.

("With Trumpets and Zithers," CP 199)

A biegnie się i żegluje z archipelagu na archipelag w nadziei że jest
gdzieś miejsce niewzruszonego posiadania.

In these poems we find that Milosz's key words for Eros—"know,"
"take," "place of immutable possession"—are above all a metaphor
for cognitive passion, the desire to take in with a single glance all the
variety and richness of reality. A decade later Milosz confirmed the
helplessness and limitation of the senses when faced with a vast and
polymorphous reality, but in a contemplative attitude toward existence he detects a moral ambiguity. Adoration of being is, after all, a
rare privilege; it separates individuals from the collective and renders
them insensitive to its problems. Once again, from behind a moral
reproach emerges what in the poet's mind are unfulfilled obligations to
society. That is why his alter ego hurls this accusation:

A spirit pure and scornfully indifferent,
You wanted to see, to taste, to feel, and nothing more.
For no human purpose.

("From the Rising of the Sun," CP 303)

Duch czysty i wzgardliwie obojętny
Chciałeś widzieć, smakować, doznać i nic więcej.
Dla żadnych ludzkich celów.

In *Visions from San Francisco Bay* Milosz laments:

If it were only possible to give oneself, to trust and be trusted, lose
yourself in the other. But how, if the other, like nature, is elusively
alluring and, though it arouses the desire to be rid of consciousness, will
not be possessed except by conscious violence? The heavenly valley—to
plunge into it, to forget, but no, it is waiting for the hunter's spear, the
plow, the grotesque act of the conqueror, who, when he aspires in his
initial happiness to pass beyond thought and control, is not free to
abandon either thought or control.

(V 27)

In other words, every longing carries within itself an insoluble contradiction: the sexual act shows an elemental desire to give up one's own
subjectivity; it is an escape into a prenatal state and a total immersion in
existence. This desire cannot be satisfied because of the barrier prevent-

ing the union that occurs by means of woman (again identified as nature) and the "not-I." Every single crossing of this boundary must of necessity have recourse to force—something Milosz does not want to accept. Yet any attempt of this kind is doomed to failure from the beginning since self-control paralyzes it: rape is "grotesque" because it is "conscious." Nevertheless, the overwhelming "desire to be rid of consciousness" necessitates continual attempts, a running "through room after room" and sailing "through archipelagoes" in pursuit of a receding vision, a vague sense of completion. Images of regression, of withdrawal into an embryonic stage, express this sense:

> Our own when we are asleep, devoted but to ourselves,
> In love with the scent of perishable flesh,
> With the central warmth under the pubic hair,
> Our knees under our chin, we know there is the All
> And we long in vain. An animal's: that is, our own.
>
> ("Heraclitus," CP 130)

> Swoi we śnie i sobie już tylko oddani,
> Z miłością do zapachu zniszczalnego ciała,
> Do centralnego ciepła pod włosem pubicznym,
> Z kolanami pod brodą, wiemy, że jest Wszystko
> I tęsknimy daremnie. Swoi, więc zwierzęcy.
>
> ("Heraklit," 1960)

A sense of identity, then, can only be achieved in sleep, which partially snuffs out conscious awareness and returns us to our animal state. Still, consciousness—however limited—continues to function. Hence we "know" that it is "the All," the difficult-to-imagine identification with the universe, the state in which the division between the universal and the personal disappears; but we "long in vain."

Longing to return to the womb, the "central warmth under the pubic hair," promises not only a safe and mindless vegetation but the fulfillment of delight as well, that merging with another human being:

> The dream shared at night by all people has inhabitants, hairy animals.
> It is a huge and snug forest and everyone entering it walks on all fours
>   till dawn through the very thick of the tangle.
> Through the wilderness inaccessible to metal objects, all-embracing
>   like a warm and deep river.
>
> . . . .
>
> All are quadrupeds, their thighs rejoice at the badger-bear softness,
>   their rosy tongues lick each other's fur.

. . . .
Nor would the skin guarding a different essence trace any boundary.
("With Trumpets and Zithers," *CP* 201)

W jednym wspólnym śnie ludzi mieszkają włochate zwierzęta.
Jest to las duży i bezpieczny, a każdy kto tam wejdzie czołga się aż do
   rana samym środkiem gęstwiny.
Matecznikiem niedosięgalnym dla przedmiotów z metalu,
   ogarniającym jak ciepła i głęboka rzeka.

. . . .
Wszyscy są czworonożni, ich uda radują się natrafiając na miękkość
   borsuko-niedźwiedzia i różowe języki liżą sierść wzajemnie.

. . . .
Ani pilnująca innej esencji skóra jego czy jej nie postawi granicy.

These images easily translate into the language of depth psychology or
psychoanalysis. Freud would certainly say that the linking of erotic
symbols (forest, tunnel, hairiness, crawling, thickets) with hazy recollection of the primeval womb signified by the warm river is proof that
the libido is directed incestuously toward the mother. For Jung, by
contrast, this passage would reveal the archetypes rooted in the collective unconscious, one of the most important of which is the anima, the
feminine part of the male persona. Fromm would point out that man
flees from consciousness of self into a state of safe ignorance when the
threatening abyss between the "I" and the "not-I" still has not
emerged (hence the line "Nor would the skin guarding a different
essence trace any boundary").

Psychoanalytic imagery is, of course, nothing new in poetry. Poetry
draws on these images, consciously or unconsciously tracing the path
to a lost Paradise of oneness free of cultural bonds, a return to the
primitive. The mother complex is also considered one of the variants
of the agrarian myth, bringing to mind the idea of a return to the
maternal womb of Earth. In the context of this archetypal tendency
Milosz is distinctive in that he is not an uncritical apologist for a so-
called happy unconscious naturalness; in his poetry the desire to withdraw into a primitive or prenatal state is, as I have said, immediately
contradicted and travestied. Milosz does not piously attend to his own
inner self in an effort to imitate in language the inexpressible subconscious or illustrate its voice with symbols from a psychoanalytic textbook. Rather, intuition derived from inner experience corrects prior
knowledge. In his works symbolic images appear in a kind of encoun-

ter with released consciousness and psychoanalytic study. Extraordinarily vivid, striking in their visual and emotional clarity, they shine with meanings that require a knowledge of the theories of depth psychology to be understood.

The association of the sex act with a journey into the land of archetypes presumes certain limitations from the beginning. The first line of the above selection, "The dream shared at night by all people has inhabitants, hairy animals," introduces a distance: the dream is both described and interpreted; it develops in a sequence of images subject to the rules of poetry. It contains as much imitation of psychic processes as cultural fact. It should be understood in two ways: as an attempt to imitate the content of the collective subconscious (hence one dream shared by all) and as a poetic record of scientific research into the subconscious. Imagery imitating the properties and mechanisms of dreams—fluidity and confusion of events, suspension of physical laws, the precarious status of the subject (man, who at the same time is an animal, a "badger-bear")—is submitted to objective judgment. In the expression "the wilderness inaccessible to metal objects" a clear opposition arises between the cold and neutral world of things that may hurt us and the safety and intimacy of the maternal womb. Milosz's "mother complex" cannot be taken with absolute seriousness. It is only discreetly suggested and is shrouded in signs of distance. The word *wilderness* (*matecznik*) refers to both mother and forest, and the comparison "like a warm and deep river," linking a series of vegetable and water associations, emphasizes the literary conventionality of the content.

Is the sexual act thus a kind of dream in which a return to mindless unconsciousness constitutes, paradoxically, the attainment of perfect knowledge and complete identification with one's partner? An expansion of the "I" into the entire world then occurs: "The 'I' is felt with amazement in the heartbeat, but so large it cannot be filled by the whole Earth with her seasons." This expansion, however, only seems limitless since the individual discovers a limit in himself or herself, in the conflict between the excess of one's own consciousness and the insufficiency of external reality, which cannot satisfy its needs. In "Heraclitus" the reverse had been true. The subject felt the discrepancy between the surfeit of the universe (hence the helpless generalization "All") and the insufficiency of the ego held fast by animality.

Consequently, the "I" does not "fill up" reality since it is as different from it as the world of animals is from that of human beings. Nor does reality "fill up" the "I" since its expectations of "I" reach beyond what is seen. Milosz reminds us that human subjectivity is formed in these constant struggles between intellect and instinct, the subjective and the objective, consciousness and dream.

It is not surprising that Eros leads these clashes because without this challenge the individual's libido would remain buried, safe but passive, and would never achieve self-definition. Eros arouses fear of the unknown, the other, the external. It brings perplexity and a painful craving at the same time as it arouses the need for self-improvement, an irresistible desire to break out of a well-defined circle and constantly cross barriers. From Plato and Saint Augustine the image of Eros is accompanied by a rising movement, an upward drive. Predictably, Eros is the patron of art and philosophy, the god of artists, thinkers, and scholars. The human cognitive drama is acted out in the setting of Eros, as Milosz explains:

> Later on, in crude light, separated into you and me, they try with a
>   bare foot pebbles of the floor.
> The two-legged, some to the left, some to the right, put on their belts,
>   garters, slacks, and sandals.
> And they move on their stilts, longing after a forest home, after low
>   tunnels, after an assigned return to It.
>   ("With Trumpets and Zithers," *CP* 202)

> A potem, w jarym świetle, podzieleni na mnie i ciebie, bosą stopą
>   próbują kamyków posadzki.
> Dwunodzy, jedni na prawo, drudzy na lewo, wkładają pasy,
>   podwiązki, spodnie i sandały.
> I posuwają się na swoich szczudłach tęskniąc do leśnego domu, do
>   niskich tuneli, do wyznaczonego im powrotu w to.

A return to reality after the transports of love restores the basic flaw: sex separates from sex, the human from the animal, nature from culture, dream from reality. Clothing again sets up a barrier authorized by the collective and shaped by custom. The shift from an intimate "you and me" to a neutral "they" indicates both the universality of this experience and the immediate appearance of otherness. The longing for an original unity, felt but verbally inexpressible, does not die out.

A similar opposition, but in a slightly different version, appears in the passage of "From the Rising of the Sun" cited earlier. Here Eros does not lead man into a love-dream phantasmagoria but into a world of idealized nature:

> It was Eros who plaited garlands of fruit and flowers,
> Who poured dense gold from a pitcher into sunrises and sunsets.
> He and no one else led us into fragrant landscapes
> Of branches hanging low by streams, of gentle hills,
> And an echo lured us on and on, a cuckoo promised
> A place, deep in a thicket, where there is no longing.
>
> (CP 257)

> Eros to był, który splatał nam girlandy z kwiatów i owoców,
> Lite złoto sączył ze dzbana w zachody i wschody słońca.
> On to prowadził nas między słodkie krajobrazy
> Nisko nawisłych gałęzi u strumieni, wzgórz łagodnych,
> I wabiło nas echo dalej, dalej, kukułka obiecywała
> Miejsce gdzie nie ma tęsknoty, w gęstwinie schowane.

This passage is a veiled reference to late Renaissance painting, indicated by the spectrum of colors and the placement, as in Titian or Giorgione, of mythological figures against the background of a stylized landscape, all bathed in the light of the rising or setting sun. In addition, Milosz endows the god of love with attributes traditionally ascribed to Bacchus—garlands of flowers and a jug of wine—as if to emphasize that the madness of unfettered sensuality lies dormant beneath the intimacy of love. He rejects comforting illusions and poses a question to which he never gives a final answer:

> "Should we then trust
> The alchemy of blood, marry forever the childish earth of illusion?
> Or bear a naked light without color, without speech,
> That demands nothing from us and calls us nowhere?"
>
> (CP 257)

> "Więc krwi alchemiom zawierzyć,
> Dziecinną ziemię ułudy poślubiać na zawsze?
> Czy znosić gołe światło bez barw i bez mowy
> Które niczego nie chce, do nikąd nie wzywa?"

The bright colors of the love banquet grow pale in the "crude" or "naked" light of rational knowledge. The inevitable contradiction remains between the freshness and naiveté of the child's vision, which is impossible for us to regain, and the heartless, adult knowledge we cannot forget and cannot deny. Sometimes that contradiction kills the imagination, leading it to indifference and resignation, rendering both art and poetry impossible.

In other words, the childlike Eros of Milosz's hero instinctively seeks out a mother who simply signifies—aside from all the possible mythographic explanations—safety, identification with oneself, and an "at-homeness" in existence. That interpretation is supported not only by the above passage from *Visions from San Francisco Bay* but also by a crucial scene in *The Issa Valley* where the hero meets his mother, whom he has not seen for a long time. Mother love prefigures perfect, divine love. That is why in the poem "Conversation at Easter 1620" ("Rozmowa na Wielkanoc 1620 roku") the nobleman from Wędziagoła seeks the protection of the Blessed Virgin when he is tempted by the devil. Milosz's hero longs for his mother but finds another woman instead. She cannot take the place of the mother because love for her is necessarily colored by sensual desire, which objectifies and divides. Her otherness submits only (and always incompletely) to an act of more or less masked force, whereas the love union remains only a momentary illusion leaving behind dissatisfaction.

The need to cross that chasm between the objective and the subjective, always so painful for Milosz—the chasm between what belongs to culture and what is still a part of nature, between the power of instinct and the responses of the heart, between the constant feeling of being threatened and the inexorable search for home—inclines him to a return to an earlier stage of childhood, to the period when this dichotomy had not yet been discovered. Not surprisingly, in the margins to his readings of Schopenhauer Milosz wrote:

> No one has ever so forcefully explained the genius of children: they are onlookers, avid, gluttonous, minds not yet caught by the will of the species, though I would add, led too by Eros who is still free and dances, knowing nothing of goals and service. And the gift of the artist or philosopher likewise has its secret in a hidden hostility toward the earth of the adults.
>
> (SN 39)

SELF-KNOWLEDGE

Although giving up the safe position of a spectator and settling down in the service of Eros undoubtedly brings fear and disillusionment, it also provides certain consolations. In Milosz the erotic always combines with the cognitive, and knowledge not only comprises the world around us but also enables a deeper penetration into oneself. The motif of divided self-knowledge, of an unexpectedly discovered knowledge, always accompanies Milosz's love scenes. This accompaniment is already apparent in "You Strong Night" ("Ty silna noc," 1934) where it takes the form of a generalization; the phrase "the crowd will disregard and fame will pass by" ("ominie plebs, a sława przejdzie obok") can apply equally to the future fate of the hero and to all artists faced with the approaching war. The final stanza raises the question:

> Superior wisdom, a non-feminine goodness
> Reside in your hands, o Mortal.
> And the glow of knowledge on your brow
> Is a folded moon, an unopened diadem.
>
> Ogromna mądrość, dobroć niekobieca
> jest w twoich kruchych rękach, o Śmiertelna.
> I blask poznania na czole prześwieca:
> stulony księżyc, nierozwita pełnia.

Thus the pleasures of love conclude with a noble apotheosis of femininity, justifying a pathos that is somewhat inappropriate to the scene, which, after all, takes place in bed. Where do the heroine's "superior wisdom" and "non-feminine goodness" come from? The apostrophe to the "Mortal" woman, recalling an epithet (now negated) ascribed to goddesses in ancient times, indicates that while the entire scene is saturated with symbolic meanings, ordinary everyday reality is imperceptibly being transformed into myth. The moon has often been associated with a need to shield the earth from the threatening danger of the cosmos and has been synonymous with defense against evil demons. Placed on Diana's forehead and then later beneath the feet of the Virgin Mary, the moon symbolized both virginity and maternity.[1] These rich and far-reaching mythological connotations are only suggested in the poem and remain distant. The "wisdom" of the female lover is "superior," but her "goodness" is "nonfeminine" because these are not so much her own personal attributes as qualities attributed to benevolent female goddesses such as Athena and Rhea. Although she almost embodies a myth, the heroine does not lose either her autonomy or her living essence. Not without reason does Milosz emphasize her mortality, her fragility, and her limitations.

"The glow of knowledge" and of self-knowledge explain almost all the love encounters in Milosz. In "Bobo's Metamorphosis" ("Gucio zaczarowany," 1962), "humanness" and "tenderness" are born from the common knowledge of the ill-fated lovers:

> But she, too, looked at me as if I were a ring of Saturn
> And knew I was aware that no one attains.
> Thus were affirmed humanness, tenderness.
>
> (CP 166)
>
> Ale ona też patrzyła na mnie jak na pierścienie Saturna
> I wiedziała, że wiem jak nikt nie dosięga.
> Tak stanowiona byla człowieczość i tkliwość.

The moving "Elegy for N. N." ("Elegia dla N. N."), whose subject carries on an imaginary dialogue with a lover now distant in time and space, closes with the words:

> From year to year it grows in us until it takes hold,
> I understood it as you did: indifference.
>
> (CP 240)
>
> Z roku na rok w nas dojrzewa aż ogarnie
> Tak jak ty ją zrozumiałem: obojętność.

By contrast, a poem entitled significantly "Initiation" (CP 430; "Wtajemniczenie") is framed by the opening and closing lines: "Vanity and gluttony were always her sins / . . . / In an instant, not judging anymore / I saw two sins of mine: vanity, gluttony" ("Próżność i łakomstwo były jej grzechami / . . . / Aż nie sądząc już więcej nagle zobaczyłem / Dwa moje grzechy: próżność i łakomstwo").

Intimacy, then, enables us to better recognize our own faults and virtues, to make moral evaluations, arousing in us hidden feelings. It is an old truism that by remaining with a beloved person we become better, more human. Only in the eyes of someone who is close to us can we see our own character clearly. The process works both ways: reflection returns a reflection. Humanness and tenderness allude to indifference, emptiness, and greed that are as much ours as our partners', for such qualities appear in relationships. Vanity and greed have, of course, been themes in the love lyric throughout the centuries. Milosz's originality lies in the fact that in his poetry the transition from the animal to the human occurs suddenly and without any idealization. Milosz would rather speak of desire than of love. Moreover, this transition is connected with a cognitive revelation: knowledge of the futility of striving for existential completeness unites partners instead of dividing them, as is best shown in the poem "Elegy for Y. Z." ("Elegia dla Y. Z.").

Milosz's skill at combining is indeed amazing. From a limited number of recurring concepts and motifs he composes new and startlingly fresh images, even in his descriptions of the sex act. In a condensed form and a different configuration, "Elegy for Y. Z." repeats the already described motifs of flight, loss of consciousness, and submersion into animality according to the law of nature:

> And our past moment: the mating of birds
> Without intent, reflection, nearly airborne
> Over the splendor of autumn dogwoods and maples . . .
> (CP 431)

> A nasza dawna chwila: parzenie się ptaków,
> Bez intencji, namysłu, prawie napowietrzne,
> Nad splendorem jesiennych dereni i klonów . . .

From here the road leads directly to initiation:

> I am grateful, for I learned something from you,
> Though I haven't been able to capture it in words:
> On this earth, where there is no palm and no scepter,
> Under a sky that rolls up like a tent,
> Some compassion for us people, some goodness
> And, simply, tenderness, dear Y. Z.
> (CP 431–432)

> Jestem wdzięczny, bo wziąłem od ciebie nauki,
> Choć nigdy ich nie mogłem ogarnąć słowami:
> Na tej ziemi, gdzie nie ma palmy ani berła,
> Pod niebem, które było jak namiot zwinięte,
> Jakaś litość dla nas, ludzi, jakaś czułość.
> I po prostu dobroć, droga Ygrek Zet.

This passage not only depicts the act of self-knowledge but also puts forth a definition of the inalienable attributes of the human condition in the contemporary world. The interpretation is supported by the carefully chosen signs in the poem, which render it a text for the initiated. The palm and the scepter appear because, as the epigram from Martin Buber reminds us, in Christian tradition each person is "a son of the King." The line "Under a sky that rolls up like a tent" suggests that we live in the age of the Apocalypse by alluding to the Revelation of Saint John, in which heaven is compared to a rolled-up scroll (Revelation 6:14). In addition, in the context of a hidden and silent God (as in "*Oeconomia Divina*") signs of meaning and value scatter and fade. But in the vacuum left by declining faith an ethics of compassion and interpersonal kindness is born, growing out of the most extreme loneliness and humiliation.

It would be a mistake, however, to think that Milosz deplores only the fading of the Christian *topoi* or the decline of religion. In his poetry sacral terminology takes on an entirely secular significance without losing its religious meaning—something indeed rare. This semantic ambivalence signals the erosion of the *sacrum*, an erosion that affects not only the world that the poet presents but also the worldview of the subject and to a great degree the worldview of Milosz himself. Note, for example, the postscript appended to "Elegy for Y. Z.":

> Really I am more concerned than words would indicate.
> I perform a pitiful rite for all of us.
> I would like everyone to know they are the king's children
> And to be sure of their immortal souls,
> I.e., to believe that what is most their own is imperishable
> And persists like the things they touch.
>
> (CP 431)

> Ale naprawdę bardziej mnie to przejmuje niż dowodzą słowa.
> Nad nami wszystkimi odprawiam gorzkie żale.
> Chciałbym, żeby każdy i każda wiedzieli, że są dziećmi Króla
> i byli pewni swojej duszy nieśmiertelnej,
> to znaczy wierzyli, że co najbardziej ich własne jest nie do zniszczenia
> i trwa jak rzeczy, których dotykają.

Milosz readily translates the theological into the philosophical. What matters here is not just one more illustration of the conviction that Catholic dogma is losing its former clarity and comprehensibility (hence the conditional mood and the use of postulates rather than affirmations). More important, the immortal soul is becoming a synonym for the substance or essence of humanity. In this way human nature, constant in its components and common to all members of the species, takes on a singular significance when revealed in the individual.

ANDROGYNY

Interestingly, what follows in Milosz's poetry is a major shift in accent. Appealing to religious contexts, the eroticism of Milosz's poems in *Unattainable Earth* (1986) ceases to appear in the shadow of sin. Expressions of condemnation no longer accompany raptures over the sensual beauty of woman. The rebellious pupil has drawn entirely different conclusions from Father Prefect's lessons. Even though he really "recognized the nothingness of enticing forms" ("poznałem nicość form powabnych"), he would not now cast aside the "joys of bodies, joined with water and fire, / with a bird soaring upward, with a fish diving downward" ("wesele ciał, złączonych z wodami i ogniem, / górą lecących ptakiem, rybą mknących dołem"; "To Father Ch.," "Do księdza Ch.," 1934). Beyond the fascination with youth he has discovered for himself that current of Christianity where the erotic inseparably intertwines with the religious. The path to transcendence need not pass through asceticism, which turns its eyes away from the beauty of the world and presumes the mortification of the body. The tradition of religious reflection stemming from the Song of Songs, which produced so many works of art and literature, teaches this lesson. Hieronymus Bosch, for example, has attracted Milosz's attention. Milosz's carnal metaphysics is not only a transmission of religious content with the aid of erotic allegories (the esoteric deductions of the Scholastics do not appeal to the sensualism of his imagination) but also an attempt to rehabilitate the sphere of sensual experiences. In the section "Summer" ("Lato") from the poem "The Garden of Earthly Delights" ("Ogród ziemskich rozkoszy") we find the following admission:

> I was old but my nostrils craved new scents
> And through my five senses I received a share in the earth
> Of those who led me, our sisters and lovers.
>
> (CP 389)

> Byłem stary ale nozdrza moje pożądały nowych zapachów
> I przez pięć moich zmysłów dostawałem udział
> W ich ziemi, prowadzących mnie, sióstr naszych i kochanek.

The "sisters and lovers" are the same ones that are displayed in the Prado on the canvases of the Dutch master Hieronymus Bosch. Their costumes have changed—"Their hips in trousers, not in trailing dresses, / Their feet in sandals, not on cothurni" ("Biodra ich w spodniach, nie w powłoczystych szatach, / stopy bose w sandałach, nie na koturnach")—but the festival of intoxicated senses, the affirmation of the charm and transient beauty of youth, remains the same: "Yet constantly the same, renewed by the moon, Luna, / In a chorus that keeps praising Lady Venus" ("Ale te same, odnawiające się, pod znakiem Luny, miesiąca, / W korowodzie, który sławi panią Wenus"). Subject to destruction by time and threatened by change, they endure in that which preserves the ideal of femininity in itself, in a new way expressing again the antinomy and ambivalence of human nature. This ideal is incarnated in both motherhood and virginity, supernatural love and sensuality, and it unites inseparably Eros and Charitas, Venus and the Moon.

There are some obvious reasons why Milosz "recognize[s] [him]self" in this particular painting. The moment at which the Middle Ages tilted toward the Renaissance probably best harmonizes religious themes with the wonder at all those things that eye, ear, and touch experience. That moment established a delicate balance between the two dimensions of reality such as art has never again achieved. That is why Bosch's work amazes us even today with its combination of sensual clarity and religious content. What could be closer to Milosz, who wants to return sensual tangibility and realistic value to the erotic-religious *topos?* The coexistence of antiquity and Christianity also elicits a positive response from his imagination, especially in a painting from a period when neither of those traditions had yet lost its life-giving power or turned into decorative ornament. In Bosch's paintings associations with Italian Neoplatonism appear on an equal footing with biblical motifs and symbols derived from folklore, alchemy, and astrology—a situation that presents no small problem for contemporary critics.[2] Hidden there is an ancient model of symbolic language based on a stratification of the senses and the principle of correspondences, the very qualities Milosz strives to renew in poetic speech. But such an explanation is only partially satisfactory, particularly since similar situations occur, with a different intensity and in a different configuration, in the baroque and romantic periods. What, then, is the motif that lies behind this choice?

The section "Paradise" ("Raj") puts us on the right track, for there Milosz describes the left panel of Bosch's *Garden of Earthly Delights*. The following passage warrants particular attention:

> Adam sits astonished. His feet
> Touch the foot of Christ who has brought Eve
> And keeps her right hand in his left while lifting
> Two fingers of his right like the one who teaches.
> Who is she, and who will she be, the beloved
> From the Song of Songs? This Wisdom-Sophia,
> Seducer, the Mother and Ecclesia?
>
> (CP 391)
>
> Adam siedzi w zdumieniu. Jego stopy
> Dotykają nogi Chrystusa, który przywiódł Ewę
> I trzyma jej rękę w swojej lewej a dwa palce prawej
> Podniósł jak ten, co naucza. Ewa spuszcza oczy.
> Kim jest i kim będzie ta umiłowana
> Z Pieśni nad Pieśniami? Ta Mądrość-Sofija,
> Uwodzicielka, Matka i Ecclesia.

This scene, like the entire triptych, arouses controversy and debate even today. Initially considered to be an illustration of the biblical story of the creation of Eve, it has been interpreted by modern scholars as a depiction of the marriage of Adam and Eve,[3] an illustration of the ceremony of initiation for Brothers and Sisters of the Free Spirit,[4] or as the marriage of Christ and the church.[5] But the difficulties do not end here, for even the separate gestures of the characters in the painting have been variously interpreted. One Bosch expert maintains that "Eve, whom God brings to Adam, is no longer a woman created from his rib, but an image of temptation. Hence, the amazed glance that Adam casts upon her constitutes the first step in the direction of sin."[6] Elsewhere it has been maintained that Adam is looking at the Creator, contemplating his image or, more precisely, reexpressing it in himself ("sich ihn 'ein-zu-bilden' "),[7] whereas a comparison of a frontal view and a profile expresses the conviction of the Adamites concerning the corporeal similarity of man to God. Yet another interpretation asserts that

> not Adam, but Christ—the second Adam—grasps at the wrist of Eve, who kneels before him. A clearly palpable spiritual bond, emphasized by the painter, exists between Christ and Eve. Christ, the second Adam, at that moment weds Eve, who, raised to this position of honor, no longer is the first sinful mother of mankind, the wife of the first Adam,

but is the second Eve, the Mother Church, the bride and wife beloved of Christ. In this way Bosch depicted the theological doctrine of the union of Christ-Adam with Eve-the-Church.[8]

Even this brief review of critical opinion gives an idea of the difficulties in trying to understand Bosch's triptych. Its contemporary interpretations constitute a unique survey of twentieth-century philosophical trends and fashions: here traditional historicism vies with depth psychology and comparative anthropology. Milosz avoids the arbitrariness typical of Bosch critics. Instead, without concealing his own doubts, reservations, or ignorance, he limits himself to objective description of the painting, using the conditional mood and posing numerous questions. It is generally thought that Christ raises his hand in a gesture of blessing or of taking an oath. But could it not also be a gesture of instruction? Who is Eve? Is she the mother of humankind? The church? The focus of contradictory attributes of an ideal femininity? Interestingly, the question is posed in such a way as to contain its own answer as well as to indicate its inadequacy since both the character on the canvas and the meaning it conveys elude simple and succinct definition. Surely, considering Bosch a member of the Adamite sect is rash and based on too little data,[9] but the question of the source of God's human form is not entirely unwarranted:

> Thus he created her who will conceive him?
> Where then did he get his human form
> Before the years and centuries began?
> Human, did he exist before the beginning?
> And establish a Paradise, though incomplete,
> So that she might pluck the fruit, she, the mysterious one,
> Whom Adam contemplates, not comprehending?
>
> (CP 391)

> Utworzył oto ją, która go zrodzi,
> Skądże więc dostał swoją ludzką postać
> Zanim zaczęły się lata i wieki?
> Człowieczy, istniał tedy przed początkiem?
> I ustanowił Raj, ale niepełny,
> Aby zerwała jabłko, ona, tajemnicza,
> Na którą patrzy Adam, nie pojmując.

A picture referring to this biblical story can be explained in various ways, for the story touches on the mystery of humanity's origins and essence, the fundamental obscurity and incomprehensibility of which do not diminish but rather grow as the number of scholarly hypotheses and conceptions increases. It may well be that the significance of Bosch's triptych is unclear to us because we have lost the key to symbolic speech used in the painter's own day.

Who, then, is the persona? He is both Everyman, whose fate reflects that of the human race, and a contemporary viewer contemplating Bosch's painting. At the beginning of the poem Milosz discreetly hints at a link between the subject of the poem and himself when he recalls that he was born under the sign of Cancer and introduces a series of motifs typical of his own work: the intensity of human existence, revulsion at "the moving jaws of crabs," scenes of cruelty and death in nature. But Milosz also finds all these motifs in the painting itself. "The Garden of Earthly Delights" might then somehow summarize Milosz's own most important convictions. The conclusion of the poem, just like his descriptions of the panels in the triptych, is deceptive in its apparent simplicity:

> I am these two, twofold. I ate from the Tree
> Of Knowledge. I was expelled by the archangel's sword.
> At night I sensed her pulse. Her mortality.
> And we have searched for the real place ever since.
>
> (CP 392)
>
> Jestem ich dwojgiem, podwójny. Jadłem z drzewa
> Wiadomości. Byłem wygnany mieczem archanioła.
> W nocy czułem jej tętno. Jej śmiertelność.
> I szukaliśmy odtąd miejsca prawdziwego.

I might conclude these lines with a hypothetical theological commentary: We all are descended from Adam and Eve, and thus we bear the burden of their transgression. Alongside it an anthropological commentary could appear: The fall of our first parents is a figure of the moment when man, emerging from a state of animal unconsciousness, enters a phase of moral distinctions and an intellectual subordination of the world to himself but without ceasing to long for a lost unity. Or, in the language of depth psychology: The biblical Eden contains the archetypal record of the two poles of human consciousness, where the male element constantly clashes with the female, intellect with impulse, the progressive tendency with the regressive. Other hypothetical interpretations could be added to this list, but that is not the point. What is crucial is that the text of the poem contains a kind of nucleus

of such interpretations and that in the course of reading the poem no
one interpretation is privileged. Digging deeper into the poem, we
should ask what the phrase "I am these two, twofold" means. Beyond
the interpretations indicated above, the phrase seems to refer to the
concept of divine androgyny, which appears in many religions. Anna
Boczkowska contends that

> Christ, the Christian Eros, became the religious type of a man whose
> personal model could be recognized by everyone in himself and in oth-
> ers. . . . Man and the virgin became "one in Christ." For this reason as
> well we frequently meet the concept of Christ-Logos as a bisexual, male
> and female, yet one indivisible personality in the esoteric speculations of
> medieval philosophers, theologians, alchemists, and astrologers who
> tried to fathom the laws of nature by seeking their secrets in religious
> manifestations. . . . We find reflections on the theme of the mystical
> androgyny of Christ in the writings of Saint Gregory, Saint Teresa of
> Ávila, and Duns Scotus Erigena. According to Duns Scotus, Christ and
> every human being unite the male and female sexes in their nature.
> Many centuries later, during the Renaissance, Leone Ebreo in *Dialogues
> on Love* connected the Platonic idea of hermaphrodite as a perfect being
> with the biblical tradition of the Fall as the cause of the separation of the
> two sexes. The metaphysical goal of humanity was the achievement of a
> renewed unification of the male and female sex.[10]

Contrary to first appearances, these ideas are not distant from
Milosz's own reflections. The inexplicable arbitrariness of the division
into two sexes constitutes a problem that exasperates him. Already in
"Sentences" ("Sentencje," 1963–1965), where we hear the echoes of
Platonism, he writes:

> Still it's just too great a responsibility to lure the souls
> From where they lived attentive to the idea of the hummingbird, the
>   chair, and the star.
> To imprison them within either-or: male sex, female sex,
> So that they wake up in the blood of childbirth, crying.
>
> (CP 176)

> A jednak za duża odpowiedzialność zwabiać dusze
> Stamtąd gdzie mieszkały razem z ideą kolibra i krzesła i gwiazdy.
> Więzić je w albo-albo: płeć męska, płeć żeńska,
> Żeby we krwi narodzin budziły się z płaczem.

As a reflection of the image of God, man also duplicates the divine
androgyny, but—like everything else—in a misshapened, imperfect,

and disguised form. Constant defects and divisions are the fate of man; they give birth to a nostalgia for a variously understood completion. The traditional problem of *felix culpa* returns here, in a different light, however. Original sin was a "happy fault" not only because it enabled the mystery of redemption to be accomplished but also because through it the need was born to transcend man's actual condition in the pursuit of the "true place," a desire to nullify even the difference between the sexes. Herein lies the paradoxicality of human nature, that it leaves Paradise—understood in various ways—and then unceasingly desires to return to it. But it is from this paradox that all philosophy, science, art, and religion stream forth.

For Milosz, divine androgyny seems to be a poetic hypothesis of a complete humanity, just as *apokatastasis* is a hypothesis for the fullness of existence. In fact, they may be simply two statements of the same problem. It is surely no accident that as a commentary to his 1986 collection of poems Milosz quoted a note Oscar Milosz had written in the margins of a copy of Swedenborg's *Vera Christiana Religio:* "Consequently, the whole of Creation is FEMALE and the love of the Lord for Himself in Creation is the love of *Man* for *Woman,* and the return to God is Conjunction or Marriage . . . (Creation is also the Church)" (*UE* 95).

Here the idea of androgyny takes on a cosmic and metaphysical dimension. This is, after all, the intellectual tradition that is close to Milosz—Swedenborg and Oscar Milosz, as well as Saint Gregory and Duns Scotus. Milosz, however, brings this entire line of thought down to earth.

In *Visions from San Francisco Bay* Milosz wrote: "The mind never ceases transcending itself and is always pursuing the receding heaven of the idea; and the body, the abode of Eros, the god of all the creative impulses, never escapes the necessity of physiology" (*V* 191).

Beneath the scepter of Eros a struggle occurs between obedience to the dictates of nature and the ardent desire to free oneself from them. Eros stages a drama of cognition that ends in the catastrophe of disinheritance. While in the power of Eros, man seeks the unattainable synthesis of what in himself belongs to nature, history, and culture. In other words, Milosz reminds us that each one of our lives is worked out, consciously or not, according to archetypal models preserved in the Scriptures. We must return to those texts and pore over the works of ancient masters in order to fill our own personal existence with the rich content of the most ancient symbols, at the same time illuminating those symbols with the help of twentieth-century theories about man. Poetry plays a fundamental role in this two-way process. It calls up forgotten signs out of nonexistence as a means of understanding them in the process of revivifying their content and, indirectly, of promoting the self-understanding of the poet and the reader. Jan Błoński is correct when he states that "Milosz's recent work is the huge undertaking of socializing and sacralizing his own personal experiences."[11] I would add that this sacralization occurs largely through contemporary anthropology, while the undertaking itself dates from the beginning of Milosz's writing. A significant example is the collection of poems *Three Winters* (*Trzy zimy*), an attempt at interpreting both private and collective events by means of the sacral symbolism of Mediterranean culture. It is an attempt as yet not fully conscious of its own assumptions and not completely successful artistically. Such interpretation is perhaps the deepest current in all of Milosz's poetry. It sometimes recedes because of the pressure of his own historical experiences, but then it stubbornly rises to the surface again.

Still, one might question why Milosz grants Catholicism such a privileged position in this process. In his own words the answer is that "Catholicism is the most anthropocentric of religions, and in some sense, through its own excess of divine humanity, it resists the exact sciences which annihilate the individual, and thus, paradoxically, is less susceptible than other religions to the disintegrative influence of science and technology" (V 82). Catholicism preserves the concept of the unchangeableness of human nature, and its centuries-old tradition provides the idea of humanity with a wealth of meanings. From it as well, according to Milosz, flows the most stimulating impulse for the poetic imagination. The question whether "the God-man existed then before the beginning" only seems naive, for it is not simply the way in which past artists envisioned the eternal Creator. Milosz says elsewhere that "God should have a beard and stroll the heavenly pastures. . . . Only a Creator resembling man can make an exception of us here among the rocks, the waters, and other living organisms; only from his lips can a meaningful voice issue, only his ears can hear our words" (V 77–78). Milosz says this with a distance that is the sign of loss, but also with the conviction that a human image of God is the highest embodiment of the anthropocentric myth. Only such a conception of the Creator gives human existence a safe shelter, ennobles man, and returns meaning to morality and art.

6

The Identity Game

According to Witold Gombrowicz, the ego exists in a hard-to-define sphere between unconscious impulse and the invasions of form. For him, nature remains indifferent and impenetrable, and history reveals itself only in the guise of irresistible ideas. Transcendence is, at most, a postulate. The self interprets its own presence and traces its contours by means of those imprints made on it by another self. For Gombrowicz, "to be" means "to be with Others and to confront Others."

By contrast, Milosz, as I have shown, grants no dimension a privileged place, nor does he limit human nature to any one dimension. According to Milosz, definitions of human nature have always depended on the particular perspective from which an individual is observed. Experience teaches that man is simultaneously—but not exclusively—a historical, social animal and a metaphysical being. Therefore, none of these dimensions should be given priority, and man should not be reduced to any one of them. All dimensions collide and intersect with one another in the mind of each human individual. Man may, however incompletely and imperfectly, attempt to approach his own essence, never for a moment forgetting its entanglement in nature, historicity, other persons, and the *sacrum*. Such efforts at self-definition must be individual, momentary, and unique: individual because only what is refracted through the experience of one man, immersed in his own existence, is considered to be true by the poet; momentary because such an act is defined by the time and place in which it occurs; unique because only one distinct aspect of the above-mentioned entanglement can be elucidated at one time. Milosz's hero discovers himself through contact with a bird, a beaver, or another man; through his presence in the ruins of a town; and through ardent prayer to a silent God.

Does the hero really appear in the poem as a different entity? What suppresses the threat of relativism and protects *humanitas* against its diffusion into these diverse relations? Milosz's answer sounds somewhat provocative in the context of the fashionable theories of today, but it is in keeping with a centuries-old tradition. He seeks to persuade us—in spite of numerous doubts and reservations on both sides—to believe in the existence of an undiminished element in human nature. Furthermore, this belief should remain the keystone of man's self-definition. Derived from the doctrine of the immortality of the soul, the belief of course cannot be maintained in its former shape. Its base has been effectively undermined by the theory of biological evolution, by psychoanalysis, and by historical determinism.

Milosz seems to suggest, however, that such faith can be saved at least in the form of an axiological postulate. But here too the crisis of ethical norms and the increasing dehumanization of life and art impinge. As a result, Milosz's poetic attempts to establish what in human nature resists reduction are marked by uncertainty and indecision. Dramatically suspended between the elusiveness of the object and constantly changing criteria, these attempts seek justification as much in the needs of the individual as in the history of the culture that testifies to these efforts. In other words, Milosz's writing can be read as a record of the devastating test to which the Christian conception of the human person has been submitted. This concept has been tested most acutely by those modern scientific theories, philosophical systems, and sociopolitical doctrines whose nihilistic implications are evident in both the idea of man and his imagination.

These beliefs are naturally not present in all of Milosz's poetry. All four dimensions of human existence cannot be traced in every poem, and the poet shifts emphasis in successive periods of his writing. However, with striking insistence he returns to the questions of what constitutes human nature, what marks its limits, and how it manifests itself. In addition, he multiplies the signs of the dissociation, sprinkles in paradoxes, and piles up contradictions. In defining the particularity of the relations between man and nature, the narrator of "Treatise on Poetry" says: "You say Kingdom. We belong and do not belong to it at the same time" ("Królestwo mówisz. My nie należymy, / Choć równocześnie do niego należąc"). One of the interlocutors in "I Sleep a Lot" (*CP* 177; "A Magic Mountain" in 1980 Ecco Press ed. of *SP*; "Dużo śpię," 1962), who is probably Mexican, seriously maintains that women have only one soul, whereas men have two. In other poems the soul argues with the body in the manner of a medieval dispute ("From the Rising of the Sun," *CP* 302) or blames human nature for its own shortcomings ("To My Nature"; "Do mojej natury"). In other words, outdated concepts of man are as valuable as contemporary ones; folk-religious ideas are intermingled with echoes of psychoanalysis; the poetic imagination competes with scientific theory; and all is treated half-jokingly, half-seriously.

Milosz seems to be asking, What can be said about that which constitutes human nature? In spite of scientific progress it remains an unsolvable puzzle. Any definition of man can easily be challenged by juxtaposing another definition. Such notions as *homo faber, homo ludens, homo ritualis,* and so on grasp no more than a part of the phenomenon and tend toward generalization. Traditional theological and philosophical systems also diminish in importance. What can be done besides listening intently to the voice of intuition, comparing it with knowledge and experience, and always doubting the resulting conclusions? As in Milosz's poem "Consciousness" (*CP* 420; "Świadomość"), humanness (*człowieczość*), veiled in negation and trapped in paradox, can be sensed but not expressed; separated from its potentiality, humanness congeals immediately into yet another formula. "Our humanness becomes more marked then" (*CP* 422; "Człowieczość nasza wtedy wyraźnieje") when we are in contact with nonhuman reality, specifically expressed in this poem when the speaker reflects on the essence of a dog's nature. Milosz even coins the word *psiość*—"doggishness." Here a direct sensation is reinforced by philosophical knowledge, in this case the knowledge of universals. The claim that "humanness *becomes* more marked" (emphasis added) seems to indicate that cognition can be described as a continuous and infinite process, simultaneously open to past and future. This process combines the insistent question, Who am I? which everyone asks privately, with a variety of ready-made answers furnished by the history of mankind.

Milosz is as interested in the phenomenon of aspiring to self-knowledge as he is in the forms in which this aspiration expresses itself in the cultural tradition of a given time and place. His poetic imagination animates the multiplicity, diversity, and richness of forms, at the same time strongly emphasizing their mutability. He achieves this animation by distancing himself from forms and juxtaposing them. Perhaps the true subject of his poems is not the finished *concept* of human nature but the *process* of attaining that concept. Each time the process occurs, it is different and unique. Milosz reminds us that human nature does not inhabit the heaven of abstractions but rather evolves in history, suffused with new meaning in different periods. The innumerable formulas and images with which man through the centuries has tried to illuminate his own uniqueness in the cosmos may sometimes seem ridiculous and naive. However, something elementary is present, beyond the language of ideas, that cannot easily be questioned: the dualism of human nature. Referred to variously throughout history, it can be reduced, as Milosz states, to the basic opposition between what is "the divine in man" and what is "the natural in him," or more explicitly: "Consciousness, intelligence, light, grace, the love of the good—such subtle distinctions are not my concern; for me it is enough that we have some faculty that makes us alien, intruders in the world, solitary creatures unable to communicate with crabs, birds, animals" (V 175–176). Embodied in the signs and symbols of culture, the divine in man changes and at the same time endures throughout history owing to collective memory. This divine is opposed to the natural in man, that which obeys mathematical necessity and the laws of instinct and is excluded from the spheres of sense and value.

Milosz adds:

> We are unable to live nakedly. We must constantly wrap ourselves in a cocoon of mental constructs, our changing styles of philosophy, poetry, art. We invest meaning in that which is the most purely human of our activities. For the threads spun by our ancestors do not perish, they are preserved; we alone among living creatures have a history, we move in a gigantic labyrinth where the present and the past are interwoven.
>
> (V 176)

The problems with which we deal here could be, and perhaps should be, provided with a comprehensive theological and philosophical commentary. Yet Milosz's reflections are impossible to contain in the framework of a single philosophical school or explain through a single philosopher's system. The poet asks questions rather than gives answers, sharpens contradictions rather than resolves them. Instead of tracing the philosophical sources of Milosz's poetry, we should more closely observe the tension between the scope of the basic questions implicit in his poems and the variety of answers those texts give. In addition to the concept of meditation on existence, the problem of humanness is also important. Logically speaking, these are two sides of the same issue: as the world cannot be imagined without human presence in it, human nature is equally unable to exist without acknowledging the world's reality.

To assume that only what has passed through the filter of individual experience is important has another consequence that deserves mention. Namely, the silent question in Milosz's poetry, Who is man? corresponds to the questions spoken by his heroes and personae: Who am I, unique and placed in a particular historical age, a certain space? in short, questions concerning individual identity, or rather, doubts about identity. In these poems one often finds such statements as: "The same and not quite the same" ("Ten sam i nie ten sam"; "Magpiety," *CP* 120); "I do not remember who I am and who I was" ("nie pamiętam kim jestem i kim byłem"; "With Trumpets and Zithers," *CP* 197); and "a young man, my ancient self, incomprehensibly identical with me" ("młody człowiek, ja dawny, niepojęcie ze mną tożsamy"; "The Separate Notebooks," *CP* 379, "Osobny zeszyt").

How to be oneself, then, is a serious question and the answer is not at all self-evident. The ego of the character in Milosz's poems is still threatened by the passage of time, the pressure of his subconscious, the burden of heritage, social milieu, and caprices of memory. He searches for his own identity by delving into his personality or projecting his cognitive uneasiness on the environment. Milosz expresses all these problems simultaneously through the complicated network of three entities: the implied author, the speaker, and the lyric hero.

THE NONINDIRECT MONOLOGUE

Milosz's juvenilia exhibit a marked tendency of the poet to create characters whose connection with their creator is both suggested and evaded. A link is suggested because the heroes appear in roles and situations in which the author could have participated. But the author also evades this link by clearly distancing himself from these characters. This tendency goes hand in hand with an invasion of dramatic forms of expression, whether as a microdialogue or as a lyric in the second person interspersed with the collective "we." Beginning with "Three Winters," all dramatic forms undergo a gradual refinement and intensification. In his prewar poetry, written between 1934 and 1939, there is a blurring of the lines between the implied author, the speaker, and the hero. They become embodiments of the same person, who in different ways prophesies to the world its own destruction. This blurring is signaled by a stylistic unity of utterances connected with biblical rhetoric and the fluctuating status of the speaker. Suspended between reality and myth, realism and terrifying phantasmagoria, the "I" of the speaker easily turns into "you" or "he," as in "Birds" or "Slow River." These transformations are aided by the relatively small number of autobiographical allusions or by camouflaging so that they become imperceptible. Incomparably more important is Milosz's extensive use of the device of the microquotation so that the identity of the actual speaker remains an open question. When evaluating *Three Winters* in retrospect, Milosz pointed out something essential:

> We should also remember that ultimately that book is full of playful elements and self-contained phrases which have their own autonomy. I would call them emotional operations, because lines like the ones you quoted are very dramatic and seem automatically to express the tragic side of life. Various lines can be extracted from that poem and analyzed as gestures of dramatic speech.
>
> (CCM 107)

Milosz's entire poetic discourse echoes with such autonomous phrases or voices.

Milosz questions the identity of the person who speaks in a poem as well as the distinctness of his act of enunciation: the direct monologue in his poetry constantly leans toward the indirect monologue and the dramatic monologue. This is achieved through various kinds of stylization, by transforming some of the poet's personal experiences into parables and traveling freely through the time and space of someone similar to him. The reader armed with scholarly definitions of direct monologue, indirect monologue, and dramatic monologue will have trouble categorizing Milosz's poetry. The problem cannot simply be reduced to determining the distance between the implied author and the speaker. Milosz undermines the tacit basis of that classification system, namely, the fact that in its reference to popular psychological and sociological knowledge that typology presumes the coherence of the human personality and homogeneity of character. The speaker must be endowed with features of his own character and grounded in a precisely defined milieu; he would then command a certain store of knowledge, system of values, language, and so on. In other words, his "portrait" is constructed rather arbitrarily at the intersection of the poet's strategy and the reader's expectations, erudition, and attitudes.

The case of the implied author is similar. His image is comprised of both statements from outside the text made by the writer and information about his life. Clearly, to distinguish three types of monologue we must presume the relative stability and coherence of both the speaker and the implied author; without it there is no way to determine their mutual distance or the degree of their identification. In short, they must be hypostases of a homogeneous and internally cohesive personality. But it is precisely this conception that Milosz questions. Psychological unity is not a given but is itself problematic.

There are, of course, poems by Milosz that can be considered within the framework of the traditional direct monologue; for example, "Introduction" ("Przedmowa") in the collection *Rescue* (*Ocalenie*, 1945), religious lyrics such as "On Angels" ("O aniołach"), and the epistolary poems "Elegy for N. N.," "To Robinson Jeffers" ("Do Robinsona Jeffersa"), "To Raja Rao," "To Joseph Sadzik" ("Do Józefa Sadzika"). Their number increases in *From the Rising of the Sun* and *Hymn of the Pearl* (*Hymn o perle*), but even here, with the growing intimacy of tone or allusion to his own life, Milosz still aims at generalization. The speaker becomes more an exponent of a certain worldview, moral attitude, and philosophical choice than a medium for private confidential disclosures. Milosz achieves distance in various ways, but first of all by means of stylization or use of traditional literary genres. Stylization lends a timelessness to the experiences of the speaker while preserving his essential grounding in the here and now.

There is a second way in which Milosz shifts his private experiences, even trivial ones, to the universal: he encloses them in the form of moral or philosophical maxims. For example, in "Rivers Grow Small" (*CP* 167, "Rzeki maleją") his recollections of swimming in a lake in his youth conclude with the line "What was individual becomes a variety of a general pattern" ("Co było indywidualne staje się odmianą ogólnego wzoru"). His poetry contains a host of such formulations.

Finally, Milosz's third method relies on endowing the subject with the ability to move about freely in time and space. Here Milosz seems to develop and modify the conception of the eschatological "I" from *Three Winters*, in which the wanderings of the hero-speaker are motivated by a mythological context or prophetic vision. After the war similar wanderings are presented without such clear fabular motivation. A notable example is the beginning of "From the Rising of the Sun":

Whatever I hold in my hand, a stylus, reed, quill or a ballpoint,
Wherever I may be, on the tiles of an atrium, in a cloister cell, in a
    hall before the portrait of a king,
I attend to matters I have been charged with in the provinces.

                                                    (*CP* 252)

Cokolwiek dostanę do ręki, rylec, trzcinę, gęsie pióro, długopis,
Gdziekolwiek odnajdą mnie, na taflach atrium, w celi klasztornej, w
    sali przed portretem króla,
Spełniam, do czego zostałem w prowincjach wezwany.

                            ("Gdzie wschodzi słońce i kędy zapada")

Who is speaking here? An eternal poet? The high and pathetic style
of speech might indicate that. In the next lines, however, the speaker's
language becomes more concrete, and pathetic and colloquial expressions are intermingled. Loftiness changes into triteness. Thus, after
praising the poet's eternal vocation, the persona says: "Odious rhythmic speech / Which grooms itself and, of its own accord, moves on"
("Obrzydliwość rytmicznej mowy, / Która sama siebie obrządza, sama
postępuje"). And, "a flu like the last one . . . / When, looking at the
futility of my ardent years, / I heard a storm from the Pacific beating
against the window" ("Grypy jak ta ostatnia . . . / Kiedy wpatrzony w
daremność moich zaciekłych lat / Słuchałem jak bije w okno sztorm od
Pacyfiku"). The speaker is a contemporary poet in exile, perhaps
Milosz himself. At the same time one can easily recognize in his stance
the gestures and expressions of the heroes of Polish romanticism,
Mickiewicz's pilgrim poets. What is characteristic here is the constant
oscillation between the present and the past, tradition and novelty,
private and public (captured by conventions), the futile and the eternal. Thus, in addition to the storm from the Pacific, there is "the
neighing of the red horse" ("rżenie konia rydzego") from the Revelation of Saint John. Besides Milosz's reminiscences of his childhood
("Vast lands. Flickering of hazy trains. / Children walk by an open
field, all is gray beyond an Estonian village" ["O równiny. Błyskające
pociągi mgliste. / Idą dzieci pustkowiem, szaro za wioską czu-
chońców"]), there are verses that seem to echo Mickiewicz:

> Never again will I kneel in my small country, by a river,
> So that what is stone in me could be dissolved
> So that nothing would remain but my tears, tears.
>
>   (*CP* 252)

I nigdy już nie uklęknę nad rzeką w maleńkim kraju
Żeby co we mnie kamienne rozwiązało się,
Żeby nic już nie było prócz moich łez, łez.

This example shows how Milosz's direct monologue leans toward the indirect monologue and the dramatic monologue of masks and roles. As in the poetry of Konstantine Cavafy, the "I" is expanded to historical dimensions, but Milosz's unique approach is to have that "I" wander not only in human history but also within his private autobiography. Whereas Cavafy reconstructs situations primarily from antiquity, evoking ancient personages and judging their behavior with contemporary distance, Milosz expands the amount of time and space traversed by the speaker while remaining ever mindful of the penetration into his experience of various temporal and spatial dimensions. He accomplishes this in two ways. The sensations and experiences of the lyric hero, with whom he identifies to a large extent, are an individual variation of the paradigm of the human condition (such as exile in "From the Rising of the Sun" or "Greek Portrait" ["Portret grecki," 1948] or temptation by the devil in "Temptation" ["Pokusa," 1982]). Or the childhood and youth of the hero may be presented from the vantage point of later knowledge. "Bobo's Metamorphosis" is the first of such evocations of oneself long ago that appear particularly in Milosz's California period. Milosz's choice of this vantage point can be explained by the passage of time, which removes the poet from past times and places and arouses nostalgia for them. He also consciously detaches himself from the American environment (except for the American landscape) and draws on an earlier period for poetic material. The following passage proves that these evocations are not merely sentimental reminiscences:

I walk about. No longer human. In a hunting outfit.
Visiting our thick forests and the houses and manors.
Cold borscht is served and I am abstracted
With disturbing questions from the end of my century,
Mainly regarding the truth, where does it come from, where is it?
Mum, I was eating chicken with cucumber salad.
                          ("The Hooks of a Corset," *CP* 399)

Przechadzam się. Już nieludzki. W myśliwskim stroju,
Tam gdzie nasze puszcze i domy i dwory.
Podano chłodnik, a ja w abstrakcji,
Przy zapytaniach z końca mego wieku.
Głównie o prawdę: skąd ona, gdzie ona.
I milcząc jadłem kurczaka z mizerią.
                          ("Haftki gorsetu")

Besides the temporal leaps between the present and the past, it is vital to note the visual clarity of past events that now take place afresh, as if in the present. Something like a fourth dimension arises: the persona who is remembering does not summon up an irrevocably past and finished time but exists in two time dimensions simultaneously. He is the young hunter but also possesses a wisdom acquired much later; or perhaps when young he had asked himself questions the answers to which he would seek again only toward the end of his life. In these two ways we may understand the line "With disturbing questions from the end of my century." In short, whereas Cavafy meditates on man in general, with concrete realizations of that idea as a subject for meditation, Milosz ceaselessly tests that idea out on the material of an individual life. For Cavafy, the basic unifying hypothesis is the constancy of human nature and the unity of Mediterranean culture; for Milosz, it is the individual, personal biography, in which human nature and culture are refracted in a unique way. This is true not only of Milosz's poetry but also of *Native Realm*, where he examines himself as a "sociological object," and *The Land of Ulro*, where the physical and intellectual adventures of the author immediately take on the dimensions of a model and a generalization.

The last example compels us to devote more attention to the nature of Milosz's autobiographical allusions, the purpose they serve, and the degree of identification between the author and the subject. These questions are crucial since the allusions encompass both past and present time. The person seduced in "Temptation" (*CP* 324) is placed "On a ridge overlooking neon cities" ("Na skraju góry skąd widać neonowe miasta"). The real locale is easy to guess: one need only stand on Grizzly Peak, where Milosz lives today, and from there gaze down on the cities of Oakland, Berkeley, and El Cerrito (mentioned by name in "With Trumpets and Zithers," *CP* 200). It is possible, then, that other scenes in Milosz's poems also have counterparts in actual locations. This supposition is supported by the fact that in his conversations with Ewa Czarnecka, Milosz persistently emphasizes that he takes his descriptions from personal observation.[1] It does not preclude, however, their far-reaching transformation. Saturated with vivid visual details, the descriptions are also generalized: they are reduced to their constituent elements and marked by an extreme typicality (a mountain and cities are described without mentioning their names).

The suggestion of autobiographism has become most evident since Milosz has been in America. All of his poetry, of course, contains many references to his own private life; we can reconstruct from them the precise places where he has lived, and sometimes their names become titles in his record of successive impressions: "A Notebook: Sanary" ("Notatnik: Sanary"); "A Notebook: Bon by Lake Leman" ("Notatnik: Bon nad Lemanem"); "A Notebook: Pennsylvania" ("Notatnik: Pennsylvania"). But in his California period the number of references to significant persons increases, although Milosz does not divulge their identities. The reader will certainly never learn who the "young lady with a curl on her ear" ("panna z kosmykiem na uchu") is, or the identity of the painter who "did not look for an ideal object" ("co nie szukał idealnego przedmiotu"; "Bobo's Metamorphosis," CP 162). Likewise unknown will remain Anna and Dorcia Drużyno ("City Without a Name"), Lisabeth (Alżbieta, "From the Rising of the Sun"), Filina ("Filina"), and many other characters. This privacy, something new in Milosz's poetry, lends his descriptions an air of authenticity and attests to that authenticity. Milosz is never indiscreet; proof of his sensitivity is that his most intimate poems are designated only with initials: "Elegy for N. N." and "Elegy for Y. Z." He even tries to endow privacy with the quality of generalization.

IN SOMEONE ELSE'S SHOES

In Milosz's poetry not only the direct monologue leans toward the indirect monologue, but also the dramatic monologue. There are poems in which the speaker is undoubtedly someone other than the author and with whom he cannot be identified in any way. To this category belong poems with a female narrator and, for example, "Siegfried and Erika" ("Siegfried i Erika"), "Carolers" ("Kolędnicy"), "Conversation at Easter 1620" ("Rozmowa na Wielkanoc 1620 roku"), "The Master" ("Mistrz"), "Peasant into King" ("Z chłopa król"), "On the Other Side" ("Po drugiej stronie"), and "Higher Arguments in Favor of Discipline Derived from the Speech Before the Council of the Universal State in 2068" ("Wyższe argumenty na rzecz dyscypliny zaczerpnięte z przemówienia na radzie powszechnego państwa w roku 2068"). But even in these poems the author more or less discreetly indicates his presence. For example, in "The Master" (CP 134) Milosz puts his own artistic credo in the mouth of a seventeenth-century German or Italian composer: "What comes from my evil—that only is true" ("Co z mego zła powstało, to tylko prawdziwe"). Not by coincidence does the Calvinist who returns to Rome during the Counter-Reformation hail from Wędziagoła, the family home of Milosz's father. It is as if Milosz would like to suggest that the fate of this Calvinist is in some way his own. Even where the subject is unquestionably someone other than the author, Milosz deals with the same problems that in other works he examines openly and without disguise.

"Siegfried and Erika" is a case in point. Here a Nazi pilot, inadvertently demasking fascist ideology, at the same time lays bare the myth-creating veil that covers every totalitarian system. In the eyes of a fanatic, Nazism constitutes the embodiment of man's eternal desire to discipline body and soul and bend the course of history to his own will. Recalling the Polish campaign of September 1939, Siegfried tells his sister with almost unconcealed pride:

> Yes, I was killing. Was I wrong, Erika?
> A highway sped towards me in the shriek of my rudder,
> And there was chaos, you know, columns
> Of carts, bundles, dirt, heat, crawling, fear,
> A shattered will unable to cling to its design.
> The lethal sparks that flew into that crowd
> From under my wings, were so pure.

> Tak, zabijałem. Czy to źle, Eriko?
> Szosa szła do mnie z gwizdem moich sterów,
> A tam był chaos, rozumiesz? Kolumny
> Wozów, toboły, brud, skwar, czołganie się, strach, rozprzężona
> Wola niezdolna utrzymać zamiaru.
> Śmiertelne iskry które w ten tłum biegły
> Spod moich skrzydeł, były takie czyste!

Genocide is easy to condemn, and expressions of moral outrage are numerous, not only in Polish literature. Hence Milosz's voice sounds all the more original and fresh. Clearly, neither the pathology of crime nor the psychological motivations that created indifference to mass death interest him. According to Milosz, the sources of that explosion of destructive instincts lie elsewhere. The satanic force of nazism was expressed primarily in its striving for "purity," as opposed to the "crawling," "chaos," and weakness of will. In this context, the Nazi love of orderliness takes on a new meaning. As Milosz says elsewhere: "Diabolical temptation may take different forms. When it is associated with the person of Lucifer, the aspects of pride and purity come to the fore, for Lucifer is a pure and haughty spirit . . . [and] this is the case for the majority of the reformers of humanity in our century. They

themselves are so pure, they love purity" (*PS* 169). The short-lived
social, legal, and behavioral order that Siegfried laments is a defense
against the degradation and demoralization that beset man when he
falls prey to the brutal struggle for survival. Proof of this is the scene at
the beginning of the poem that sketches German life just after defeat at
the end of World War II. But when such order is too rigidly conceived
and given over to the incompetent, it brings incalculable destruction.
"Social hygiene" that aims at the elimination from the collective of
anything that is not in line with the utopia, that opposes the system of
official beliefs and resists uniformity, is essentially inhuman. It not
only negates the existence of an aspect of humanity that is confused
and dark but also violates an elementary principle that every person
must remain himself, even at the price of his own errors and weak-
nesses. According to Milosz, every totalitarian ideology that promotes
the supremacy of some group—whether race, nation, or class—over
the individual is based on a hidden deception, a paradox. On the one
hand, it grants the prerogative of infallible knowledge and absolute
power to a group of individuals that, entrusted with the fulfillment of
a supposedly historical mission, secretly despises the collective—hence
the poem speaks of the undifferentiated "crowd" ("tłum"). On the
other hand, it rules out those moral principles that are based on, and
justified by, a recognition of the dignity and sovereignty of the individual. That is why the poem concludes with a warning addressed to all
"reformers of humanity" ("naprawiaczy ludzkości") who advise us to
consider qualms of conscience as just a "liberal fallacy" ("przesąd
liberalny").

Whereas Siegfried erred in his misconceived preference for purity,
the representative of the "Council of the Universal State in 2068" (*CP*
213) errs in his Luciferian pride. The logic of his argument seems
irresistible, much like that of the Grand Inquisitor in *The Brothers
Karamazov*. Since man is too weak to bear the burden of his freedom,
and left to himself becomes lost in contradictions and reaches far
beyond his own capabilities, he must be taught his own limitations.
"The Law of Blackout" ("Prawo Zaciemniania") frees him from intellectual anxiety, and "the Law of Diminished Goals" ("Prawo Zmniej-
szonych Celów"), paradoxically, preserves his idealism: "For a necessary condition of happiness is poverty and rancor" ("Ubóstwo i gorycz
albowiem są koniecznym warunkiem szczęścia").

The real political import of Milosz's futurological fantasy, the reason for its references not only to Dostoevsky but also to Witkiewicz and Orwell, is easy to see. Once again, Milosz shows that the realization of social utopias contradicts their idealistic premises. Such utopias can be attained only at the price of destroying the spiritual aspirations and metaphysical needs of the individual and usurping the right to decide what is best for people. Milosz nevertheless avoids facile condemnations, for although the logic of totalitarianism is based on false premises and its reasoning fatally flawed, the supposedly superior arguments it employs warrant attention. Can the charge be denied that bread had no taste: their bakeries were filled with it ("Chleb nie smakował im, bo dość go było w piekarni")? There is evidence enough that a life-style based on consumption, having satisfied the population's greatest needs, creates conditions for the legal incapacitation of the individual. Similarly, there is some truth in asserting that state pressure, while both arousing idealistic aspirations and hindering their achievement, creates a medium for compensatory processes—hence those "who curse interdictions / Afraid that interdictions might disappear" ("złorzeczą zakazom, / Już boją się, że mogłyby zniknąć zakazy"). On the other hand, Milosz perceptively observes that in a world that has destroyed absolute values, truth too may only be one member in a dialectical opposition, a "truth versus" some other truth or lie. Thus, even the praise for "censorship and scarcity" ("cenzura i niedostatek") is not simply derision. In a degraded reality axiology becomes stunted. The diagnosis of our culture ultimately reveals its fundamental dilemma, one that leads to a growing attraction to totalitarian ideologies: either safety for everyone at the price of obedience and discipline of its citizens or free choice with all its attendant discomforts.

These examples show that for Milosz, more important than the creation of individualized speakers is an analysis of the problems that preoccupy him. It is easy to show that the various aspects of totalitarianism as well as the dialectic of seeing oneself and being seen by others invariably absorb his attention. Unlike other masters of the dramatic monologue, such as Jules Laforgue,[2] Robert Browning, or Ezra Pound,[3] Milosz is little interested in a detailed recreation of the social context or the personality features of his narrator-characters. He reduces such information to an essential minimum that allows recognition but at the same time hinders concretization. All we know about Siegfried is that he served in Hitler's army during the war and that he later contemplated the defeat of his nation. Nor is it clear who is the representative of power in the state of the future who, not by accident, speaks in the plural. Milosz also avoids, with some exceptions, creating characters with real or fictional names or a legitimizing historical, mythological, or literary genealogy. The reader can learn about the qualities of the speaker—his fate, attitudes, values, and background—only indirectly from his speech. But even language does not completely solve the problem of identity, for the ability of language to characterize is limited, as can be seen in the above examples. Milosz's techniques are probably intended to reflect in poetics the process of interiorizing the points of view of others. Milosz not only universalizes private experiences but also acknowledges the convictions and experiences as partly his own.

That acknowledgment does not mean, of course, that the implied author loses his independence to his speakers. They remain separate from him both physically and spiritually. In the constant game of apparent identifications and immediate dissimulations, approaches and retreats, the authorial "I" takes care to mark the distance from the external attributes of the narrator as well as from his worldview. The simplest means of preserving distance is irony. In the examples cited, irony appears on several levels of the text simultaneously. Not only does the author, for the purposes of his own ironic attacks, get the better of his subject (who unmasks himself by his own speeches), but the subject speaks ironically of the heroes. Siegfried derides the "reformers of mankind" ("naprawiacze ludzkości") who, as he foresees, "will exclaim: We? We are innocent, we did not know" ("krzykną: My? My niewinni! Myśmy nie wiedzieli!"). The representative of a totalitarian state ridicules its citizens: "The land of Cockaigne allures them and repels; / They would find there nothingness, i.e., themselves" ("Kraj pieczonych gołąbków nęci ich i odpycha. / Spotkaliby tam tylko nicość, inaczej: siebie").

Thus, the ironist who directs his barbs at other objects may easily become the subject of irony, and vice versa, particularly since the author himself is not immune to its sting. Irony is aimed not only at certain views but also at the one who holds them, although what on one level seems to be an ironic unmasking is on another level completely serious.[4] If we look at only the passages already cited, we can see that they lay bare a certain hypocrisy, a cowardly conformity, society's delusion in the face of the historically changing forms of authoritarian systems. However, a sociopsychological diagnosis inscribed in objections raised by that fact does not lose its accuracy. That is all the more true since it concerns the state of mind of a collective, living throughout the centuries in a world that has now become unhinged. Irony presumes the right to have the last word, and in Milosz's poetry no one is able to boast of this right.

MASKS OR ROLES?

Milosz particularly favors forms of expression somewhere between the direct monologue and the dramatic monologue. To term his favorite forms of expression indirect monologue would mean to diminish their richness and reduce their variety.

Thus far our discussion has led to the conclusion that Milosz's poetry displays some new quality that is outside traditional categories and for which there is no accurate name. As a first example, to consider "The World" an indirect monologue is perhaps too hasty, since when examined more closely, the image of the speaker in the poem exhibits a subtlety and complexity that escapes simple formulas.[5] But what is striking is that the points of view of the adult and the child interpenetrate in both the emotional outpourings of the main narrator and the utterances of the characters, the father and the mother. This effect can be observed on the level of linguistic style (poetic metaphors and philosophical and religious terms exist alongside simplified syntax and diminutives), categories of thought (abstraction alongside depiction), and modes of understanding (a vision from down low, as if through the eyes of a child, alongside a vision from above, from the universe, that takes in—as in "A Parable of the Poppy"—the whole of existence). In addition, a perceptible gradation of the level of knowledge occurs, starting with that of children and proceeding to that of the parents and finally that of the author. More crucial, however, is that both approaches to the world are simultaneously affirmed and questioned.

In this juxtaposition a vision of the world as it ought to be, using models taken from Saint Thomas Aquinas, turns out to be either an illusion the poet defends despite the facts or itself a desperate attempt to defend threatened values, a therapeutic measure or an act of heroic choice. Hence the Polish subtitle, "poema naiwne," "a naive poem," may be interpreted in two ways: as an affirmation of an attitude with a long and noble tradition (Christ himself taught his followers to be like little children) or an ironic unveiling of a conviction that is both anachronistic and based on delusion. This variation of meanings is even suggested by Milosz's choice of words. In Polish the term *poema* is associated with past literary forms, whereas the epithet *naiwne* may, depending on the intent of the speaker, have positive associations as a synonym for purity, innocence, and trust, or negative ones, signifying foolishness and limitation.

Who then does the author purport to be? Is he donning the mask of a child or the mask of a sage extolling a holy naiveté? How might we establish the degree of identification between the author and these points of view when he alternates between them, constantly balancing on the borderline between irony and nonirony? What type of utterance is it—indirect monologue, or perhaps a creation independent of the author, an internally divided speaker? The very possibility of posing these questions indicates how inapplicable the traditional typology is to Milosz's poetry.

Indeed, not without reason does Milosz warn in his "Semi-Private Letter on Poetry" ("List pół-prywatny o poezji") against treating these creations as "his own disguises" (*K* 73). The crucial issue is no longer the distance or the emotional relation of the author to the speaker but the speaker's ontological status. In other words, both the identity of the persona and the nature of the lyric situation are called into question. This is a result of the increase in the number of persons speaking in the poem combined with an effacement of the distinctions between their utterances (facilitated by both the lyric "you" and the quotation of other voices) and also the endowing of the speaker with qualities of at least two different personalities, one of which shows certain similarities with the authorial "I." More simply, until the end of the poem it is not clear who the speaker is, whether he is always the same character, and where his utterance begins and ends. Precisely this vagueness and fluidity is, we may presume, one of the rules of a conscious game that the poet plays with the reader, a game all the more risky and dangerous because by means of direct and indirect autobiographical allusions it involves the person of the creator himself.

Milosz's postwar poetry provides abundant examples in which the identity of the speaker and his relation to the implied author constitute an extremely difficult problem to disentangle. Practically every work presents a unique situation. The clearest example is "I Sleep a Lot," where the question of who is speaking at any given moment is difficult to answer:

I sleep a lot and read St. Thomas Aquinas
or *The Death of God* (that's a Protestant book).
To the right the bay as if molten tin,
beyond the bay, city, beyond the city, ocean,
beyond the ocean, ocean, till Japan.
To the left dry hills with white grass,
beyond the hills an irrigated valley where rice is grown,
beyond the valley, mountains and Ponderosa pines,
beyond the mountains, desert and sheep.

When I couldn't do without alcohol, I drove myself on alcohol,
When I couldn't do without cigarettes and coffee, I drove myself on
    cigarettes and coffee.
I was courageous. Industrious. Nearly a model of virtue.
But that is good for nothing.

Please, Doctor, I feel a pain.
Not here. No, not here. Even I don't know.
Maybe it's too many islands and continents,
unpronounced words, bazaars, wooden flutes,
or too much drinking to the mirror, without beauty,
though one was to be a kind of archangel
or a Saint George, over there, on St. George Street.

Please, Medicine Man, I feel a pain.
I always believed in spells and incantations.
Sure, women have only one, Catholic, soul,
but we have two. When you start to dance
you visit remote pueblos in your sleep
and even lands you have never seen.
Put on, I beg you, charms made of feathers,
now it's time to help one of your own.
I have read many books but I don't believe them.
When it hurts we return to the banks of certain rivers.
I remember those crosses with chiseled suns and moons
and wizards, how they worked during an outbreak of typhus.
Send your second soul beyond the mountains, beyond time.
Tell me what you saw, I will wait.

(CP 177–178)

Dużo śpię i czytam Tomasza z Akwinu
albo "Śmierć Boga" (takie protestanckie dzieło).
Na prawo zatoka jak odlana z cyny,
za tą zatoką miasto, za miastem ocean,
za oceanem ocean, aż do Japonii.
Na lewo suche pagórki z białą trawą,
za pagórkami nawodniona dolina gdzie uprawia się ryż,

za doliną góry i sosny ponderosa,
za górami pustynia i owce.
Kiedy nie mogłem bez alkoholu, jechałem na alkoholu.
Kiedy nie mogłem bez papierosów i kawy, jechałem na papierosach
    i kawie.
Byłem odważny. Pracowity. Prawie wzór cnoty.
Ale to nie przydaje się na nic.

Panie doktorze, boli mnie.
Nie tu. Nie, nie tu. Sam już nie wiem.
Może to nadmiar wysp i kontynentów,
nie powiedzianych słów, bazarów i drewnianych fletów,
albo picia do lustra, bez urody,
choć miało się być czymś w rodzaju archanioła
albo świętego Jerzego na Świętojerskim Prospekcie.

Panie znachorze, boli mnie.
Zawsze wierzyłem w gusła i zabobony.
Naturalnie że kobiety mają tylko jedną, katolicką, duszę
ale my mamy dwie. Kiedy zatańczysz,
we śnie odwiedzasz odległe pueblos
i nawet ziemie nigdy nie widziane.

Włóż, proszę ciebie, amulety z piór,
poratować trzeba swojego.
Ja czytałem dużo książek ale im nie wierzę.
Kiedy boli powracamy nad jakieś rzeki,
pamiętam tamte krzyże ze znakami słońca i księżyca,
i czarowników, jak pracowali kiedy była epidemia tyfusu.
Wyślij swoją drugą duszę za góry, za czas.
Powiedz, będę czekać, co widziałeś.

In creating a mood of intimate confession, the first line evokes the traditional model of lyrical poetry. To reinforce the realistic features of his vision, the author exploits his own California setting: the San Francisco Bay area, the Sacramento valley, and the dry landscape of Nevada. Even the references to the books read by the speaker recall Milosz's own reading. Certainly, their choice and interconnection bring the poem additional, symbolic meanings. In his own books, such as *Native Realm* and *Visions from San Francisco Bay*, Milosz often refers to Aquinas, and in an interview he reiterated his interest in Gabriel Vahanian's *Death of God*.[6]

Starting with the plaintive cry "Please, Doctor, I feel a pain," the speaker separates himself gradually from the author. The only remaining aspects of their former resemblance are the confession of the pain of existence and an allusion to Vilnius (Saint George Street was one of the main streets in the city). The identity of the man who addresses himself to the Medicine Man is not certain. It might be the same person, but it could also be the Mexican peasant who "believes in spells and incantations" and is sure that "women have only one, Catholic, soul" but men have two. It could even be a disappointed intellectual who has read many books but no longer believes them.

In "I Sleep a Lot" it is not difficult to recognize some of the recurrent motifs of Milosz's poetry. He returns often in his imagination and memory to the banks of the river of his childhood. Those "crosses with chiseled suns and moons" appear in "To Robinson Jeffers" (*CP* 224–225). Milosz solemnly declares his own belief in "spells and incantations" in "Bypassing Rue Descartes" (*CP* 382–383; "Rue Descartes").

Milosz has created a character who is separate from himself but has endowed him with many of his own qualities; he has embodied himself in someone entirely different without giving up his own sovereignty. Hence, both the speaker and the author—as in the poems previously analyzed—suffer from a strange kind of split personality.[7] Moreover, the suggestion of their being identical, strongly stressed at the beginning of the poem, is undermined at its end. This undermining is promoted both by the contradictory attributes with which the speaker is endowed and by the changes in his own utterance. It gradually moves from a direct lyric to a form combining features of both the lyric of masks and roles. From a first-person utterance, it moves through the lyric "you" toward a hidden dialogue revealed both in verbal replies to the silent questions of an interlocutor and in commands addressed directly to him: "Put on," "Send," "Tell me."

Thus, "I Sleep a Lot" can be viewed as a model of the evolution of Milosz's poetry as a whole. That evolution fluctuates between two major poles: identification of the speaker with the author, and their total separation. To be more precise, it proceeds from a rather unclear distinction between the author, the speaker, and the hero, through a growing independence of the speaker until the moment when the speaker's identity and the degree of his identification with the author become a structural feature of the text. This movement is characteristic of the majority of Milosz's California poems.

Let us once again return to "From the Rising of the Sun." The part entitled "The Accuser" ends with a chorus of voices whose origin is unknown:

—Yet I have learned how to live with my grief.

—As if putting words together has been of help.

—Not true, there were others, grace and beauty,
I bowed to them, revered them,
I brought them my gifts.

(CP 306–307)

—Nauczyłem się jednak żyć z moją zgryzotą.

—Jak gdyby coś pomogło układanie słów.

—Nieprawda, byli inni, łaska i uroda,
Pokłoniłem się im, uwielbiłem ich,
Dary przyniosłem.

Perhaps the best commentary on this passage is the confession of one of Milosz's personae in "The Wormwood Star" from "The Separate Notebooks":

He hears voices but he does not understand the screams, prayers, blasphemies, hymns which chose him for their medium. He would like to know who he was, but he does not know. He would like to be one, but he is a self-contradictory multitude which gives him some joy, but more shame.

(CP 374)

Słyszy głosy, ale nie pojmuje tych krzyków, modlitw, bluźnierstw, hymnów, które jego obrały za medium. Chciałby wiedzieć kim był, a nie wie. Chciałby być jeden, a jest wielością w sobie sprzeczną, która go trochę tylko cieszy, a bardziej zawstydza.

Thus Milosz creates a new type of lyric poetry while retaining the traditional *topos* of the poet as seer. But—and this is his innovation—the seer not only resembles the author in many respects but also is uncertain about his identity. We can sense different and unidentified voices within his speech, voices that often cannot be distinguished from his own. The result of this multiplicity is the speaker's interior diffusion. The identity of the persona is no longer obvious but has become a conflict the reader himself must resolve. In short, this kind of monologue not only provides an exceptional opportunity to see the world from various viewpoints but also has become a way to restore the poet's ego. This restoration, however, can be as hypothetical and momentary as the very definition of humanness is hypothetical and momentary.

DISINHERITANCE

The problem of who is speaking is usually resolved by appealing to the author. He is the court of last resort, deciding which of the utterances we may validly recognize as his and which we are to consider the opinions of others. Yet here the implied author too is "a self-contradictory multitude." It is not enough to repeat that in Milosz's case the image of the author is based on antinomies expressed not only in references to opposing points of view to which the author subscribes to some degree, or in the utilization of styles and genres belonging to different periods. Equally important is the setting aside of the possibility of the author's direct intervention. For example, Milosz's poem in praise of intellect is entitled "Calling" ("Zaklęcie," 1968). He entitled his poetic credo, in accordance with classical tradition, "*Ars Poetica*" (1968), but then added a question mark. He has written his own commentary to "*L'Accélération de l'histoire*" (1971) and "Three Talks on Civilization," not to mention his self-evaluations in "From the Rising of the Sun" and "The Separate Notebooks." In these poems, to the extent that commentary appears in dialogue (whether quoted directly or paraphrased), and in the longer poetical works, the author sometimes changes places with the narrator or the hero, judging his own emotions and experiences with the distance proper to a fully autonomous literary character. The result is that the authorial word is given the same hypothetical and relative quality that the utterances of the subject have.

This is also true, though it may seem surprising, of the moralizing instructions. These do not appear frequently, and they are voiced by someone who only resembles the author slightly (as in "Treatise on Morals"). They are either camouflaged by irony that discredits convictions alien to Milosz (as in "Higher Arguments") or cast in an elevated rhetorical tone (as in "To a Politician" ["Do polityka"]), introducing a bit of distance almost spontaneously. In the Czarnecka interview Milosz admits that he responds with open aversion to those of his works that "arose as a moral response" at a given moment, saying that "writing such poems always affected me badly" (*PS* 64). To some extent he is justified because those poems are not as a rule his greatest artistic achievements. The moral creed contained in his poetry is accepted by virtue of an unspoken understanding with the reader rather than open authorial declarations. His affirmation of values is not connected with self-affirmation but arises more from an excessive tendency to self-criticism and a sense of guilt and an aversion to excessively noble rhetoric. Perhaps the feeling of guilt stems, as Harold Segel suggests, from the fact that after the war Milosz worked with the government of the People's Republic of Poland.[8] In view of the fact that many suffered at that time for their political views, Milosz now considers this a consciously chosen dishonorable activity. It is not out of the question, however, that his conscience is disturbed by the fact that he did not take part in the Warsaw Uprising of 1944 and perish as did so many poets.

Clearly, the portrait of the author that develops during the course of a reading does not disintegrate into disparate fragments. The creator's memory stands behind them, and the choice of problems, symbols, motifs, and key words that recur in Milosz's poems is easily recognizable. Without a doubt, Milosz's worldview constitutes a cohesive whole marked by inner logic, although not without dramatic tensions. That is what I have sought to demonstrate in the preceding chapters, deliberately setting aside the question of the poet's masks and disguises, passing over the polyphony of his poetry, and temporarily disregarding (sometimes considered methodologically inadmissible) the distinction between Milosz's poetry and his prose. The word expressed in verse has a more hypothetical nature, but that word is reinforced by the word that is directly expressed. The guarantee of unity is also the poet's voice breaking through the voices of others. One might say that just as the point of reference for the metamorphosis of the subject is the authorial "I" in poetry, so too the crystallizing means for that authorial "I" is the subjectivity of the creator himself. In other words, whereas in Milosz the Christian idea of the person focuses the various definitions of man, a dynamic conception of personality based on a fragile equilibrium of contradictory elements makes the profiles of the speaker and the implied author similar.

Although that is true when considering Milosz's output as a whole, in individual poems these profiles are sometimes clear, at other times blurred. The reader must not only distinguish those personality features that belong to the speaker and the implied author but also, more important, construct their identities. These are determined each time by the point of view and the selection and arrangement of information. The task is further complicated since the reader is presented with a chorus of mingled voices, incomplete utterances the origin of which is difficult to determine, and the divided subjectivity of the speaker. The reader has few clear directions, and those he possesses are often contradictory. This situation causes extraordinary problems when the reader must determine the distance dividing the "I" of the speaker from the "I" of the author and assess the degree of their identification. Mistakes can easily be made.

Similar situations arise when interpreting other poets. Milosz, however, invests them with particular significance, incorporating the process of discovering and constructing identity into the very construction of the poem. This occurs primarily because the speaker-medium is not only transmitting the word of others but also betraying a similarity with the implied author. The originality of this device is perhaps best seen if we compare Milosz with T. S. Eliot. The clearest example is *The Waste Land,* a text likewise interlaced with heterogeneous quotations and citations of the speech of others. It is well known that Eliot also employs dialogue forms and a constantly shifting speaker. But Eliot's interpolations are signaled by either quotation marks or the clear use of an alien style. Their source is known (with the aid of Eliot's meticulous footnotes), and Tiresias is beyond doubt someone other than the authorial "I." In Milosz, by contrast, just as the word of another imperceptibly penetrates the author's speech, so too another personality imperceptibly becomes part of his own. This takes place, moreover, not without conflicts and reflexes of self-defense. As Milosz says, he is "a medium, but a suspicious one" (*PS* 175).

The conclusion seems to be that the concept of polyphony can be accurately applied to Milosz's poetry but remains inadequate.[9] The process in which the individual points of view become independent halts at the moment when they are to break away from the author. The acts of enunciation constantly oscillate between polyphony and monophony: the voices separate from the voice of the author and then rejoin it, though he does not lose control over them.[10] Despite all the divisions in the ego of the subject, the various "you"s to whom he entrusts judgment of himself, the person of the author remains ultimately the same. Even the autonomy of characters who represent convictions that are contradictory to the author's is, as I have tried to show, limited. Precisely the internal dynamics of the speaker, the ceaseless centrifugal and centripetal movement, endow Milosz's poetic word with a flickering ambiguity. On the level of worldview, this movement is perhaps a function of relativism or an expression of struggle with doubts that press from all sides.

Attempts to create a subject different from the author (something with which the dramatic monologue is connected) were, as Robert Langbaum observed, a reaction on the one hand to the autobiographism and confessional tone of romantic poetry and on the other to its concomitant faith in the existence of an unchangeable self.[11] The social sciences and the discoveries of psychoanalysis, however, effectively shook that faith. Consequently, contemporary advocates of the ego seek support primarily in the theories of Jung and his break with the vision of subjectivity as only an individual and conscious creation. Also no longer tenable is the idea of the self as separate from the world and constituting an autonomous source of values the world does not possess. The comparison with romanticism in Langbaum's study is particularly interesting. Twentieth-century romantics, as Langbaum terms T. S. Eliot, Thomas Mann, D. H. Lawrence, and William Butler Yeats, among others, differ from their predecessors primarily in the fact that they no longer oppose a sovereign ego to culture. Quite the reverse, they consider the ego to be the creation of culture, as much internalized as existing objectively in the form of symbols reflecting archetypes. Finding his dim image in cultural symbols, the individual, instead of losing his identity, regains it anew.

That train of thought is certainly close to Milosz; there are numerous arguments in favor of including him among the restorers of romanticism. But here too Milosz introduces his own features. Breaking with naive, superficial autobiographism, he at the same time returns to a poetically created and rendered biography the value of a system of signs explaining an individual human existence. In a single life remnants of ancient myths and archetypes appear and crystallize in a unique and unrepeatable model, whereas biography fills mythic stories with living content. Milosz undoubtedly would consider Eliot's "archetypal identity" to be just one more inconclusive concept referring to man in general and ignoring the specificity of the individual.[12] We need only recall "Paradise," where the speaker, who says, "I ate from the Tree / Of Knowledge. I was expelled by the archangel's sword" (*CP* 392; "Jadłem z drzewa / Wiadomości. Byłem wygnany mieczem archanioła"), is both a representative of humanity who recounts his cognitive adventure in the language of symbolic parable and one who finds an entirely personal meaning in biblical history, an alter ego of the author. He is also a connoisseur of art, who digresses while viewing Hieronymus Bosch's triptych. This last aspect of the speaker diminishes the seriousness of his reflection and suggests it is conventional.

Why, then, is identity such an agonizing problem for Milosz, his ceaseless pursuit, and not something obvious, something given? What is the source of his feeling of division and lack of identity? His use of personae, which not only appear in individual poems but also wend their way through his entire oeuvre, undergoing various transformations, provides a clue. We can easily distinguish the most important personae: the pupil, the witness, the pilgrim, the prophet. Just enumerating them alerts us to the scale of experiences they represent and the different traditions from which they stem. The search for authority, for refuge in the shadow of a master's wisdom—this is the classical tradition. The pilgrim and prophet point to romanticism. Giving witness, crucial after great historical cataclysms, acquires unusual significance in twentieth-century literature.

Authorial personae usually take the form of a pair of oppositions that exchange features and functions, ultimately merging into other oppositional pairs. Thus, the pair pupil–teacher is accompanied by two further pairs, child–adult and simpleton–wise man, all of which appear in "The World." The witness easily becomes prosecutor and judge; the pilgrim is now an exile, now an inhabitant of the entire earth. Not only do the roles undergo constant change, but the values associated with the roles also shift. For example, learning may be pursued in good or bad faith; the teacher may be an advocate of fundamental values or their cynical manipulator. Thus, the Bible and catechism inspire "To Father Ch." and "Dialogue" ("Dialog"), whereas Enlightenment faith in the power of reason controls "Treatise on Morals" and "To Jonathan Swift." But even reason, it turns out, may lead one astray, as in "Child of Europe" ("Dziecię Europy," 1946); thus "Readings" refers back to the wisdom of the Gospels.

In addition, an independent inner evolution occurs in these pairs, leading them throughout the development of Milosz's poetry to the edge of self-contradiction. Thus, as in "With Trumpets and Zithers," the pupil turns away from his master and has no confidence in the usefulness of knowledge: "Beyond seven rocky mountains I searched for my Teacher and yet I am here, not myself, at a pit of tangled bones ("Za siedmią skalistych gór szukałem Nauczyciela, aż jestem tutaj, nie ja, przed jamą splątanych kości"). The witness sits in the condemned man's box, doubting his ability to know and the reliability of his testimony. From "Letter of January 1, 1935" through "In Fever, 1939" to "From the Rising of the Sun" the poet-prophet or bard is tormented by the sin of pride, by shame at his incomprehensible superiority toward others and the deafness of his listeners to his prophecy. In the end the pilgrim wanders aimlessly, fixing his attention only on movement in space: transcendence turns out to be elusive and the Homeland–Holy Land has been wiped from the face of the earth.

Viewing one's own biography through the prism of inherited models of attitudes and behaviors drives Milosz to verify literary tradition. This is especially true of romanticism, where not only the pilgrim and prophet but also the witness and the pupil were important characters. All these characters really can be considered variants of the romantic hero, components in the romantic biography. Milosz is certainly conscious of this, repeatedly emphasizing that the stages of his own life seem to follow those of Adam Mickiewicz's.[13] Both poets are linked by Wilno, the city of their university studies and their youthful friendships, the course of their foreign wanderings (France, Italy, and Switzerland), and finally their lecturing on Slavic literatures at a foreign university. In this way Milosz transforms his own biography into a kind of personal myth.

Milosz attaches such significance to biography as a hypothetical unity, a system of signs that illuminates the meaning of an individual life, and a personal myth because biography legitimizes a personal existential perspective. Faced with the ruins of concepts purporting to explain all human history, concepts like Hegelianism or dialectical materialism, and the threat of bending history to immediate needs or even its falsification, the individual biography seems the sole trustworthy means of reconciling accident with necessity. In addition, the individual biography promises refuge from the strangeness of the environment. Probably for this reason, particularly in California, Milosz's major source of material for his poetry has been his recollections of childhood and youth. The poet's biography is open to the whole world, or conversely, it may incorporate the world into itself.[14]

In pushing the components of romantic biography to the verge of self-destruction, Milosz also includes its myth-making function. Biography aids in the search for meaning, the reason for life, and its values beyond itself in the erotic, patriotic, moral, and religious spheres of ideas. The compensatory mechanism in the romantic biography is all too obvious. At the same time the life of the individual human being appears in different aspects simultaneously, as if along different lengths of ribbon. Its meaning seems now clear and comprehensible, now dark and obscure.

Milosz's personae are one more reflection of his striving to find his own place in a community and achieve wholeness. The pupil craves unshakable knowledge; the witness, participation; the pilgrim, a clearly marked road and a destination worthy of his efforts;[15] the prophet, faith and obedience. Each of them, more painfully than his romantic predecessor, experiences loss, isolation, and division. Each is stripped of all illusions and given over to the heroic effort of opposing the nothingness that presses from every side. Perhaps that is the reason he must search for his own identity.

With the passage of time it is increasingly clear that through his writing Milosz relates the history of his own disinheritance, and not just his alone. He is reminiscent of Zbigniew Herbert, in whose poetry, as Stanisław Barańczak has shown, the fundamental opposition is that of "the realm of inheritance" ("obszar dziedzictwa") versus "the realm of disinheritance" ("obszar wydziedziczenia").[16] Herbert's hero is always suspended between East and West, between the past and the present, between myth and empiricism, primarily because of historical events in which the biographical peripeteia of the poet coincides with the fate of Poland: the loss of his own native land is caused by Poland's loss of independence. In a larger dimension, for Herbert, the history of the twentieth century exemplifies the dynamic of civilization that has abandoned its Mediterranean past. For Milosz, disinheritance is an inevitable part of the human condition, an in-between state natural to every inhabitant of the earth: man is always between nature and culture, history and transcendence, Christian tradition and its negation, religion and science. For that reason Herbert and Milosz interpret the Fall differently. For Herbert, it is a symbol of the loss of an idyll—personal, patriotic, cultural. For Milosz, it is the image of existential division. Herbert sees himself outside the gates of Paradise; Milosz, in the shadow of the tree of knowledge.

7

Palimpsest

Mimesis clearly has two aspects. One concerns the tangible, visible world, and the other concerns the various ways it is presented. An attempt to reflect in poetry an individual sensual experience or some particular that historical memory fills with meaning immediately finds itself located in the context of similar attempts. The poet's language not only struggles with the inexpressible and with his own limitations but also must resist the pressure of other formulations, his own and those of other poets. To some extent aside from, or even contrary to, "the passionate pursuit of the Real" a work is born that with increasing persistence makes its own inner laws known.

In his Nobel Prize speech Milosz asserts that

> every poet depends upon generations who wrote in his native tongue; he inherits styles and forms elaborated by those who lived before him. At the same time, though, he feels that those old means of expression are not adequate to his own experience. When adapting himself, he hears an internal voice that warns him against mask and disguise. But when rebelling, he falls in turn into dependence on his contemporaries, various movements of the avant-garde. Alas, it is enough for him to publish his first volume of poems to find himself entrapped. For hardly has the print dried when that work, which seemed to him the most personal, appears to be enmeshed in the style of others. The only way to counter an obscure remorse is to continue searching and to publish a new book, but then everything repeats itself, so there is no end to that chase. And it may happen that leaving behind books as if they were dry snake skins, in a constant escape forward from what has been done in the past, he receives the Nobel Prize.
>
> (NL 5–6)

The poem "No More" perhaps best reflects the duality of mimesis and Milosz's own inner turmoil. We immediately see that Milosz is able to turn apparently obvious truths into an authentic drama, extracting from it a gamut of shades and subtle complications. Two kinds of poetry are opposed in this poem. The first, which is best exemplified by the art of Japan and symbolically represents this type of poetry, gives up the cognitive, the ambition to discover, and is content with repeating conventional aesthetic models. It is marked by the use of customary emotional expressions, facile imitation, and faithfulness to artistic canons hallowed by centuries-long tradition. The poet ceases to be someone extraordinary and raised above the crowd, a demiurge or a prophet. Any merchant or artisan may play this role—in a word, anyone who is able to write "verses about cherry blossoms, / Chrysanthemums and the full moon" ("wiersze o kwitnieniu wiśni, / O chryzantemach i pełni księżyca").

The second variety of poetry is not satisfied with the *making* of verse on a given theme. Quite the contrary, it measures its value according to the skill of *description* of reality in its moment-by-moment flow. The poet's ambition is to grasp the essence of phenomena, go beyond the limitations imposed by the linear sequence of words, and finally attain an understanding that preserves the indissoluble essence of a thing and yet retains some influence on the attitude of the viewer. Milosz says:

> If only I could describe the courtesans of Venice
> As in a loggia they teased a peacock with a twig.
> And out of brocade, the pearls of their belt,
> Set free heavy breasts and the reddish weal
> Where the buttoned dress marked the belly,
> As vividly as seen by the skipper of galleons
> Who landed that morning with a cargo of gold . . .
> (CP 123)

> Gdybym ja mógł weneckie kurtyzany
> Opisać, jak w podwórzu witką drażnią pawia,
> I z tkaniny jedwabnej, z perłowej przepaski
> Wyłuskać ociężałe piersi, czerwonawą
> Pręgę na brzuchu od zapięcia sukni,
> Tak przynajmniej jak widział szyper galeonów
> Przybyłych tego ranka z ładunkami złota . . .

Thus, the two theories of poetic art, based on two different conceptions of the world, the subject, truth, and language, are placed side by side here. Subjectivity is opposed to objectivity and cold distance; the elusive quiver of a passing moment, to the eternal; the individual, to the collective; doubt and hypothesis, to certainty; invention and innovation, to esthetic norms; the cognitive value, to the aesthetic value;

and so on. This series of oppositions could be extended, but what is more important is that the second type of poetry, as the use of the conditional mood indicates, remains solely in the realm of projection. It is an unrealized postulate. Hence the speaker's declaration that he has chosen the first kind of poetry is not surprising because he has been unable to meet the demands of the second kind. That choice is at the same time an admission of the defeat of poetry in its confrontation with the world, the defeat of language that cannot bear the weight of existence. The word is helpless in the face of the simultaneous existence of distant moments in time because it itself unfolds in time. Moreover, evaporating in the air, language turns out to be less enduring than material objects, more open to destruction:

> And if I could find for their miserable bones
>
> .   .   .   .
>
> A word more enduring than their last-used comb
> That in the rot under tombstones, alone, awaits the light . . .
>
> > (CP 123)

> I gdybym równocześnie mógł ich biedne kości
>
> .   .   .   .
>
> Zamknąć w słowie mocniejszym niż ostatni grzebień
> Który w próchnie pod płytą, sam, czeka na światło . . .

The aesthetic values of poetry are then only an insignificant attribute, a small compensation for an unattainable truth. For

> > Out of reluctant matter
> What can be gathered? Nothing, beauty at best.
> > (CP 123)

> > Z opornej materii
> Co da się zebrać? Nic, najwyżej piękno.

The phrase "at best" expresses both irony directed toward the poet-aesthetes and helplessness in the face of the process of knowing.

Nevertheless, the poet's choice of his arguments and their hidden significance undermines the entire logical course of this argument. The first paradox is that contrary to solemn assurances, the speaker in the poem—who only partly coincides with the author—has not changed his opinion about poetry nor taken the victor's laurels away from the second kind of poetry. At most, he has only pointed out its limitations.

The description of the fluid matter of the world is never completely free and unfettered. The limping repetitiveness of the word corresponds to the unrepeatable phenomena of existence. Any presentation of external reality must of necessity be expressed through stiff conventions, schemata, and symbols. They can be modified but not avoided altogether.

The second paradox is that at the moment when the persona states "If only I could describe . . ." he does exactly that and fulfills the conditions claimed to be impossible. The vividness and precision of the description are clearly tinged with the erotic, as befits the viewer, "the skipper of galleons." In his mind's eye he undresses the courtesans, delighting in the intimate details of their bodies. Instead of their complete image we see "heavy breasts" and "the reddish weal / Where the buttoned dress marked the belly." What is interesting is that this is not merely a rendering of the deformation that the world undergoes in a subjective view. The speaker wants to describe things "as vividly as seen" by a hero who is separate from him, rooted in a concrete time and place. He wants to render the subject and the object in their interdependence, their mutual conditioning. As a result the world rendered is neither a neutral background for the experiences of the characters nor simply a projection of the speaker's imaginings, a stream of flickering, random impressions. It is sufficiently objectified that organization can be perceived in the picture, and yet the details are based on a deformation so that the picture is marked by the presence of the viewer.

Here further complications arise, for the poet attempts to incorporate himself somehow into the viewer. He would like to see through the eyes of the skipper of galleons; he would like to attain that minimal faithfulness proper to an individual point of view. In short, he wants to record one more moment of seeing so that he might have his own part in it. The use of the conditional mood—the third paradox—unexpectedly makes it possible to suspend time, and moments vastly distant from one another may be spoken of as if they were simultaneous. Hence the courtesans appear at the height of their physical charms (at court) and in mortal decay (in a cemetery). Moreover, the very composition of the poem is eloquent proof of faith in the immortality of poetry, even based as it is on the erosion of time and the changeability of speech.

My somewhat rambling interpretation should be supplemented at this point by Milosz's own explanation. In *The Witness of Poetry* he writes:

> It would seem that the description of Venetian courtesans provides a valid proof of language's capacity to encounter the world. But immediately the speaker undermines that conclusion. This he does most obviously by referring to a painting by Carpaccio, which depicts a yard in Venice where the courtesans are sitting and teasing a peacock with a twig. Thus not only language changes reality into a catalogue of data, but reality appears as mediated by a work of painting—in other words, not in its original state but already well ordered, already a part of culture. If reality exists, then how are we to dream of reaching it without intermediaries of one or another sort, whether they are other literary works or visions provided by the whole past of art? Thus the protest against conventions, instead of taking us to some free space where a poet can encounter the world directly, as on the first day of Creation, again sends us back to those historical strata that already exist as form.
> (WP 74–75)

Grossly simplified, the hidden meaning of the poem can be expressed as follows: the poet's eternal drama played out between realism and classicism has become particularly intense. A hitherto unknown sensitivity to the conventionality of language now exists, together with the idea that the subject is hypothetical and, even more generally, with an awareness of the artificiality of art. It would seem, then, that a weakness should be turned into a strength, to lay bare the limitations of form and come closer to the unnamable through conscious play with those limitations. Each component, each layer of the poem ought to be both the subject and the object of interpretation. In "No More" the skipper interprets the courtesans, the speaker interprets the character of the skipper, and the author-poet interprets the painting by Carpaccio. Beyond this, the art of Japan illuminates European art, and classicism carries on its debate with realism. In working through to reality, one must always bear in mind the presence of a foreign style, the presence of another person, and the presence of works not one's own.

MIMICKING THE VOICES OF OTHERS

It is well known that Milosz manipulates various genres, poetics, and styles with extraordinary agility. In his early work this skill resulted in what may have been an almost unconscious imitation of different twentieth-century styles, from expressionism through futurism and the avant-garde to late symbolism. With time, however, it has become an inherent property of Milosz's poetic speech. A conviction of the changeableness of history accompanies imitation, as well as a sense of the arbitrariness of all rules. The poet is fully aware that whether writing or speaking, he is determined by time and place of birth, milieu, personal experiences, and national culture. Contrary to the claims and delusions of the avant-garde, language is to a great extent ready-made, resistant to the writer's manipulation of it. At the moment of utterance each word immediately begins to fade into the past. The reverse also occurs, however, and voices from the past demand consideration of their circumstances, a reconstruction of the context in which they appeared.

Convention leaves its mark on both ancient and contemporary utterances. The norms by which we interpret tradition are conventional. It is impossible to draw on the rich storehouse of tradition neutrally, for even our gestures are immediately marked both semantically and axiologically. Though easy to formulate intellectually, this situation is difficult to grasp poetically.

As has been frequently noted in this study, Milosz's poetry is full of echoes of the canon of Polish poetry: Bible translations and the poetry of Jan Kochanowski, Mikołaj Sęp Szarzyński, Jan Andrzej Morsztyn, and Adam Mickiewicz. And yet in Milosz's poetry a discreet allusion to rhythm or versification is enriched by a startling break in intonation, a subtle shift in accent, or an original rhythm. As Jerzy Kwiatkowski observes: "The primary device of artistic play here is a certain asymmetry between suggestive but traditional versification and—what is far more modern—frequent utilization of colloquialisms, an immensely individual and extraordinarily supple syntax."[1] That is not all. A similar asymmetry appears elsewhere—between the style and the content it expresses, between the genre norm and its realization, between the traditional versification model and Milosz's use of it.[2] So many variants exist that it is difficult to enumerate them. In "Ballad" ("Ballada," 1958) the expressed monologue (addressed, moreover, to a dead person) fulfills the dramatic function. In "Ode to a Bird," where the very object of adoration is astonishing, philosophical reflection is intertwined with an erotic plot. In "To Laura" ("Do Laury," 1949) a pastoral idyll clashes with history, and a sentimental style is tinged with an ironic distance. Finally, in "Dithyramb" (*CP* 179;

"Dytyramb," 1965) ecstasy at sheer existence is reconciled with the thought of the insignificance of all things. In a word, the models that Milosz uses are subject to varied interpretations. More important, these interpretive manipulations do not appear separately on different levels of the work. On the contrary, a poem by Milosz sets up its own system for interpretation: the style is confronted with the versification; the imagery detaches itself from the general meaning of the poem; genre determinants are transformed by an intention contradictory to them; the message of a treatise is expressed in an ironic tone; a meta-physical discourse is couched as a tale for children; a long poem simul-taneously becomes a *silva rerum,*[3] an essay, a meditation, or a memoir. Of course, Milosz's style, versification, and genre can be studied sepa-rately, and such study yields a considerable number of surprises. But it is striking that all the elements of a Milosz poem refer to something beyond themselves, constructing an entire series of references and at the same time mutually illuminating one another, establishing their own unique context.

As regards stylization alone, its presence and frequency in Milosz's poetry has been explained by Jan Błoński as an effort toward "a full-ness of speech" ("pełnia mowy") and a resistance to the corruption of everyday language.[4] Stanisław Barańczak sees it as a reflection of "the proliferation of various mutually supplementing testimonies about re-ality."[5] But stylization may with equal justification be considered an offshoot of a "mediumistic" understanding of poetry. Someone who is the medium through whom others speak must remain faithful to the characteristics of their speech, which is both individual and dependent on a historical epoch. Milosz often repeats that other *voices* speak through him; he does not mention *texts.* Of himself he says, "I, one voice, no more, in the vast theater" ("An Appeal," *CP* 243; "Ja, głos, nic więcej, wielkiego teatrum"). This probably explains Milosz's sensi-tivity to the acoustical properties of quoted utterances, their awkward-ness, and their distinctive features of personality or milieu.

The question is whether this relation between voices and stylization can be reconciled with the idea, to some extent justified, that the entire culture is like a huge text requiring a sympathetic reading, or even that stylization constitutes one form of such a reading. After all, writes one critic, "stylization presumes that a specific style we consider to be its basis has been understood by us as a sign of certain attitudes, the result of choices that bear traces of someone's preferences and, as such, have been presented in both their essential and recognizable features."[6] This sign, it should be added, causes stylization to appear in two contexts simultaneously and fulfills its interpretive function in two directions, in relation to both the original style and the contemporary rules of speech. Such rules or norms exist in the stylized utterance like an awareness of something missing, a significant silence. What is hidden behind the style of another can only be reconstructed secondarily, by a comparison with the contemporary literary language.

Milosz's emphasis on the spoken rather than the textual nature of his stylizations enriches these general characteristics. Aside from utterances actually quoted, there are no attempts in Milosz's poetry to imitate the language of a single writer, a specific social group, or an isolated milieu. The context for his stylization is not an idiolect or specific work but a historical epoch—more precisely, the language of an era as it is refracted in the speech of a single person. And the dispersion of stylizations in Milosz is immense. There is practically no historical period in Polish literature whose language Milosz has not echoed. Let us take as one example, "Conversation at Easter 1620," which opens with the following question:

> Sir, now you are like a fly in a pitcher.
> Drunk with wine it rows with its legs.
> As much will remain of it, as of you, sir.
> In vain hope sweetens your anguish.
> Golden buttons, capes, ceremonial clothes
> Glimmer in the coffers while death says: it's mine.

> —Waść teraz jesteś jako mucha w dzbanie.
> Winem opita łapkami wiosłuje.
> Z niej tyle samo co z waści zostanie,
> Darmo nadzieja frasunki cukruje.
> Złociste guzy, kiereje i stroje
> W skrzyniach jaśnieją a śmierć mówi: moje.

Although the English translation does not convey it, the reader can be assured that Milosz has captured the flexible syntax of the baroque style in Polish—its typical choice of words and its vivid imagery. But this seemingly authentic passage is linguistically finer and clearer than the actual poetry of the period. We have only to dip into the works of Samuel Twardowski, Hieronim Morsztyn, or Daniel Naborowski to see this. Milosz introduces anachronism in such a way that the text does not lose its comprehensibility for the contemporary reader. He achieves the effect of faithfulness more through inflection and syntax than through lexicon. The words he chooses are archaic but generally familiar to, and understood by, the average educated reader. Only rarely does he employ an obscure expression. Though imitating Latin syntax, he does not violate the norms of twentieth-century Polish. His poetic filter lets through completely different elements of the baroque than do the filters of other Polish poets who imitate the baroque, such as Jerzy Harasymowicz or Stanisław Grochowiak.

Milosz's poetic filter is composed, in part, of the norms of modern Polish, but it also includes interpretations of the baroque known through scholarly or popular studies of the period and implied in the historically different imitations of the style. Stylization cannot be reduced simply to a more or less successful imitation of an ancient form of speech. Surely just as important is the re-creation of the meanings intended by the ancient model. Thus, attitudes formulated in a past period meant something different than they do now because the very act of reconstructing them affects their value. In a word, Milosz's filter is on the one hand common and on the other hand individual. Current opinions create it, but so do Milosz's own innovations. The romantics understood the baroque poets one way, and we understand them in another.

Milosz's complex and multileveled poetic reading of the baroque primarily seeks out the religious themes of the period. Hence "Conversation" seems to refer to two popular literary models of the baroque period: the theological dispute with the heretic and scenes of temptation by the devil. The first voice, in the above passage, is surely the devil's. The second, below, probably is that of a heretic who has not completely returned to the fold. Contrary to the teachings of the Roman church, he does not believe in an immortal soul and in earning merit on earth; rather, he puts all his faith in predestination. One of his prototypes could be, as the author suggests, Janusz Radziwiłł, a Calvinist who on his deathbed appealed to the Blessed Mother.

A difference in style and rhetoric influences the speech of both interlocutors. The language of the devil, betraying his low social status, favors blunt expressions and imitates a little of the carelessness of ordinary speech. The devil is vulgar and coarse; he constantly deprecates and offends his interlocutor. He is extremely deceitful, for in order to make his case, he employs the arguments of Lenten sermons. Taking examples from daily life, he demonstrates the futility of human pursuits, pleasures, and values in the face of man's inevitable end. Making lavish use of the macabre, the church employs a similar line of reasoning to oppose the transience of earthly existence with eternal happiness. In the same way Satan proves that religion is an outgrowth of fear of death.

The second voice in the poem, however, sounds completely different:

> I neither believe in the immortal soul
> Nor await a reward for my merits.
> My name and memory will be cast off like my dress,
> My age is over and my age was short.
> And when, vacuous, I will lie alone in the grave
> It is for infinite time, not for a moment.

> —Ani ja wierzę w duszę nieśmiertelną,
> Ani nagrody czekam dla zasługi.
> Imię i pamięć z szatą mi odejmą,
> Wiek mój skończony i wiek mój niedługi.
> A kiedy, pusty, legnę sam w mogile,
> Na nieskończone czasy, nie na chwilę.

Here Milosz's careful choice of words and limpid syntax go hand in hand with disciplined thought and speech, attention to precision, and logically cohesive exposition. This utterance, significantly closer to contemporary Polish, is remarkable for its noble tone and utilization of conventional figures of speech. It approaches a short, fervent prayer or a psalm. The dialogue between strongly individualized characters, styles, and views enriches and animates the meanings of both utterances. Naturally, a stylized utterance is basically more limited in its possibilities to transmit new content. It is made up of frozen signs and stamped with the memory of its textual origin. Precisely the continual effort to push stylization in the direction of living, spontaneous, personal speech is, in my opinion, one of the most important features of Milosz's poetic language.

This intuition could be proved only through laborious examination of his works; consequently, I will confine myself to the observation that this entire process comes to a halt midway, as it were. Milosz neither succumbs to the elemental force of the spoken word nor passively repeats fixed models. Even his texts closest to colloquial speech preserve the delicate trace of the word of the other in the background. This undoubtedly explains the impression that Milosz's language gives of being slightly archaic.

Milosz adopts two strategies to ward off the stiffness, foreignness, and even artificiality that stylization always risks. He tries to create an impression that the utterances in his poems are unrepeatable and unique. This impression is fostered by dialogicality, imitation of actual living speech by interjecting colloquialisms, a conspicuously casual syntax, and a clear and concrete presentation of the situation in which the given utterance is made. At the same time Milosz emphasizes his personal relation to the problems the poem treats, either by allusions to his other works or by autobiographical interpolations. When questioned about "Conversation," Milosz characteristically replied: "I am not a writer of historical poems that re-create a particular period. The poet clearly identifies with the nobleman here" (*PS* 141).

Because of Milosz's own biography and poetic output, which create unusual contexts for stylized utterances, the process of adapting tradition becomes imperceptibly internalized. The distinctiveness of "Conversation at Easter 1620" from other poetic readings of the baroque lies in the fact that this interpretation of the period is a truth that is Milosz's own, personally experienced, and not a display of technical skill or a disinterested literary game.

THE INTERNAL DIALOGUE

Milosz, to perhaps a greater degree than Zbigniew Herbert, is a poet of dialogue. At first glance Milosz's poems are not remarkable for extraordinary richness, variety, and flamboyance of dialogical forms. Moreover, he goes back to the oldest traditions: his "Antigone" ("Antygona") travesties the famous dialogue between the Sophoclean sisters; in "The Song" (*CP* 7; "Pieśń," 1934) and "The Unveiling" ("Posłuchanie"; the introductory section of "From the Rising of the Sun") the elevated commentary of a chorus takes second part to a lone voice. In addition, certain of Milosz's poems written many years apart reflect a conflict between two different, often opposing, attitudes, positions, or points of view, such as "Dialogue," "Conversation at Easter 1620," "Frivolous Conversation," and "Three Talks on Civilization." In truth, in Milosz's poetry it is hard to find a single work that is not colored by dialogue or does not contain at least a portion of a reported exchange of opinions. Along with dialogue, though not always concurrently, different personal forms are at play in Milosz's "theater of speech":[7] the "I" almost spontaneously is transformed into "you" or "he."

Dialogue has customarily been understood and considered in three ways: as a rhetorical form, as a compositional element of the literary work, and as an expression of philosophical premises. The first meaning of dialogue refers to ways of communicating, the second to literature and theater, and the third to the ancient philosophical tradition reflected in Plato's *Dialogues*. Milosz's "Conversation at Easter 1620" illustrates the great extent to which these concepts, so different from each other, may be mutually complementary. Milosz conceives of dialogicality in these three ways simultaneously, as "Conversation" generally confirms: here dialogue is at once a method of understanding, a form of poetic construction, and a philosophical attitude.

Milosz stubbornly returns to one type of dialogue, the conversation. The word even figures in the title of the Easter poem. He prefers conversation to dialogue because the latter tends to generalize, objectify, and theatricalize a host of particulars; he prefers it to discussion because in discussion the struggle over arguments leads to a change of opinion and a joint effort to establish a certain truth; and he prefers it to allegory or to crushing irony or diatribe. Conversation, after all, is a free encounter in which respect for another person's differentness presumes a certain distance and at the same holds out the possibility of a close relationship and the tightening of bonds. Whimsical, open to both the past and present exchange of thoughts without a predetermined goal or the compulsion to convince, partly for amusement and partly for learning—conversation is the ideal of Milosz's dialogic poetry, one it either cannot attain or does not want to attain.

For example, despite its title, "Three Talks on Civilization" is not a sequence of dialogues but a lyric in the second person. All we know about the concealed addressee is that her name is Hermantia. She is referred to by name in the first and third parts of the poem; in the second part her presence is indicated only by phrases directed toward her and replies to her unuttered questions. The fact that the three talks take place with the same person in different historical periods precludes our treating the poem as a fictional dialogue. Furthermore, their setting in time clearly influences their style of expression: the first talk is the most rhetorical, the second is close to contemporary colloquial speech, and the third is a discreet stylization of nineteenth-century language.

But that is not all. Dialogicality also penetrates the speech of the narrator himself. In his exposition each argument immediately meets a counterargument, each thesis an antithesis. The theme of "Three Talks" is difficult to pin down, but it is something reflected in the experience of the individual, of society, and of all human civilization. Most simply stated, it is the relation between that which belongs to nature and that which belongs to culture, a sort of review of Milosz's poetic anthropology. The narrator shows that man must accept his dependence on nature even though it degrades him. He must accept a chemically polluted nature although he would want it to be pure and undefiled. He must give up his dreams of unlimited freedom although that relinquishment relegates him to social bondage. Civilization calls into existence the state, which restrains the animal instincts of its citizens and creates an institutional framework for individual activity, thus allowing culture to develop:

> if people (instead of everyday necessity and the, so to speak,
> hairy pleasures proper to the flesh)
> spick-and-span, pretending they do not stink at all,
>
> nibbled chocolates in a theater,
> if they were moved by the loves of Amyntas,
>
> . . . .
> none would be fit for the barracks. The State would fall.
> (CP 173)

> gdyby zamiast codziennego musu, oraz, że tak powiem,
> włochatych rozrywek należnych cielesności,
> zbyt umyci, udając, że wcale nie śmierdzą,
>
> ludzie w teatrum gryźli czekoladki
> i wzruszali się miłością pasterza Amyntasa
>
> . . . .
> nikt nie nadawałby się do koszar. Państwo by upadło.

Does the state, whose model and quintessence are barracks, preserve us from our own bestiality? Evil exists, but is it inevitable? The irony here is easy to detect, and it once again expresses helplessness in the face of contradictions that cannot be resolved.

The meaning of the second talk is ambiguous. Nature, which we shape according to our needs, seems to some to be crippled and deadly. But does that mean that if left alone it would be worthy of admiration?

Probably only in the Garden of Eden, that is, in nature's ideal state, when "the beasts licked the air and yawned, friendly, / While their fangs and their tails, lashing their backs, / Were figurative . . ." (*CP* 174; "zwierzęta oblizywały pyski ziewając przyjaźnie / a kły ich tudzież ogon smagający boki / były figuratywne . . ."). Thus, neither an affirmation of nature and a naive dream of returning to its womb, nor condemnation of its brutality, is the right answer. Is the fault, then, in ourselves?

The third talk is an attempt at an answer that resorts to the language of dream symbolism and through that language approaches the deepest levels of the subconscious. In a nightmare recollections of a crime committed and scenes of pursuit, capture, and a disgraceful death recur obsessively. The question insistently repeats:

> If I only knew one thing, this one thing:
> Can contrition be just wounded pride?
>
> (*CP* 174)
>
> Gdybym wiedział to jedno, nic, tylko to jedno:
> czym różni się żal za grzechy od urażonej ambicji.

The murderer is tormented not by qualms of conscience but rather by the inability to define his own attitude. Sorrow for sins presumes implicitly both an eternal system of ethical norms and a suprahuman court of last resort that can judge the morality of human acts infallibly. But ambition and honor have only a social use and in addition have taken historically different forms. What is this voice that responds in us? Does it represent a metaphysical order or a social norm? The soul or the unconscious tormented by a feeling of guilt? The very formulation of this doubt rules out faith in the inherent nobility of human nature.

Meanwhile, the belief of "these pups of foolish Jean-Jacques" ("uczniowie głupiego Jana Jakuba") in their own innocence resulted from their delusions or, simply, ignorance based on faith in the harmonious symbiosis of man with nature. But is not such a conviction enviable? After all, it not only returns to the individual his sense of being at home in the world but also indirectly extols protest against all forms of coercion created by the state, power, and civilization. Only in this context is the meaning of Milosz's paragraph of commentary to the poem clear. That commentary is omitted in the English version in *The Collected Poems:*

The name Hermantia is chosen randomly and does not signify any historical personage. In Part III, however, it is certainly Metternich relating his dreams as a pessimistic defender of the political order during the period of the Holy Alliance, since it was he who in 1820 wrote a letter to Tsar Alexander I containing an accurate analysis of the political consequences of romanticism (although he did not use this term).[8] The thought also occurred to me that the content of my poem is rather reminiscent of a conversation in Słowacki between Tsar Nicholas and the Grand Duke Constantine about a strangled English girl.[9]

Thus, not only the speakers change; their entire imagined dialogue is also somehow reflected in other dialogues that differ from one another in genre (epistle, play), content, and time. And so still another hall of mirrors appears in Milosz's poetry where reflections refer to one another. The meaning of this excursion into the past, the poet says, is that faith in man's goodness threatens every absolute order, for the foundation of such orders is the opposite conviction, that of the weakness and baseness of human nature, which is defenseless against the brutality of nature and submissive to all sorts of manipulation. Consequently, is there on one hand rational order, discipline, and (disregarding the value of human life) clearly established goals for the collective, and on the other hand blind instinct, unbridled bestiality, and individual aspirations that upset the clear order of the state? But it is enough to bracket the entire opposition and, referring to metaphysical values of an individual, reveal the constraint, difficult to bear, and oppression of any absolute order or totalitarian system.

What is to be done, however, when the metaphysical basis of ethical norms crumbles? This question is not foreign to the reader of Milosz's poetry; "Three Talks" simply focuses and intensifies philosophical dilemmas that are consistently there. I have reconstructed the talks in order to show that they pervade the speech of the poem's narrator regardless of whether his interlocutor is present. One could say that dialectic on contradictory arguments supplants a dialogical exchange of opinions. This supplanting is, it seems, consonant with a general tendency in Milosz's work. The poems we have examined here show that an evolution takes place, one beginning with independent dramatic characters and moving to more or less anonymous voices that seem to echo in the speech of the author. The character of the partner gradually dissolves; his voice subsides and is finally silent.

We do not know who the speaker is in "Frivolous Conversation" or who Hermantia is. At least the former takes an active part in the conversation, but we can only indirectly conjecture about the existence of the latter. A word directed toward someone who listens fits in, moreover, with the context of the author's biography, his own output, and his literary and philosophical tradition, just as in the case of stylization. In short, beyond—or, more precisely, through—dialogue between the characters, the author enters into a dialogue with himself and, of course, with the reader.

To find the reason for this shift we must look at the lyric "you" that appears in Milosz's work with remarkable frequency. The two poles of this type of monologue are the addressee who is distinct from the subject of the poem and the addressee who is a projection of the subjective "I." Between these two extremes there exists a gamut of variations. Remember that the relations between "I" and "you" in Milosz's poetry are unusually refined and complex because they intersect (although they do not always coincide) with the use of the lyric mask and the lyric role. Milosz's poetry exhausts all, or almost all, possible variations: hence the "I" and "you" that are different from the author; the "I" partially identifiable with the author; and the "you" distinct from him and referring to a concrete person ("you" functioning as "he"). At the same time the second person may be a historical personage ("To Jonathan Swift"), someone real but without proof of identity ("Elegy for Y. Z."), or someone suprahuman, as in his religious poems ("*Veni Creator*"). There are many examples of traditional lyrics that have a "you" describing phenomena and abstractions. A combination is also possible where the "I"—with respect to the attitudes expressed—differs from the author but the "you" can be identified to some extent with him; recall the passage in "Child of Europe" where the disciple of the New Faith delivers a lecture on cynicism to the heir of Mediterranean culture. The "you" may be either the reader, subjected to the tricks of persuasion ("Treatise on Morals"), or partly the reader and partly the author ("Readings" ["Lektury," 1969] or "Proof" ["Dowód," 1975]).

A presumed addressee appears, as has often been noted, not only in phrases directly addressed to him but also on the stylistic level itself. Milosz increasingly anticipates possible reservations, counters conjectured charges, or supports his own arguments. Acknowledging the young poets, he admits in "Counsels" (*CP* 208, "Rady"), "It's true, I did not happen to see the triumph of justice" ("To prawda, nie zdarzyło mi się oglądać triumfu sprawiedliwości"). The concluding passage of "*Ars Poetica?*" (*CP* 212) begins, "What I'm saying here is not, I agree, poetry" ("Co tutaj opowiadam, poezją, zgoda, nie jest"). "Sentences" (*CP* 176) repeats someone's—the author's or the reader's—question, "What constitutes the training of the hand? / I shall tell what constitutes the training of the hand" ("Na czym polega zaprawa ręki? / Powiem na czym polega zaprawa ręki"). Finally, there is the last variant of the lyric "you": "you" as a projection of "I," which is the most identical with the author ("Not This Way" ["Nie tak"], "Poet at Seventy" ["Poeta siedemdziesięcioletni," 1984], "Paradise").

The situation in Milosz's poetry, however, is considerably more complex than can be deduced from such an overview. Milosz very seldom maintains the entire narration in the second person. "I," "we," and "he" consistently appear alongside "you." The status of the speaker wavers and is misleading. His identity at one moment can be grasped, only to then dissolve and vanish. Moreover, the speech of the subject includes allusions, citations, and fragments of anonymous dialogues. Practically every poem has its own score and should be examined individually. I will therefore confine myself to only the two most extreme variants of lyric "you."

In Milosz's poetry there is a relatively high number of poems addressed to a person referred to by first or last name, often someone famous. Sometimes, as in "To Father Ch.," "Letter of January 1, 1935," and "To Raja Rao," they are verse epistles, as indicated by the title or some reference in the poem itself. The letter in verse has, of course, its own long tradition. The subject of the epistle is either a moral-philosophical discourse or an intimate outpouring of feeling. Its patrons in antiquity were Horace (*Epistles*) and Ovid (*Heroides*), whose works constitute the basic models of the form. The neoclassicists and the romantics wrote such epistles too. In reading Milosz's epistles, it is interesting to note with whom he carries on his poetic correspondence and how he transforms this somewhat archaic genre.

Above all, Milosz clearly erases the barrier between the epistle and other variants of the lyric of appeal. The personal tone of the outpourings, the questions directed toward an addressee, and references to times experienced together are all elements that can be found in the poems mentioned above. The reverse also holds true: in Milosz's works the epistle is transformed into a discourse that combines philosophical reflection with a settling of accounts with himself, and intimacy of tone with the need to generalize his own experiences.

The group of addressees is admittedly varied. It includes friends from youth like Jerzy Zagorski and Father Prefect, as well as Jonathan Swift, Tadeusz Różewicz and Robinson Jeffers, Albert Einstein, and Raja Rao and Father Józef Sadzik. The list includes both the living and the dead, persons from the past and present, those personally known to the poet and those known only from his reading. Despite the heterogeneity of their ways of thinking and their professions, we can divide them into protagonists and antagonists of the poet. The latter group is not numerous, for only Robinson Jeffers and Raja Rao belong to it. But "To Robinson Jeffers" and "To Raja Rao" are two extraordinarily important poems in Milosz's output, presenting both the fundamental outlines of his worldview and his conception of poetry in a dense summary. The shape of Milosz's universe looms in both poems. That is certainly why "To Robinson Jeffers" constitutes a key to *Visions from San Francisco Bay,* while "To Raja Rao," written in English, is a continuation of an hours-long discussion with the Hindu philosopher.

The historical personages who appear in Milosz's poems are often acknowledged and respected authorities who, however, seem to be denied their autonomy. These personalities appear to the poet as ossified, fixed within formulas. Their portraits in verse do not arouse doubt; they are markedly static and not mysteriously intriguing. Perhaps that is because the response of the one to whom the poet is speaking is not foreseen ("To Jonathan Swift" is the one exception here), particularly since he is a character from the past. It is enough that this person represents a model for imitation, a moral authority. He is thus a sign of a certain attitude rather than a complete personality. Hence instead of a polemic, the evolution of the speaker's position is shown. A description of the internal changes in the speaker takes the place of the dynamic of mutual relations between partners in a dialogue.

The "you" consequently fulfills two functions at the same time: it characterizes the addressee and is a means for the speaker to characterize himself. However strongly individualized, the second person is still just another mask of the persona, emerging partly from the consciousness of the speaker and having limited autonomy. That is why instead of debate, it is acceptance and coming to an agreement that predominate in Milosz's poetry, but in his polemical poems the views contained therein are more strongly expressed.

The well-known phrase *style is the man* is directly confirmed here. The coming together of points of view is manifested in the coming together of styles of expression, as can best be seen in "To Father Ch." This example is all the more interesting since the addressee turns from an opponent into an ally. In reality the addressee did not change, but rather the relation of the poet to the prefect evolved from revolt and conflict to agreement and understanding. This change was determined by the experiences that broke down the hero's illusions.

In accepting the position of the prefect, the speaker begins to speak in his style, full of pathos, bristling with visions of annihilation, and readily employing biblical stylization. More exactly, the style of the character (the object of description), the manner of characterization, and the language of the persona become a complete unity.

The reverse occurs in the polemical poems. Sticking with one's argument is simultaneously a defense of the distinctness of one's own language, one's past, and one's cultural tradition. Here Milosz presents Robinson Jeffers's vision of a lifeless world in terrifying but gripping images of the cosmos:

> Above your head no face, neither the sun's nor the moon's,
> only the throbbing of galaxies, the immutable
> violence of new beginnings, of new destruction.
>
> ("To Robinson Jeffers," CP 224)
>
> Nad twoją głową żadnej twarzy, ni słońca ani księżyca,
> tylko skurcz i rozkurcz galaktyk, niewzruszona
> gwałtowność nowych początków, nowego zniszczenia.

To this vision Milosz opposes a Polish-Lithuanian image of nature harmonized, calm, and friendly to man, an echo of Mickiewicz's *Pan Tadeusz* with its praise of the provinces and "society," an ecstasy over the particular in which one sees the metaphysical order of creation. The Polish poet comments:

> What have I to do with you? From footpaths in the orchards,
> from an untaught choir and shimmers of a monstrance,
> from flower beds of rue, hills by the rivers, books
> in which a zealous Lithuanian announced brotherhood, I come.
>
> (CP 225)

A mnie co do ciebie? Z drobnych stecek w sadach,
z nieuczonego chóru i jarzeń monstrancji,
z grządek ruty, pagórków nad rzekami, ksiąg,
z których gorliwy Litwin wieścił braterstwo, przychodzę.

The convictions of partners as well as adversaries thus only have significance to the extent that they pass through the filter of the personal experience of the poet and are internalized, as happened with their language.

Dialogue conceived as a meditation on universal problems, a spectacle both intimate and public since it takes place on the borderline of the subjective and the objective, of one's own opinion and that of another, suggests a model in the soliloquy. Since the 1970s Milosz seems consciously to link himself with this tradition: I have in mind poems like "Calling to Order" ("Przywołanie do porządku"), "Proof," "A Boy" ("Chłopiec"), and "Poet at Seventy." It is clear that the number of dialogues with himself increases as autobiographism intensifies.

Saint Augustine, considered the creator of the soliloquy, meditating on the roads to knowledge of God and of one's own soul, called into existence a personified Reason. He carried on lengthy debates with him, responded to his doubts, damped his excessive emotions. For Milosz, too, the essence of the soliloquy—just as of every conversation—is a search for truth. Naturally, truth for Milosz is not as unswerving and universal as it was for the medieval philosopher. The existence of God and the voice of faith no longer guarantee truth, and that influences both its meaning and the means of attaining it. The ideal would be truth as a spontaneous harmony of word and factual state, guaranteed by elementary experience. In reality, however, even this brief outline of the problem reveals a web of complexities: both the subject and the object and the language betray their relative character. Hence knowledge must be uncertain and constantly threatened with error in the process of discovery of meaning. Truth cannot manifest itself other than in dialogical entanglement; meaning, however, becomes movement itself, energy that flows within the text and beyond it. Without recalling the various contexts that elucidate its text, a Milosz poem would be a dead letter.

But even this fictional "you" is not reason, whose perplexities are effectively silenced by faith. At one point an angel speaks up inside the poet, summoning him to "do what you can" ("zrób co możesz"; "On Angels," CP 249). At another point a satanic voice ironically says:

You would like to lead a gathering of people
To a ritual of purification through the columns of a temple.

A ritual of purification? Where? When? For whom?
("From the Rising of the Sun," CP 307)

Ty chciałbyś na rytuał oczyszczenia
Lud zgromadzić prowadzić między kolumny świątyni.

Rytuał oczyszczenia! Gdzie? Kiedy? Dla kogo?

Thus, the soliloquy is not only the image of division so frequently described. It is also an expression of the existence of subjectivity, or more precisely, the expression of its existence in language. The speaking "I" does not possess substance in and of itself but rather constitutes a hypothetical personal perspective that another point of view defines. It emerges from the relation between "you" and "he," which fills it with meaning. The soliloquy most easily allows us to see that the "I" is an effort to assimilate a view of oneself from another angle. That is why Milosz's dialogues are really self-reflexive: their various projections come from subjectivity in order, after their enlargement, to return to that subjectivity. The process is somewhat analogous to the suspension of the poet's speech between monophony and polyphony, discussed earlier.

In the last analysis dialogue is an attempt to objectify one's own "I" or distance oneself from it. Retracing, it would seem, the road that his own life took, Milosz writes, not without irony:

Thus, brother theologian, here you are,
Connoisseur of the heavens and abysses,
Year after year perfecting your art,
Choosing bookish wisdom for your mistress,
Only to discover you wander in the dark.
("Poet at Seventy," CP 439)

Tyżeś to, bracie teologu,
Znawco niebiosów i otchłani,
Spodziewający się co roku
Kiedy ślęczałeś nad księgami,
Że dotkniesz ostatniego progu.

The title, the personal feelings expressed, and the standard motifs indicate that the poem is a kind of inner monologue of the poet. In reality the speaking "I" appears in disguise; the addressee could just as well be someone else, and the entire poem recalls the Faust myth. In a word, the dialogue with oneself is at the same time a dialogue with an entire cultural tradition conducted in the presence of witnesses.

The awareness that his poetry might not reach Polish readers undoubtedly influenced Milosz's use of this device in his poetry, particularly in works written during the years when his books were forbidden in Poland. But equally important is his summoning spirits of the past as witnesses to his inner struggles, giving his inner dialogues a timeless dimension. In addition, such a form of expression obscures the border between what is seen and what is imagined, between what is thought and what is said. It is not enough to repeat that for Milosz poetry is above all the domain of speech—not writing, not the word, not the letter. It also contains confidence in the possibility of questioning reality and faith in the usefulness of language. Thus, absent in Milosz's poetry are scenes of two distinct consciousnesses unable to come to an understanding and conversations between the "deaf" and those who lack faith in the word, situations characteristic of contemporary Polish poetry. That is how Milosz avoids dry, intellectual, objectified discursiveness. He wants to combine vivid imagery and elements of a microplot with profound reflection. He "thinks in poetry"—but also in images that cannot be translated into concepts.[10]

Dialogicality, together with stylization, thus serves Milosz's "mediumistic" concept of poetry. It is yet another way to cross the barrier between poetry and nonpoetry, a roving along the periphery of different genres. Dialogue seems to be the ideal form of expression to transmit in descriptive language the clash between the subject and the object. It is open, dynamic, incomplete. In the dialogical word the momentarily revealed subjectivity and essence of a thing are embodied in the equally momentary word.

CIRCLES OF ALLUSIONS

Milosz's poetry—sensitive to the striking detail, the suggestive and tangible concrete—is also, as I have mentioned *en passant,* interlaced with countless allusions, quotations, paraphrases, excerpts, and references to other works. "Treatise on Poetry" is a particularly subtle and refined construction of literary and extraliterary reminiscences. The history of Poland and Europe, philosophical works, Polish national literature, details of everyday life, and exalted theories all comprise its circles of allusions. Thus, the reader must have the patience of a scholar and the passion of an archaeologist who, from a few traces, can decipher the outline of a past civilization irrevocably lost—even if less than a hundred years have passed. One might say that "Treatise on Poetry" concentrates and raises to the level of a compositional principle the distinctive quality of all Milosz's poetry. The poem requires continuous commentary and glossing; it sends the reader to ancient works, dictionaries, and encyclopedias. Yet its erudition seems effortless and carefully masked. Even in the choice of readings the poem appears to be ruled by caprice rather than the great care of a collector. Scholarly works appear alongside products of mass culture, fairy tales and children's stories alongside philosophical and theological treatises, lyrics of forgotten songs and private chronicles alongside references to the Bible and the classics.

Milosz's journeys amid the relics of the past do not go beyond the boundaries of Mediterranean culture.[11] Rarely, and rather unwillingly, does he express himself about other cultures, and then only to emphasize their foreignness. That is particularly true of cultures of the East— see "No More," "To Raja Rao," and "Reading the Japanese Poet Issa (1762–1826)" ("Czytając japońskiego poetę Issa [1762–1826]"). His recalling of ancient symbols, signs, or verbal expressions is not a display of empty erudition or superfluous ornament but simply and entirely a search for another form of expression with which to name contemporary reality. In his allusions Milosz utilizes metaphor rather than simile. He does not compare distant things or problems with one another for entertainment or for learning but instead braces elements together with a metaphoric clasp. Here is one example: "Cities will be extinguished by a stream of hot lava / and no Noah will escape in a boat" ("miasta strumień wrzącej lawy / zgasi i żaden Noe nie ujdzie na łodzi"; "To Father Ch."). The lines are not merely a fresh version of the hackneyed biblical image but also a vision of the annihilation that awaits people of the twentieth century. If in these times the end is near, then language too must be apocalyptic. In substituting boiling lava for the waters of the deluge and prophesying that no one will be saved, Milosz not only modernizes the ancient *topos* of extermination but also reinterprets it. When presenting the visual world, this poet of metonymy is, in his appeal to the collective memory, a poet of metaphor.

Judging by the allusions that appear in the poems written in his youth, the horizon of Milosz's readings did not exceed the level of knowledge of the average prewar intellectual with an education in the humanities: the Old and New Testaments, ancient history and the classics, Dante's *Divine Comedy*, Goethe's *Faust*, and of course the literature of the romantics. This syllabus is not much different from that of, say, Adam Mickiewicz. Twentieth-century traces appear only in Milosz's reading (probably as a result of proximity to the Soviet Union) of Mayakovsky and Esenin, alongside the poetry of the avant-garde, late symbolism (Oscar Milosz), and Paul Valéry. Milosz's lycée syllabus remains, in principle, the basis for his later readings, which followed his own tastes, chance, and sometimes necessity. The fact cannot be underestimated that Milosz spent twenty years as a professor of Slavic literatures, lecturing not only on Polish literature but also on Manichaeanism and Dostoevsky. Undoubtedly, he is someone who simply enjoys reading, as lines in his poetry frequently indicate. More important, however, and probably more interesting, are those references that are cleverly camouflaged and difficult to decipher.

As is often emphasized, Milosz employs the gamut of allusions to other literary texts. It is to those allusions that I now turn. They include genre indicators, stanzaic construction, theme, character, motif, and even individual lines—in fact, practically all elements of a literary work.

Milosz's quotations, like his allusions, can be divided into the overt, the hidden, and the only apparent. Stanisław Barańczak states that in Milosz

> the line between quotation and allusion on the one hand, and stylization on the other, is deliberately vague. In other words, quite frequently what matters is not a precise reference to this or that literary predecessor but rather the general suggestion of "the word of another," a transmission from the depths of the past, recognizable more by its distinctive stylistic features than by its clear "return address."[12]

The suggestion of stylization and allusion reinforces the suggestion of concreteness and autobiographism in an effort to recall a certain whole—some visible reality, the life of an individual, the style of an era, the universe of culture. Through these emerges the outline of a sought-after truth and wholeness, themselves only an imperfect realization based on the principle of analogy. The "transmission," however, comes not only from the "depths of the past" but also from the present, to which Milosz's cultural resources are also readily inclined. What is more, "the word of another" echoes in Milosz's own language, becoming an integral part of his speech, not an alien interpolation. Milosz makes this "word of another" his own in diverse ways. He avoids lengthy literary quotations, confining himself to those that memory can contain and everyday speech can employ, as if he would like to imitate the natural gaps and deficiencies of the average reader's mnemonic mechanism. Correspondingly, he strives to shift a text that sounds too bookish toward the spoken language. "Treatise on Poetry" in particular is filled with such imprecise or parodied quotations.

Milosz adapts, and makes his own, quotations not only from works of literature but also from the Bible. In "A Notebook: Bon by Lake Leman" Milosz speaks out in these words: "If I forget thee, Jerusalem, / Says the prophet, let my right hand wither" ("Jeśli zapomnę ciebie, Jerusalem, / Niech, mówi prorok, uschnie mi prawica")—words taken, of course, from Psalm 137. But the interpolated "says the prophet" effectively dilutes the pathos of the language, rendering it more prosaic and accessible, almost ordinary. A quotation from the same psalm, incorporated into "On a Certain Book," rings ironically: "A pitiful sight—that lament by the Babylonian waters, / Intellectuals in baggy trousers resurrecting the new Middle Ages" ("żałosny widok—ten płacz nad rzekami Babilonu. / Inteligenci w opadłych portkach wskrzeszający nowe średniowiecze"). Not so much the source itself counts as the concrete context in which the quotation appears. Even sacred speech may sound now elevated, now flat; now ceremonial, now prosaic. It may be tinged with religious fervor or with sarcasm. Everything depends on who is speaking and the circumstances in which the words are used.

The variety and immediacy of the functions that quotations fill can best be observed in the microquotations that appear as titles in Milosz's works. In "Treatise on Poetry" where these quotations are countless, they are, in addition to biographical information and a survey of typical motifs, fragments of particular portraits. In "On a Certain Book" Berdyaev's *New Middle Ages* is a signal evoking a certain worldview (without, however, losing its literal significance). In "Conversation at Easter 1620" a book entitled *Bird Shooting* (*Myślistwo ptasze*), by the Polish nobleman Mateusz Cygański, serves to describe the hero while heightening the sense of reality. Other books include Witkiewicz's *Unwashed Souls* (*Niemyte dusze*), Dostoevsky's *Brothers Karamazov*, Daniel Halévy's *L'accélération de l'histoire,* and John Steinbeck's *Grapes of Wrath.*

Such a cursory enumeration does not do justice to the wealth of associations that this type of quotation evokes, especially since the titles are usually incorporated into the poem without any clear demarcation. There is an element of play in this, a common game to which the author invites the reader while testing his interpretation. But these titles, like other kinds of quotations, are not merely some anonymous "message." They are also the individual testimony of an unrepeatable person with whom the poet initiates dialogue. The very title of a work is an essence of the authorial personality—its identity card. It is unique in the same way as are a style, favorite motifs, the narrator's comments, or the details of a biography. But "the word of another," by virtue of its general use, loses its individuality. Its source is forgotten even when it is simply the title of a book. It is foreign and yet a little one's own; we both speak and "are spoken." Even our own everyday speech is a constant duel between what is original and what is borrowed, what is accessible only to some and what is accessible to all, what shines through in a single utterance and what is almost eternal because it is repeated by many people and belongs to the common treasure of culture. True, that is not always the case. We cannot underestimate the fact that Milosz consciously transforms the mechanisms and functions of language into an element of poetic strategy and makes them an outgrowth of his worldview.

An allusion, quotation, or title of some work is a gauge of the reliability of the "message" while setting into motion an avalanche of associations for the reader. They drag behind themselves, as it were, a trail of knowledge amassed in past centuries. In poetry they create still another changeable context. Edward Balcerzan once made the penetrating observation that Milosz "treats the poetic text like a multi-leveled construction of allusions that are like discreet suggestions on the topic of the *possibility* of extracting 'the word of another' from Milosz's words."[13] His emphasis on possibility seems particularly important, for the message of the poet is hidden precisely in those possibilities. They call on the reader's resources of intellect and knowledge as well as patience and persistence in discovering meanings. They invite the reader to join with the poet in a game and at the same time constitute a unique model of meaning. What is hidden beneath a seemingly transparent surface is elusive but historically measurable.

The fourth part of "Treatise on Poetry" is an interesting example of allusion. The words "Sint mihi Dei Acherontis propitii / Valeat numen triplex Jehovae! / Ignis, aeris, aque, terrae spiritus, / Salvete!" are Faust's incantation from Marlowe's *Doctor Faustus*.[14] The phrase "the Socrates of snails" is an allusion to the poem "The Comedian as the Letter C" by Wallace Stevens. Both works expand the field of meditation contained in this part of "Treatise on Poetry." Their use by Milosz is all the more significant since they express a concept of man and nature that is different from the poet's own.[15]

In this way Milosz wards off loss of memory, preserving not only the individual moments of vision, fragments of the visual world, but also certain individuals' testimony about them, a testimony, according to Barańczak, "belonging to different dimensions of values, to different voices," times, and places.[16] Just as these moments refer to the unfathomable essence of existence, testimonies of culture bring to mind the limitless stores of tradition. Both elements combine in the text of the poem, creating a delicate design. Were I to describe this design in the most general terms, I would say that the choice of both is dictated by metaphor, whereas their arrangement is determined by metonymy. In that choice randomness and uniqueness are emphasized. Simply put, the one who sees and the one who recalls words and images are the same person. In Milosz's poems, and in fact throughout all his work, the speaking persona is really the author in his various disguises. He constantly appears as both an individual "I" and a witness of a historical period, a representative of a certain sociological group or formation.

The poet indicates his personal relation to tradition not only through the choices he makes from it but also through the naming of his own existential situation, his experiences, and his reflections by means of commonly understood signs and symbols. I have already mentioned this point when discussing other aspects of Milosz's work. Here, however, we might take a look at "So Little" ("Tak mało," 1969), a poem in which this aspect of Milosz's imagination is pressed to maximum abbreviation and condensation. The situation of the hero is outlined in a series of symbolic statements:

> The jaws of Leviathan
> Were closing upon me.
>
> Naked, I lay on the shores
> Of desert islands.

The white whale of the world
Hauled me down to its pit.
(CP 247)

Paszcza Lewiatana
Zamykała się na mnie.

Nagi leżałem na brzegach
Bezludnych wysp.

Porwał mnie w otchlań ze sobą
Biały wieloryb świata.

The sources are easy to spot—the biblical Leviathan from Job, the story of Jonah, *Robinson Crusoe,* and *Moby Dick.* But the allusions are now placed in a different context, startlingly juxtaposed, and finally made to refer to the fate of someone who seems to be settling accounts with his own life (the past tense signifying distance from events long past). Contrary to appearances, the images are not randomly selected but are linked by a circle of associations with the element of water, which has primarily negative connotations for Milosz. In addition, the poet's favorite motifs return: Leviathan, in the Bible and the Cabala a symbol of unhappiness and immanent evil that for Milosz also embodies a monstrous totalitarian state; and the castaway, a sign of loneliness, rootlessness, and disinheritance. The speaker is thus as much a timeless "I", a witness to cultural changes whose own development is marked by myths and symbols, as one of the countless embodiments of the author, who is attempting to find his own identity.

The ceaseless effort to understand oneself becomes, almost spontaneously, a reinterpretation of symbols. Colliding with one another, they shine with new meanings, certainly, but they also lose something of the weight of their original genres, particularly the religious motifs and symbols. Milosz's world of allusion, like his entire poetic universe, has the Garden of Eden and the Apocalypse as its poles. It contains both the longing for rescue, for escape from nothingness, and the painful awareness of loss. Symbolic significance colors the fact that while the biblical associations center around the Apocalypse, Qoheleth, Jeremiah, and Ezekiel, the classical ones recall fallen cities and civilizations: Troy, Babylon, and Nineveh. Milosz's attitude toward classical tradition is always ambivalent. At times he heightens the import and perception of the historical chronicles of Herodotus or Thucydides; he is fond of Heraclitus. But the shadow of destruction hangs over the literature of antiquity. The contemporary poet repeats to himself with bitter derision:

> Oh yes, not all of me shall die, there will remain
> An item in the fourteenth volume of an encyclopedia
> Next to a hundred Millers and Mickey Mouse.
> ("From the Rising of the Sun," *CP* 301)

> O tak, nie cały zginę, zostanie po mnie
> Wzmianka w czternastym tomie encyklopedii
> W pobliżu setki Millerów i Mickey Mouse.

The shadow of destruction also hangs over the Christian imagination in, for example, Milosz's vision of Paradise. References to Eden are numerous in his works, so I will confine myself to the motif of the tree in the Garden. It appears for the first time in "To Father Ch."

> . . . the heavy apple, a dream of the Paradise tree
> rolls, touched by nimble feet.

> . . . ciężkie jabłko, sen rajskiego drzewa
> toczy się, potrącane końcem lekkich stóp.

Here the apple of Paradise is both a synonym for sensual temptation, rejected after the discovery of the "nothingness of seductive forms" ("nicość form powabnych"), and the prospect of the end of the world. By contrast, "Lessons" points to an entirely different meaning of this same symbol:

> I would imagine the two of them, with my guilt,
> Trampling a wasp beneath the apple tree in Eden.
> (*CP* 122)

> Wyobrażałem sobie dwoje, z moją winą,
> Jak depczą osę pod rajską jabłonią.

The search for a personal and a collective genealogy reminds us of humanity's original sin, the sin of every human being. The gesture of trampling a wasp has the symbolic significance of an act of breaking the unconscious, and therefore harmonious, link with nature, of gaining freedom at the price of disinheritance.

The apple of Eden is not only a symbol of the discovery of physical desire and the bitter taste of freedom but also the first act in the drama of knowing. As in the poem "On the Road" (*CP* 205), to find oneself "without the apple of knowledge, on long loops from earth to sky" ("bez jabłka wiadomości na wirażach od ziemi do nieba") undoubtedly means to find oneself without the ability to distinguish between good and evil. The experience of an absence of an axiological, and hence moral, basis accompanies the intense and painful awareness of committing sin.

Milosz endows this symbol with yet a different meaning in "From the Rising of the Sun":

> We were flying over a range of snowpeaked mountains
> And throwing dice for the soul of the condor.
> —Should we grant reprieve to the condor?
> —No, we won't grant reprieve to the condor.
> It didn't eat from the Tree of Knowledge and so it must perish.
>
> (CP 255)

> Lecieliśmy nad pasmem skalnośnieżnych gór
> I o duszę kondora rzucaliśmy kości.
> —Czy ułaskawimy kondora?
> —Nie ułaskawimy kondora.
> Ginie, bo nigdy nie jadł z drzewa wiadomości.

Here we must return to the neo-Manichaean theme in Milosz's writing. Nature is sinless but at the same time denied the opportunity of redemption (something Manichaeanism did not want to accept), condemned to eternal doom.

For the "disinherited mind" sacral symbols no longer reveal their value-laden power but instead recall their absence or their forgotten metaphysical foundation. Milosz turns to them with the proper respect, never just as part of a game but also not without some distance: the apple of Paradise is trampled underfoot; the imagination describes the scene in Eden; the fate of the soul of the condor is determined by a roll of the dice. Objects of faith change into tokens in the poetic game, into a part only of literature. In other words, the drama of the loss of God, constituting (not for Milosz alone) the most important drama of our civilization, is consistently enacted by his poetry in the attitudes that it directly expresses as well as in its poetics. It is precisely this drama that is, in my opinion, the great theme of Milosz's poetry, its very basis, and the source of all its other themes.

Milosz seems to say that the interpretive aspect of the religious *topos* should be made explicit and utilized artistically. Of course, the interpretive or self-interpretive value always appears in poetry, particularly when it plays on allusion. But what for other poets is a less significant feature is for Milosz one of the most fundamental principles of his poetry. He has created a new kind of poetic expression, in which all the constituent elements mutually interpret one another and thus must be examined functionally—not only in the linear order of the text but above all in their depth, in the layering of meanings created by their original usage and cultural or literary context. The trouble is that this subtle mechanism has been carefully inscribed in poetry, and every attempt to reconstruct it (including my own) inevitably reduces and impoverishes it.

THE BOOK AS A MODEL OF THE UNIVERSE

The phrase *eternal moment* in a way recapitulates, on a microscopic scale, Milosz's poetic world. It contains the fundamental tension between the present moment and eternity, movement and constancy, that which is particular and individual and that which is general, the sacred and the profane. It also refers to the knowing subject, the object, the act of cognition, and the linguistic transcription of their mutual relation. Moreover, the oxymoron captures the bipolar structure of this world, the web of dependence and autonomy of all its elements, the contradiction that cannot be unraveled. It also conveys the two fundamental rules of Milosz's thought and expression: antithesis and ambivalence. The intense condensation of meanings in the two words and the elliptical quality of "take from movement / the eternal moment" seem to indicate the breaking of barriers between the language of poetry and the language of philosophy, earthly speech and sacred speech.

Milosz does not simply use verse to illustrate philosophical, anthropological, or theological questions. Although he takes up complicated problems, he consciously and deliberately refuses to abandon the realm of poetic language. This refusal imposes a number of limitations, but it simultaneously accords certain privileges. In poetry, because of its weakened assertory capacities and its compression of meanings and ambiguity, there are no obstacles to a discussion of problems that would be beyond the power of the language of abstract theory. For example, replacing the concept of consciousness with a complex and subtle play of identifying and dissimilating the author with the speaker in the poem cleverly avoids the difficult problem of defining the subject. Milosz's poetry strips philosophical dilemmas of their veneer of excessive gravity, their turgidity, and their solemn erudition while always maintaining an element of distance, amusement, contrariness, and challenge directed toward intellectual unction. Milosz makes declarations such as "I don't want to be too deep."[17] But none of this lessens the gravity of the problem itself.

The interrelation between the language of poetry and the language of philosophy, or more precisely the specifics of that speech which unites the properties of both kinds of language, is yet to be exhaustively described. The main obstacle seems to be the lack of a language with which to render these specifics. Usually when philosophers and literary critics approach Milosz's poetry, each pulls in his or her own direction, either explaining it in terms taken from one philosophical system (for example, Heidegger's Hölderlin lecture) or avoiding the whole problem by applying the apparatus of descriptive poetics. My goal here has been to approach these problems indirectly, pointing out at least the limitations of each method.

Milosz's poetry could well serve as a prime example in a renewed consideration of the whole question because he not only philosophizes poetry but also, we might say, poeticizes philosophy. In his own words, his poetry is "thinking in verse." It returns to the very origins of philosophy, when it existed at one with poetry. That is probably why Milosz often refers to Heraclitus, and is also probably the source of Milosz's references to other authors who are close to him. Milosz writes: "Jeffers, his forerunner Whitman, and Cavafy are tangible proof for me that the poet need not yield to the scientist and the philosopher, on the condition, however, that his language, in which thought and image are fused in the high temperature of emotions, retains something of intellectual communicativeness."[18] How Milosz succeeds in this remains the mystery of his talent. He has created an entirely new quality in Polish literature—and perhaps in world literature as well. He necessarily differs from poets like Jeffers in his cultural heritage and historical experience. Milosz—and few have this honor— is at once a national and a supranational poet, a poet both Polish and universal.[19]

If Milosz seems to scoff at pseudointellectuals or simply display his own dilettantism, it should be noted how thoroughly well-read and reflective he is. His own disclosure about his process of communication is the best proof:

> A very strong poetic-cognitive experience is mute: if words accompany it, they are only a vague outline, the shadow of a rhythmic incantation. . . . The problem is that although I am involved in a language that embraces all my dependence on place, moment in history, etc., I am here, corporeal, tangible, positioned in relation to corporeal, tangible things, and I have moments of "vision" when I both transcend the relativity of language and yet at the same time am unable to transcend it. Perhaps only then does my Delphic language attain its proper balance: behind the words the reader can divine their barely intimated internal charge.
>
> I haven't been satisfied, however, with appealing to the *ineffable*. I mobilize my mind, aiming at what degree of intellectual grasp is possible, and if my language is ambiguous, it is not because ambiguity itself gives me the pleasant sensation of being in a "thicket," but because the excessively complex thought-feelings are impossible to express.[20]

In other words, profound reflection on existence leads to the creation of a distinct language. How else could these "thought-feelings" be presented? Surely an entirely new conceptual apparatus would need to be created. Milosz awaits his own interpreter, one such as Dostoevsky found in Mikhail Bakhtin.

I would like to propose one other approach to Milosz. A mode of existence dependent on being interpreted; the need to decipher signs in order to grasp their unforeseeable meaning; the hypothetical and historically shifting status of truth not expressible in words; the circumstantiality of an utterance and the weight of the speaker's intention it contains; and the view of culture as unending dialogue in which the process of seeking truth is more important than truth itself—all these concepts put Milosz close to twentieth-century hermeneutics. Obviously, I do not claim that in expressing these ideas Milosz declares allegiance to any one philosophical school, that he follows Hans-Georg Gadamer or Paul Ricoeur. He does not build a system, and in the judgments he expresses in passing he pays little heed to consistency of thought. But precisely this philosophical context illuminates his poetry.

If spontaneous, naive faith is nowadays much more difficult, if not impossible, then—as Ricoeur postulated—an understanding view of religious symbols and an internalization of their profound meaning must support faith and overcome that which has led modern culture to forget the sacred. Milosz would probably agree. After all, he relentlessly explores the phenomenon of forgetting the sacred—its genesis, various manifestations, and consequences. He sees in it the primary threat to the anthropocentric vision of the world, and he strives to oppose it. His poetry, taken as a whole, is its own kind of hermeneutics of the Christian imagination. But the meaning of Ricoeur's postulate goes much deeper, with roots in the age-old dilemma of religion versus science, or faith versus knowledge. By using scientific methods, by examining history and religion, one cannot truly reach the sacred. Faith cannot be recovered simply by recalling its testimonies. In other words, Milosz's verse indirectly communicates the idea that language that speaks about a hope in the Second Coming is afflicted with the same disease as language that announces the ultimate loss of that hope.

Having wandered through the depths of a twentieth-century hell, Milosz would like to cultivate metaphysical poetry. From this hell he reaches out to his poetic forebears, finding the essence of their work and touching its painful convolutions with unheard-of ease. For example, after so many books on Mickiewicz, Milosz's reading is revelatory because from beneath layers of commentary he reveals the eschatological pattern in Mickiewicz's poetry, a pattern veiled by messianic illusions. What is more, he shows that this veil was one of the first symptoms of the breakdown of romantic consciousness. The Moderna (the first phase of the Young Poland movement, culminating in Polish letters around 1900) inherits and intensifies this romantic breakdown, although it cannot manage to fully express it. Inheriting it from the Moderna and skillfully assimilating the achievements of the poetry termed avant-garde, Milosz finds a proper and poetically full expression of the adventures of the "disinherited mind" in his own poetry. He is thus one of the last romantics—perhaps the last romantic—and like all of us, knowingly or unknowingly, is heir to that epoch. In any case, he has comprehended and summarized romanticism best, pointing out the painful relevance of the questions it raised as well as the suitability of its artistic solutions. Romanticism, with a backward glance at baroque metaphysical poetry, and the Moderna constitute his main poetic lineage. Consideration of that lineage is more to the point than debate about whether Milosz is a classicist or a romantic.

Milosz succeeds at the impossible: he erects his anthropocentric vision of the world out of material that literally disintegrates in his hands. He accomplishes this in defiance of skepticism and unbelief, almost in spite of the terrifying knowledge of man's position. His defense of the Christian imagination is directed against the philosophy of the absurd and against despair. He asks, "What can one think about a civilization that makes breathtaking scientific discoveries, sends vehicles to other planets, and at the same time recognizes itself in a writer like Beckett?" (*PO* 10). Milosz opposes the reduction of the individual to a passive, tragicomic puppet, of language to gibberish, and of imagination to the contemplation of waning moments. At the same time he considers Samuel Beckett to be the most honest diagnostician of the twentieth century. Milosz is a poet of hope, but of a defiant hope, a tragic hope. He seeks salvation not only in contemplating the beauty of existence and in preserving works of the human mind and imagination. He also seeks it in the removal of all delusions. As he wrote, "Can something or someone be saved? Perhaps only through an awareness of one's defeats, through nakedness that causes forms to come loose and peel off like old paint" (*PO* 14).

In the end Milosz's poetic corpus can be viewed as a huge palimpsest, in which—from beneath diverse styles, dialogues with himself and with others, changing masks, and partly blurred signs—the outline of the Book shines through, a lost archetype of the unity of existence, the human subject, and language. From a distance Milosz's work looks like a single great poem or a series of versions of the same poem. Repetition and variation govern it, for "a passionate pursuit of the Real," never losing sight of its goal, cannot stand still even for a moment, and no stage is its last. Mimesis is the re-creation not so much of the world itself as of the effort and difficulty that knowing it presents. The testimonies of culture changing throughout history offer some consolation. They record the memory of a different language and a different knowledge—a true and holy one. In Milosz's poetry an intuition persistently recurs—or is it rather a hope?—that he will attain the full truth when either his own life ends or humanity ceases to exist. In "From the Rising of the Sun" he asks, "When will that shore appear from which at last we see / How all this came to pass and for what reason?" (*CP* 253; "Kiedyż nastanie ten brzeg, z którego widzieć będziemy / Jak stało się i dlaczego?"). It is no accident that in the twilight of his life Milosz began translating the Bible. His return to the source of true language, one supported by metaphysical sanction, is also a return to the origins of hermeneutics—initially the exegesis of the sacred texts.

The Book that the poet tirelessly attempts to decipher is a representation, a repetition in words of the entire universe. It is a text that discloses the method for its own reading only to the initiated. It is a prefiguration of the world that like a parchment scroll God will roll up at the end of human history. Only then will the chasm between the subjective and the objective, the sign and the signified, be bridged. Only then will nature once again become a garden. There will be no history; the clocks will stop. The multitude of languages will disappear, sensory perception will attain fullness, and the individual, overcoming his "I," will immerse himself in the perfection of the Word which was in the beginning. Then, as we read in the poem "On Prayer" (CP 424, "O modlitwie"), "everything is just the opposite and the word *is* / Unveils a meaning we hardly envisioned" ("wszystko już na opak i słowo 'jest' / Odsłania sens przeczuwany ledwo"). As the converted Calvinist believed:

> Child again, I will run in radiance to the garden
> In a clear dawn after a night of storm.
> I will receive new sight, and taste, and touch.
> I will listen to musics better than those here.
>
> Greek, Egyptian speech will resound in my mouth
> And any that has ever been spoken.
> I will read anew the book of origins
> Comprehending entangled wefts and warps.
> I will penetrate every secret cause.
> And then will disappear in His bliss.
> ("Conversation at Easter 1620")

> Dzieckiem pobiegnę w świetle do ogrodu
> Jutrzenną porą po nawalnej nocy.
> Wzrok, smak i dotyk nie takie posiędę,
> Lepszych niż tutaj muzyk słuchać będę.
>
> Grecką, egipską odezwę się mową
> I wszelką, jaka była od początku.
> Księgę rodzaju odczytam na nowo,
> Świadom splątanej osnowy i wątku.
> I każdą poznam tajemną przyczynę.
> A potem w Jego szczęśliwości zginę.

But implacably accompanying this expectation—as in all of Milosz's poetry—is a nihilistic temptation, a diabolic derision.

Appendix: A Chronology of the Life and Works of Czeslaw Milosz

1911   Born June 30 at Szetejnie (Šetainiai) in Lithuania to Weronika Kunat Miłosz and Aleksander Miłosz, a civil engineer.

1914–1918   Aleksander Miłosz is called up to serve in the Imperial Russian army in World War I and with his family travels throughout Russia, erecting bridges and fortifications behind the front lines. The Miłosz family returns to Lithuania in 1918.

1921   Czeslaw Milosz enters the Sigismund Augustus secondary school in Wilno, the historical capital of Lithuania, which after World War I became part of Poland (now Vilnius in the Soviet Union).

1929   On graduation from secondary school Milosz begins to study law at Stefan Batory University in Wilno. He becomes a member of the Creative Writing Section, an organization founded by students of Polish literature.

1930   Milosz's first published poems appear in the university newspaper *Alma Mater Vilnensis:* "Composition" ("Kompozycja") and "Journey" ("Podróż").

1931   Milosz becomes cofounder of the poetry group Żagary (Brushwood). He makes his first trip to Western Europe to meet for the first time with his distant relative, the French poet Oscar Milosz.

1933   Milosz's first volume of poetry appears, *A Poem on Frozen Time (Poemat o czasie zastygłym).*

1934   Milosz completes law studies. Having received a scholarship from the Foundation for National Culture, he leaves for France.

1935   In Paris Milosz studies at the Alliance Française and attends lectures on Saint Thomas Aquinas.

1936   After returning to Wilno, Milosz begins work at a local radio station and publishes his second book of poems, *Three Winters (Trzy zimy)*.

1937   Milosz is fired from the Wilno radio station for his leftist views. He makes a short trip through Italy and is hired to work at Polish Radio in Warsaw.

1940   Milosz secretly escapes from Wilno, now occupied by the Soviet army, and crossing the border illegally, arrives in Nazi-occupied Warsaw. He works as a janitor in the university library, then inactive, and under the pseudonym Jan Syruć publishes *Poems (Wiersze)* in the underground press.

1942   Two of Milosz's works appear in the Warsaw underground press: a translation of Jacques Maritain's *À travers le désastre* and an anthology edited by Milosz of anti-Nazi poetry, *The Invincible Song (Pieśń niepodległa)*.

1943   At the request of the underground theater committee Milosz translates Shakespeare's *As You Like It*. He takes part in clandestine poetry readings and writes "The World: A Naive Poem" ("Świat: Poema naiwne") and "Voices of Poor People" ("Głosy biednych ludzi").

1945   Milosz lives in Kraków. He publishes a collection of poems, *Rescue (Ocalenie)*, and departs for the United States to take up a diplomatic post.

1946   Milosz works at the Polish Consulate in New York. He writes "Child of Europe" ("Dziecię Europy").

1947   Milosz is appointed Polish cultural attaché in Washington, D.C. He writes "Treatise on Morals" ("Traktat moralny") and translates poetry into Polish, including works by Walt Whitman, e. e. cummings, and Carl Sandburg. His translation of T. S. Eliot's *Waste Land* appears in Poland.

1950   Milosz is appointed first secretary at the embassy of the People's Republic of Poland in Paris.

1951   On February 1 Milosz asks the French government for political asylum. He begins writing *The Captive Mind* (*Zniewolony umysł*).

1953   *The Captive Mind* appears in Polish and in French and English translations. Milosz receives the Prix Littéraire Européen for his novel *Seizure of Power* (*Zdobycie władzy*), which appears in French as *La prise du pouvoir*. He also publishes his first book of poetry written in emigration, *Daylight* (*Światło dzienne*).

1955   *Seizure of Power* appears in Polish and English (the British edition is entitled *The Usurpers*). The novel *The Issa Valley* (*Dolina Issy*) appears in Polish and French.

1957   *Treatise on Poetry* (*Traktat poetycki*) is published in Paris.

1958   *Native Realm* (*Rodzinna Europa*), an intellectual autobiography, and *Continents* (*Kontynenty*), a collection of essays and poetry translations, published in Paris. Milosz edits and translates into Polish selected writings of Simone Weil (*Wybór pism*).

1960   The Department of Slavic Languages and Literatures at the University of California at Berkeley invites Milosz to lecture on Polish literature.

1961   Milosz is offered tenure and settles permanently in Berkeley.

1962   Milosz publishes the poetry collection *King Popiel and Other Poems* (*Król Popiel i inne wiersze*) as well as a study of the distinguished Polish philosopher Stanisław Brzozowski, *Man Among Scorpions* (*Człowiek wśród skorpionów*).

1965   Milosz's seventh book of poetry is published, *Bobo's Metamorphosis* (*Gucio zaczarowany*), as well as *Postwar Polish Poetry*, an anthology of which he is both editor and translator.

1966   Milosz becomes a fellow of the Humanities Institute in Berkeley.

1967   An extensive collection of Milosz's poetry, *Poems* (*Wiersze*), appears in London, and he receives the Marian Kister Literary Award.

1968   Publication in English of *Native Realm*. Milosz receives the Alfred Jurzykowski Foundation Award.

1969   Publication of three works: *City Without a Name* (*Miasto bez imienia*), his collection of essays *Visions from San Francisco Bay* (*Widzenia nad Zatoką San Francisco*), and *The History of Polish Literature*.

1972   Publication of a collection of essays, *Private Obligations* (*Prywatne obowiązki*).

1973   Milosz's first volume of poetry in English appears, *Selected Poems*.

1974   Publication of *From the Rising of the Sun* (*Gdzie wschodzi słońce i kędy zapada*), for which he receives the I. Wandycz Award.

1976   Milosz is awarded a Guggenheim Fellowship for poetry and poetry translation.

1977   Publication of *Utwory poetyckie: Poems, The Land of Ulro* (*Ziemia Ulro*), and *The Emperor of the Earth: Modes of Eccentric Vision*. Milosz receives an honorary doctorate from the University of Michigan.

1978   Milosz receives the Neustadt International Prize for literature. He is also awarded the Berkeley Citation, the highest honor of the University of California. Publication of his second volume of poetry in English, *Bells in Winter*.

1979   Publication of *Księga psalmów,* a translation of the Book of Psalms from Hebrew into Polish, for which Milosz receives the Zygmunt Hertz Literary Award, and a new collection of essays, *The Garden of Knowledge* (*Ogród Nauk*).

1980   Publication in Polish of *Księga Hioba*, Milosz's translation of the Book of Job from the Hebrew. He receives the Nobel Prize in literature.

1981   Milosz returns to Poland for the first time in thirty years. He is awarded an honorary doctorate by the Catholic University of Lublin and meets with Lech Wałęsa and the leaders of Solidarity in Gdańsk. Successive volumes of his poetry are published in Poland, and his works are translated into many languages. Publication in the United States of his

Nobel Lecture, The Issa Valley, and a reprint of *The Invincible Song.* Milosz gives the Charles Eliot Norton lectures at Harvard University. He is awarded an honorary doctorate by New York University.

1982   Publication of a new volume of poems, *Hymn of the Pearl* (*Hymn o Perle*), a Polish translation of the Megilloth, *Księga Pięciu Megilot,* and an English translation of *Visions from San Francisco Bay.*

1983   Milosz receives an honorary doctorate from Brandeis University (Massachusetts). Publication of the Norton lectures, *The Witness of Poetry* (*Świadectwo poezji*).

1984   Publication of a bilingual edition of Milosz's poetry, *The Separate Notebooks,* as well as a new volume of poetry, translations, and notes, *Nieobjęta ziemia* (*Unattainable Earth*), in Polish.

1985   Publication of the collection of essays *Beginning with my Streets* (*Zaczynając od moich ulic*) and a translation of selected essays of Oscar Milosz, *The Noble Traveler.*

1986   Publication in English of *Unattainable Earth.*

1988   Publication of *The Collected Poems, 1931–1987.*

Notes

INTRODUCTION

1. Joseph Brodsky, "Presentation of Czeslaw Milosz to the Jury [of the Neustadt International Prize for literature]," *World Literature Today* 52, no. 3 (Summer 1978): 364.

2. Helen Vendler, "From Fragments a World Perfect at Last," *The New Yorker*, March 19, 1984, 146.

3. Good introductions to the national and cultural complexities and the social situation include Alexander M. Schenker, "Introduction," *Utwory poetyckie: Poems* (Ann Arbor, Mich.: Michigan Slavic Publications, 1976); Tomas Venclova, "Czeslaw Milosz: Despair and Grace," *World Literature Today* 52, no. 3 (Summer 1978): 391–395; Robert Hass, "Reading Milosz," *Ironwood*, no. 18, 1981, 140–170; Norman Davies, "The Making of His Mind," *New York Times Book Review*, September 2, 1984, 1, 16–17.

4. Ewa Czarnecka and Aleksander Fiut, *Conversations with Czeslaw Milosz* (San Diego: Harcourt Brace Jovanovich, 1987).

1. THE TRAPS OF MIMESIS

1. Much has been written about Milosz's ontology. For example, see Józef Sadzik, "Inne niebo, inna ziemia," preface to Czeslaw Milosz, *Ziemia Ulro* (Paris: Instytut Literacki, 1977); Krzysztof Dybciak, "'Holy Is Our Being... and Holy the Day,'" *World Literature Today* 52, no. 3 (Summer 1978): 415–420; Jan Błoński, "Poetry and Knowledge," *World Literature Today* 52, no. 3 (Summer 1978): 387–391.

2. "O niewiedzy wyuczonej i literackiej," *Kultura* (Paris), 1980, no. 6:38.

3. Stanisław Barańczak, "Język poetycki Czesława Miłosza. Wstępne rozpoznanie," *Teksty* 1981, no. 4–5 (58–59): 162–169.

4. See Bogdana Carpenter and John Carpenter, "The Ordinary Material Object: Its Extraordinary Fate," *World Literature Today* 54, no. 3 (Summer 1980): 369–375.

5. Louis Iribarne paraphrased this formula in "The Human Thing: Encomium for Czeslaw Milosz," *World Literature Today* 52, no. 3 (Summer 1978): 366: "To the extent that he uses language to circumscribe the nature of things, their essence, his poetry may be said to be metaphysical, symbolism *à rebours*, even when what the mind and word encounter does not always oblige. It is

here, at the very threshold of the ineffable, that Milosz the poet and Milosz the philosopher find themselves in alliance."

6. Jan Prokop, *Lekcja rzeczy* (Kraków: Wydawnictwo Literackie, 1972), 206.

7. Barańczak, "Język," 169.

8. Ibid.

9. See Zdzisław Łapiński, *Między polityką a metafizyką: O poezji Czesława Miłosza* (London: Odnowa, 1981), 24.

10. Both Józef Sadzik, "Inne niebo," and Krzysztof Dybciak, "'Holy Is,'" have pointed out certain similarities between Milosz and Heidegger.

11. Jan Błoński, "Epifanie Miłosza," *Teksty*, 1981, no. 4–5 (58–59): 33.

12. Marian Maciejewski, "Mickiewiczowskie 'czucia wieczności' (Czas i przestrzeń w liryce lozańskiej)," in *Poetyka—gatunek—obraz: W kręgu poezji romantycznej* (Wrocław: Ossolineum, 1977), 89.

13. Ibid., 94.

14. Stanley Rosen rightly emphasizes that the "instantaneousness of the moment" constitutes one of the central problems of twentieth-century philosophy, occupying a prominent place in the systems of Wittgenstein and Heidegger, who in turn refer to Nietzsche's concept of *Augenblick*. See *Nihilism: A Philosophical Essay* (New Haven: Yale University Press, 1969), 94.

15. T. S. Eliot, *Collected Poems: 1909–1935* (New York: Harcourt, Brace, 1936), 217.

16. Ibid., 216.

17. David H. Abrams, *Natural Supernaturalism: Tradition and Revolution in Romantic Literature* (New York: Norton, 1973). References here are to two subchapters: "Moments" (385–389) and "Varieties of the Modern Moment" (418–426).

18. Jacek Łukasiewicz, "Przestrzeń 'świata naiwnego.' O poemacie Czesława Miłosza 'Świat,'" *Pamiętnik Literacki*, no. 4 (1981): 87. Lillian Vallee has also written an interesting article about "The World," "What is 'The World'?" *Ironwood*, no. 18 (1981): 130–139.

19. Czeslaw Milosz, "Przedmowa," in Stanisław Vincenz, *Po stronie pamięci. Wybór esejów* (Paris: Instytut Literacki, 1965), 9.

20. Milosz states that in this respect Polish literature is in a privileged position: "Its hopeless entanglement in historical events . . . perhaps shapes its sense of historical detail which other 'happier' nations get along without. In other words, whoever descends from this literature is gifted with *significant time*. Even if its meaning cannot be deciphered, it has at least the interesting faculty of not being lost in apathy, the mother of boredom and grayness" (ibid., 10).

21. Oscar Milosz, *Oeuvres complètes*, vol. 7, *Ars magna* (Paris: Editions André Silvaire, 1961), 15.

2. LOVE AFFAIR WITH NATURE

1. Joseph Warren Beach, *The Concept of Nature in Nineteenth-Century English Poetry* (1936; New York: Russell and Russell, 1966).

2. Robert Langbaum, "The New Nature Poetry," in *The Modern Spirit: Essays on the Continuity of Nineteenth- and Twentieth-Century Literature* (New York: Oxford University Press, 1970).

3. These terms allude to the poetry of Wallace Stevens. See chapter 7, note 15.

4. Witold Gombrowicz, *Dziennik (1957–1961)* (Paris: Instytut Literacki, 1962), 36, 39.

5. Ibid., 36.

6. Ibid., 39.

7. Konstanty A. Jeleński, *Zbiegi okoliczności* (Paris: Instytut Literacki, 1982), 208.

8. Tadeusz Kotarbiński, *Elementy teorii poznania, logiki formalnej i metodologii nauk* (Wrocław: Ossolineum, 1961), 468.

9. Jacek Trznadel, *Płomień obdarzony rozumem. Poezja w poezji i poza poezją. Eseje* (Warsaw: Czytelnik, 1978), 238.

10. The debate over universals clearly continues to intrigue Milosz. See the poem "Consciousness" (*CP* 240; "Świadomość"), where he considers the question of "doggishness."

11. Gombrowicz, *Dziennik (1957–1961)*, 37.

3. FACING THE END OF THE WORLD

1. Milosz speaks of his relation to Marxism in *Native Realm* (see the chapters "Marxism," "Tiger 1," and "Tiger 2").

2. Kazimierz Wyka, "Ogrody lunatyczne, ogrody pasterskie," *Twórczość*, no. 5 (1946): 135–147.

3. Jan Błoński, "Aktualność i trwałość," in *Odmarsz* (Kraków: Wydawnictwo Literackie, 1978), 206. Originally published in *Miesięcznik Literacki*, no. 1 (1974).

4. See Małgorzata Szpakowska, *Światopogląd Stanisława Ignacego Witkiewicza* (Wrocław: Ossolineum, 1976); Barbara Danek-Wojnowska, *Stanisław Ignacy Witkiewicz a modernizm. Kształtowanie idei katastroficznych* (Wrocław: Ossolineum, 1976).

5. Danek-Wojnowska, *Witkiewicz*, 158.

6. Aleksander Wat, *My Century: The Odyssey of a Polish Intellectual*, with a foreword by Czeslaw Milosz, translated by Richard Lourie (Berkeley and Los Angeles: University of California Press, 1988), 4–5.

7. J. Hering, *Le Royaume de Dieu et sa venue* (Strasbourg, 1937), cited in Paul Ricoeur, *Finitude et culpabilité II. La Symbolique du mal* (Paris, 1960), 247.

8. Mircea Eliade, *Aspects du mythe* (Paris: Gallimard, 1963), 83.

9. Jan Kott, "O katastrofizmie," *Odrodzenie*, no. 18 (1945): 11.

10. Rudolf Bultmann, *History and Eschatology*, The Gifford Lectures, 1955 (Edinburgh: Edinburgh University Press, 1957), 152–154, at 154.

11. See J. E. Cirlot, *A Dictionary of Symbols*, translated from the Spanish by Jack Sage (London: Routledge & Kegan Paul, 1962).

12. Lev Shestov, *Good in the Teaching of Tolstoy and Nietzsche: Philosophy and Preaching,* in *Potestas Clavium,* translated and with an introduction by B. Martin (Chicago: Regnery, Gateway, 1970), p. xvii.

13. The latest confirmation may be the poem "Theodicy" in *Unattainable Earth:*

> No, it won't do, my sweet theologians.
> Desire will not save the morality of God.
> If he created beings able to choose between good and evil,
> And they chose, and the world lies in iniquity,
> Nevertheless, there is pain, and the undeserved torture of creatures,
> Which would find its explanation only by assuming
> The existence of an archetypal Paradise
> And a pre-human downfall so grave
> That the world of matter received its shape from diabolic power.
>
> (*CP* 434)

> Nie, to nie przejdzie, szlachetni teologowie.
> Wasza chęć szczera nie uratuje moralności Boga,
> Bo jeśli stworzył istoty zdolne wybrać między dobrem i złem,
> I wybrały, i dlatego świat w złem leży,
> To jeszcze jest ból, niezawiniona męka stworzeń,
> Która znalazłaby wytłumaczenie tylko wtedy
> Gdybyście przyjęli Raj archetypalny
> A w nim upadek praludzi tak wielki,
> Że świat materii dostał kształt swój pod diabelską władzą.
>
> ("Teodycea")

14. This applies particularly to Clement of Alexandria and his student Origen. See H. Jonas, *The Gnostic Religion: The Message of the Alien God and the Beginnings of Christianity,* 2d ed. (Boston: Beacon Press, 1972).

15. See D. B. Richardson, *Berdyaev's Philosophy of History: An Existentialist Theory of Social Creativity and Eschatology* (The Hague: Martinns Nijhoff, 1968), 84–85.

16. See John Peck, "Last Things," *Ironwood,* no. 18 (1981): 76–97.

17. Richardson, *Berdyaev's Philosophy,* 39–41.

18. Olga Scherer writes about this problem in "To Ulro Through San Francisco Bay," *World Literature Today* 52, no. 3 (Summer 1978): 408–412.

4. IN THE "INTERHUMAN CHURCH"

1. Milosz is completely conscious of these links. See Czeslaw Milosz, "Podzwonne," *Kultura* (Paris), 1969, no. 11: 6–11.

2. Ibid.

3. Jerzy Jarzębski, *Gra w Gombrowicza* (Warsaw: Panstwowy Instytut Wydawniczy, 1983), 376–377.

4. Jerzy Jarzębski, "Być wieszczem," *Teksty,* 1981, no. 4–5 (58–59): 247.

5. See also Schenker, "Introduction," and Harold B. Segel, "Czeslaw Milosz and the Landscape of Exile," *Cross Currents* 1982:89–105.

6. Stanisław Barańczak, "Czesław Miłosz laureatem Literackiej Nagrody Nobla," *W drodze,* 1980, no. 10:6.

7. Witold Gombrowicz, *Dziennik* (*1961–1966*) (Paris: Instytut Literacki, 1971), 30–32.

8. Gombrowicz, *Dziennik* (*1957–1961*), 90.

5. IN THE GRIP OF EROS

1. On the symbolism of the moon see Mircea Eliade, "The Moon and Its Mystique," in *Patterns in Comparative Religion*, translated by Rosemary Sheed (New York: New American Library, 1974), translation of *Traité d'histoire des Religions*.

2. A good introduction to this discussion of Bosch's work is *Bosch in Perspective*, edited by James Snyder (Englewood Cliffs, N.J.: Prentice-Hall, 1973).

3. Charles de Tolnay, *Hieronymus Bosch* (London: Methuen, 1966).

4. Wilhelm Fraenger, *Le Royaume Millénaire de Jérôme Bosch*, translated from the German by R. Lewinter (Paris: Editions Denoël, 1966), 78.

5. Anna Boczkowska, *Tryumf Luny i Wenus. Pasja Hieronima Boscha* (Kraków: Wydawnictwo Literackie, 1980), 40.

6. Tolnay, *Hieronymus Bosch*, 32.

7. Wilhelm Fraenger, *Die Hochzeit zu Kana. Ein Dokument semitischer Gnosis bei Hieronymus Bosch* (Berlin: Verlag Gebrüder Mann, 1950), 25.

8. Boczkowska, *Tryumf Luny*, 40.

9. The source of this idea, established and developed in a series of studies, is Wilhelm Fraenger. It has met with sharp criticism from many opponents. They include, in addition to those already mentioned, Erwin Panofsky, *Early Netherlandish Painting: Its Origins and Character*, vol. 1 (Cambridge, Mass.: Harvard University Press, 1958); and Dirk Bax, who explored the linguistic sources of Bosch's symbolism in *Hieronymus Bosch: His Picture-Writing Deciphered*, translated by M. A. Bax-Botha (Rotterdam: A. A. Balkema, 1979).

10. Boczkowska, *Tryumf Luny*, 8–9.

11. Błoński, "Epifanie Miłosza," 40.

6. THE IDENTITY GAME

1. See Ewa Czarnecka, *Podróżny świata. Rozmowy z Czesławem Miłoszem. Komentarze* (New York: Bicentennial Publishing, 1983), 192. [Henceforth *PS*.]

2. See William Ramsey, "Many Voices," chapter 8 of *Jules Laforgue and the Ironic Inheritance* (New York: Oxford University Press, 1953).

3. See Robert Langbaum, *The Poetry of Experience: The Dramatic Monologue in Modern Literary Tradition* (New York: Norton, 1963); G. T. Wright, *The Poet in the Poem: The Personae of Eliot, Yeats, and Pound* (Berkeley and Los Angeles: University of California Press, 1962).

4. This roving irony eludes classifications found in such fundamental studies as D. C. Muecke, *The Compass of Irony* (London: Methuen, 1969)

and Wayne C. Booth, *A Rhetoric of Irony* (Chicago: University of Chicago Press, 1974), probably because those critics do not consider the situation when both the subject and the object of irony remain split internally. Note that when using this device, Milosz displays a suspicious attitude toward irony.

5. See Barańczak, "Język," 171.

6. See *PS* 152. The full title of Vahanian's book is *The Death of God: The Culture of Our Post-Christian Era* (New York: George Braziller, 1961).

7. The motif of schizophrenia recurs in Milosz, as noted by Irena Sławińska, "The Image of the Poet and His Estate," *World Literature Today* 52, no. 3 (Summer 1978): 398. The poet explains it in different ways. In "Treatise on Morals" he speaks of the split of "a living thing into flower and root," that is, into aesthetics and ethics, principles and practical experience. In "To Raja Rao" (which Milosz wrote in English) he discloses:

> For years I could not accept
> the place I was in.
> I felt I should be somewhere else.
>
> . . . .
> Link, if you wish, my peculiar case
> on the border of schizophrenia
> to the messianic hope
> of my civilization.
>
> (*SP* 29)

8. Segel, "Landscape of Exile," 91–92, 100.

9. See Błoński, "Poetry and Knowledge," and Schenker, "Introduction."

10. In retrospect Milosz himself questions this approach: "Ultimately, I think that Jan Błoński wrote a very fine essay on 'Slow River' but, after Mikhail Bakhtin's book on Dostoevsky's poetics, it had become a bit fashionable to interpret works in terms of polyphony. If you read that poem closely, you'll see it's far from polyphonic. But a great many various voices really can emerge at times when a person has a great many conflicts and contradictions" (*CCM* 114). Hence Milosz is against polyphony and for a variety of voices!

11. Robert Langbaum, "The Mysteries of Identity," in *The Modern Spirit,* 168ff.

12. Ibid., 170.

13. See Segel, "Landscape of Exile," 98–101.

14. See Patricia Hampl, "Czeslaw Milosz and Memory," *Ironwood,* no. 18 (1981): 57–75.

15. Abrams, *Natural Supernaturalism,* considers the motif of pilgrimage in romantic literature.

16. Stanisław Barańczak, *A Fugitive from Utopia: The Poetry of Zbigniew Herbert* (Cambridge, Mass.: Harvard University Press, 1987).

7. PALIMPSEST

1. Jerzy Kwiatkowski, "Magia Miłosza," in *Notatki o poezji i krytyce* (Kraków: Wydawnictwo Literackie, 1975), 77–78.

2. This asymmetry may be partially the result of the struggle with the "flaw of harmony." As Barańczak aptly observes, "Milosz's most poetically outstanding works are those in which—aside from their other values—he achieved in the linguistic and stylistic realm a position that wavers, balancing along an invisible line of equilibrium: equilibrium between harmony and disharmony, regularity and irregularity, rigor and freedom, high style and low, 'poetry' and 'prose' " ("Język," 176–177).

3. Ryszard Nycz has written about the references in Milosz to this ancient genre, "Prywatna księga różności," *Teksty*, 1981, no. 4–5 (58–59): 203–233. Milosz's *Unattainable Earth* seems to confirm Nycz's intuitions.

4. Jan Błoński, "Bieguny poezji," in *Odmarsz* (Kraków: Wydawnictwo Literackie, 1978), 206.

5. Barańczak, "Język," 172.

6. Maria Renata Mayenowa, *Poetyka teoretyczna. Zagadnienie języka* (Wrocław: Ossolineum, 1974), 364.

7. The term *theater of speech* (*teatr mowy*) is coined by Aleksandra Okopień-Sławińska in "Jak formy osobowe grają w teatrze mowy," *Teksty*, 1977, no. 5–6.

8. Milosz quotes and comments on portions of this letter in *History of Polish Literature*, 2d ed. (Berkeley and Los Angeles: University of California Press, 1983), 201–202.

9. The reference is to Juliusz Słowacki's drama *Kordian*.

10. Louis Iribarne, in "The Naming of Hell," *Times Literary Supplement*, August 25, 1978, calls Milosz "a poet of instinct" and "a poet of intellect."

11. George Gömöri, in " 'Truth' and 'Beauty' in Milosz's Poetry," *World Literature Today* 52, no. 3 (Summer 1978): 414, analyzes in Milosz's poetry "two different, though equally enduring, myths: a 'myth of Troy' (although in some cases it is 'Nineveh' or 'Babylon') and a 'myth of Arcadia.' "

12. Barańczak, "Język," 173–174.

13. Edward Balcerzan, "Polaryzacje sztuki poetyckiej," in *Odmarsz*, 219–220.

14. Christopher Marlowe, *The Tragical History of Doctor Faustus*, edited by F. S. Boas (New York: Gordian Press, 1966), 69.

15. The original passage from Wallace Stevens, *The Collected Poems* (New York: Knopf, 1982), 27, is:

> Nota: man is the intelligence of his soil,
> The sovereign ghost. As such, the Socrates
> Of snails, musician of pears, principium
> And lex.

Here is Milosz's parody:

And what then should this principal phantom,
As he is called, do? More than a magician,
A Socrates of snails, he's called,
Musician of pears, mediator of orioles—man?
("Treatise on Poetry. IV. Nature")

I cóż ma począć ten, jak go nazwano,
Upiór naczelny, więcej niż czarodziej,
Jak go nazwano: Sokrates ślimaków,
Muzykant gruszek, rozjemca wilg, człowiek?
("Traktat Poetycki. IV. Natura")

Milosz's parody, framed as a question, softens the explicitness of the man–nature opposition as it expands its scope. For Milosz as for Stevens, nature is the hostile element of water, symbol of chaos and primordial power, before which men seek protection through their link with earth; but for Milosz vegetation does not provide any shelter either. The conclusions that may be drawn also differ. Milosz, in contrast to Stevens, does not discard the creations of the human mind in favor of experience but defends them as the sole refuge from the inhumanity of nature. See Hi Simons, "'The Comedian as the Letter C': Its Sense and Its Significance," in *The Achievement of Wallace Stevens*, edited by Ashley Brown and Robert S. Haller (Philadelphia and New York: Lippincott, 1962); Eugene Paul Nassar, *Wallace Stevens: An Anatomy of Figuration* (Philadelphia: University of Pennsylvania Press, 1965); Harold Bloom, *Wallace Stevens: The Poems of Our Climate* (Ithaca, N.Y.: Cornell University Press, 1977).

16. Barańczak, "Język," 169–170.

17. *Polityka* (1981), no. 3.

18. "Próba ujawnienia," *Kultura* (Paris) 182, no. 12 (1962): 43–59.

19. American critics concur; they compare Milosz's poetry with Anglo-Saxon poetry. See Louis Iribarne, "Naming"; Stephen Miller, "Writers' Choice," *Partisan Review* 44, no. 2 (1977): 318; Richard Howard, "An Heroic Apostate," *Parnassus: Poetry in Review* 7, no. 2 (1979). On the place of Milosz in Polish poetry, see Marek Zaleski, "The Place of Milosz in Polish Poetry," *Ironwood*, no. 18, 1981, 171–178.

20. Czeslaw Milosz, "Punkt widzenia czyli o tak zwanej Drugiej Awangardzie," *Oficyna Poetów* 2, no. 1 (1967): 7–17.

Bibliography

WORKS OF CZESLAW MILOSZ IN ENGLISH

Bells in Winter. Translated by the author and Lillian Vallee. New York: Ecco Press, 1978.

The Captive Mind. Translated by Jane Zielonko. London: Secker and Warburg, 1953; New York: Knopf, 1953; Random House, 1953; Vintage Books, 1955; London: Mercury Books, 1962; New York: Vintage Books, 1981.

The Collected Poems, 1931–1987. New York: Ecco Press, 1988.

Emperor of the Earth: Modes of Eccentric Vision. Berkeley and Los Angeles: University of California Press, 1977.

The History of Polish Literature. New York: Macmillan, 1969; expanded edition, Berkeley: University of California Press, 1983.

The Issa Valley. Translated by Louis Iribarne. New York: Farrar, Straus & Giroux, 1981.

The Land of Ulro. Translated by Louis Iribarne. New York: Farrar, Straus & Giroux, 1984.

Native Realm: A Search for Self-Definition. Translated by Catherine S. Leach. Garden City, N.Y.: Doubleday, 1968; new edition, 1970.

Nobel Lecture. New York: Farrar, Straus & Giroux, 1981.

The Seizure of Power. (British edition entitled *The Usurpers.*) Translated by Celina Wieniewska. London: Faber and Faber, 1955; New York: Criterion Books, 1955.

Selected Poems. Introduction by Kenneth Rexroth. New York: Seabury Press, 1973.

The Separate Notebooks. Translated by Robert Hass and Robert Pinsky with the author and Renata Gorczynski. New York: Ecco Press, 1984.

Unattainable Earth. Translated by the author and Robert Hass. New York: Ecco Press, 1986.

Visions from San Francisco Bay. Translated by Richard Lourie. New York: Farrar, Straus & Giroux, 1982.

The Witness of Poetry. Cambridge, Mass.: Harvard University Press, 1983.

Anthologies and Translations

Happy as a Dog's Tail, poems by Anna Swir. Translated by Czeslaw Milosz with Leonard Nathan. San Diego: Harcourt Brace Jovanovich, 1985.

Mediterranean Poems, by Aleksander Wat. Edited and translated by Czeslaw Milosz. Ann Arbor, Mich.: Ardis, 1977.

Pieśń niepodległa. The Invincible Song: A Clandestine Anthology. Edited by Czeslaw Milosz. Warsaw, 1942. Reprint, Ann Arbor, Mich.: Michigan Slavic Publications, 1981.

Postwar Polish Poetry: An Anthology. Selected and translated by Czeslaw Milosz. Garden City, N.Y.: Doubleday, 1965; Penguin Books, 1970; expanded edition, Berkeley and Los Angeles: University of California Press, 1983.

Selected Poems, by Zbigniew Herbert. Translated by Czeslaw Milosz and Peter Dale Scott, with an introduction by A. Alvarez. Harmondsworth: Penguin Books, 1968.

With the Skin: Poems of Aleksander Wat. Translated and edited by Czeslaw Milosz and Leonard Nathan. New York: Ecco Press, 1989.

SELECTED WORKS ABOUT CZESLAW MILOSZ IN ENGLISH

Extensive bibliographic information can be found in *Czeslaw Milosz: An International Bibliography, 1930–1980,* by Rimma Volynska-Bogert and Wojciech Zalewski, with a preface by Stanisław Barańczak (Ann Arbor: Michigan Slavic Publications, 1983).

Alvarez, A. Review of *Postwar Polish Poetry. New York Review of Books,* November 11, 1965, 24.

Ascherson, Neal. "Under Eastern Eyes." *New York Review of Books,* May 8, 1969, 27–28. [Re: *Native Realm*]

Atlas, James. "Poet, Exile, Laureate: Czeslaw Milosz." *New York Times,* October 10, 1980.

Baer, Joachim T. Review of *The Witness of Poetry. Polish Review* 29, no. 3 (1984): 97–99.

Barańczak, Stanisław. "My Part Is Agony." *Parnassus: Poetry in Review* 9, no. 2 (1981): 62–72.

———. "The Summing Up of Czeslaw Milosz." *Ironwood,* no. 18 (1981): 98–108.

———. "Hope Against Hope." *New Criterion* 1, no. 10 (1983): 84–87. [Re: *The Witness of Poetry*]

———. "In Defense of the Imagination." *Partisan Review* 52, no. 4 (1985): 448. [Re: *The Land of Ulro*]

———. "Milosz's Poetic Language: A Reconnaissance." *Language and Style: An International Journal* 18, no. 4 (1985): 319–333.

———. "A Black Mirror at the End of a Tunnel: An Interpretation of Czeslaw Milosz's 'Świty.'" *Polish Review* 31, no. 4 (1986): 273–284.

Bayley, John. "The Clear Eye of the Mediator." *Times Literary Supplement,* December 2, 1977, 1419. [Re: *Emperor of the Earth*]

———. "Return of the Native." *New York Review of Books,* June 25, 1981, 29–33.

Bell, Daniel. "Out of the Fight for Warsaw." *New Republic,* May 16, 1955, 41–43. [Re: *The Seizure of Power*]

Birmelin, Blair T. "Worlds Lost and Found: Novels by Czeslaw Milosz, Milan Kundera, and Aharon Appelfeld." *Literary Review* 26, no. 3 (1983): 460–474. [Re: *The Issa Valley*]

Błoński, Jan. "Poetry and Knowledge." *World Literature Today* 52, no. 3 (1978): 387–391.

"Books of the Times." *New York Times,* August 24, 1984. [Re: *The Land of Ulro*]

Brodsky, Joseph. "Presentation of Czeslaw Milosz to the Jury." *World Literature Today* 52, no. 3 (1978): 364. [Re: awarding of Neustadt International Prize to Milosz]

————. "Poet's View—True Child and Heir of the Century." *New York Times,* October 10, 1980.

Broyard, Anatole. "At Home Is the Exile." *New York Times,* September 4, 1982. [Re: *Visions From San Francisco Bay*]

Carpenter, Bogdana. Review of *Emperor of the Earth. World Literature Today* 52, no. 3 (1978): 489–90.

Chamberlain, Marisha. "The Voice of the Orphan: Czeslaw Milosz's Warsaw Poems." *Ironwood,* no. 18 (1981): 28–35.

Chiaromonte, Nicola. "Intellectual Under the 'System': *The Captive Mind.*" *Partisan Review* 20 (1953): 697–702.

Coleman, Alexander. "The 'Still Point' in Milosz's *Native Realm.*" *World Literature Today* 52, no. 3 (1978): 399–403.

Contoski, Victor. "Czeslaw Milosz and the Quest for Critical Perspective." *Books Abroad* 47 (1973): 35–41. [Re: *The Captive Mind, Native Realm*]

Cooperman, Stanley. "Of War and Man." *Nation,* July 23, 1955, 80. [Re: *The Seizure of Power*]

Czaykowski, Bogdan. "The Fly and the Flywheel: Some Reflections on the Poetry of Czeslaw Milosz." *Oficyna Poetów* [London] 4 (1970): 25–28.

Czarnecka, Ewa. "A Pilgrim in California: On Milosz's 'A Magic Mountain.'" *Migrant Echo* (San Francisco) 9, no. 2 (1980): 85–91.

Czarnecka, Ewa, and Aleksander Fiut. *Conversations with Czeslaw Milosz,* translated by Richard Lourie. San Diego: Harcourt Brace Jovanovich, 1987.

Czerniawski, Adam. "For an Old Bitch Gone in the Teeth. For a Botched Civilisation." *King's College Review,* June 1954. [Re: *The Captive Mind*]

————. Review of *The History of Polish Literature. New Statesman,* March 20, 1970, 414–415.

Davie, Donald. *Czeslaw Milosz and the Insufficiency of Lyric.* Knoxville: University of Tennessee Press, 1986.

Davies, Norman. "The Making of His Mind." *New York Times Book Review,* September 2, 1984. [Re: *The Land of Ulro*]

De Aguilar, Helene J. F. "'A Prince Out of Thy Star': The Place of Czeslaw Milosz." *Parnassus: Poetry in Review* 11, no. 2 (1983/1984): 127–154.

[Re: *Postwar Polish Poetry, The Seizure of Power, The Separate Notebooks, Visions From San Francisco Bay, The Witness of Poetry*]

Des Pres, Terrence. "Czeslaw Milosz: the Poetry of Aftermath." *Nation,* December 30, 1978, 741–743.

Deutsch, Babette. "To Survive Is to Sing." *Book Review,* May 9, 1965, 19. [Re: *Postwar Polish Poetry*]

Dybciak, Krzysztof. "'Holy Is Our Being . . . and Holy the Day.'" *World Literature Today* 52, no. 3 (1978): 415–420.

Edel, Leon. "Democratic Vistas." *New York Times Book Review,* October 17, 1982. [Re: *Visions From San Francisco Bay*]

Elliot, George P. Review of *Bells in Winter. New Letters* 46 (1979–1980): 118–19.

Enright, D. J. "Child of Europe." *New York Review of Books,* April 4, 1974, 29. [Re: *Selected Poems*]

Fiut, Aleksander. "Facing the End of the World." *World Literature Today* 52, no. 3 (1978): 420–425.

———. "The Poetry of Czeslaw Milosz: The Parable of the Great Disinheritance." *Cross Currents* 23, no. 5 (1983): 333–346.

———. "Reading Milosz." *Polish Review* 31, no. 4 (1986): 257–264.

Fiut, Aleksander, and Ewa Czarnecka. See Czarnecka.

Folejewski, Zbigniew. "Czeslaw Milosz: A Poet's Road to Ithaca Between Worlds, Wars, and Poetics." *Books Abroad* 43 (1969): 17–24.

"Fruits of Experience." *Times Literary Supplement* (London), July 15, 1955, 393. [Re: *The Usurpers*]

Gella, Aleksander. Review of *Native Realm: A Search for Self-Definition. Slavic Review* 29, no. 4 (1970): 756–757.

Giergielewicz, Mieczysław. Review of *The History of Polish Literature. Books Abroad* 44 (1970): 327–28.

Gömöri, George. Review of *Postwar Polish Poetry. Slavonic and East European Review* 45 (1967): 237–238.

———. "On the Collected Poems of Czeslaw Milosz." *Books Abroad* 43 (1969): 201–202. [Re: *Wiersze* (London 1967)]

———. "'Truth' and 'Beauty' in Milosz's Poetry." *World Literature Today* 52, no. 3 (1978): 412–415.

Hamilton, Carol S. "Poet Milosz as an Outsider and Insider." *San Francisco Chronicle Review,* August 22, 1982, 1, 10.

Hampl, Patricia. "Czeslaw Milosz and Memory." *Ironwood,* no. 18 (1981): 57–75.

Hass, Robert. "Reading Milosz." *Ironwood,* no. 18 (1981): 140–170.

———. "'The World': A Note on the Translation." *Ironwood,* no. 18 (1981): 37–40.

Herbert, Zbigniew. "From 'On Czeslaw Milosz.'" *Ironwood,* no. 18 (1981): 36.

Hicks, Granville. "Agony and Temptation." *New York Times,* April 17, 1955, 5. [Re: *The Seizure of Power*]

Holmes, Richard. "Innocent in a Rotten Paradise." *London Times*, January 6, 1983. [Re: *Visions From San Francisco Bay*]

Howard, Richard. "An Heroic Apostate." *Parnasssus: Poetry in Review* 7, no. 2 (1979): 44–49. [Re: *Bells in Winter*]

Howe, Irving. "Moral History of Czeslaw Milosz." *New York Times Book Review*, February 1, 1981, 3, 24. [Re: *Native Realm*]

Hyde, Lewis. "The Devil and Mr. Milosz." *Nation*, September 22, 1982, 278. [Re: *Visions From San Francisco Bay*]

Iribarne, Louis. "The Human Thing: Encomium for Czeslaw Milosz." *World Literature Today* 52, no. 3 (1978): 365–368.

———. "The Naming of Hell." *Times Literary Supplement*, August 25, 1978, 951.

Ivask, Ivar. "Czeslaw Milosz—1978 Laureate of the Neustadt International Prize for Literature." *World Literature Today* 52, no. 2 (1978): 197–198.

———. "The Endless Column: Some Reflections on East European Literature and the Example of Czeslaw Milosz." *World Literature Today* 52, no. 3 (1978): 357–362.

———. "Czeslaw Milosz: 1980 Nobel Prize in Literature." *World Literature Today* 55 (1981): 5–6.

Jaspers, Karl. "Endurance and Miracle." *Saturday Review*, June 6, 1953, 13, 30. [Re: *The Captive Mind*]

Kapolka, Gerard T. Review of *The History of Polish Literature*. *Polish Review* 29, no. 3 (1984): 99–100.

———. "Man's Need for a Sense of Place vs. The Sciences." *Polish Review* 30, no. 3 (1985): 283–289. [Re: *The Land of Ulro*]

Kavanagh, P. J. "Exorcist." *Spectator*, December 4, 1982.

Kazin, Alfred. "Writing Out of the Polish Agony." *New York Times Book Review*, May 1, 1983. [Re: *The Witness of Poetry*]

Kidd, James W. "On Poetic Imagination." *Migrant Echo* (San Francisco) 9, no. 2 (1980): 66–75.

Kryński, Magnus. Review of *The Captive Mind*. *Polish Review* 1, nos. 2–3 (1956): 141–143.

———. Review of *The Seizure of Power*. *Polish Review* 2, no. 1 (1955): 74–75.

Krzyżanowski, Jerzy R. Review of *Emperor of the Earth: Modes of Eccentric Vision*. *Slavic Review* 37, no. 1 (1978): 164.

Macdonald, Dwight. "In the Land of Diamat." *New Yorker*, November 7, 1953, 173–182. [Re: *The Captive Mind*]

McFee, Michael. "Voice of Poland." *Spectator Magazine*, no. 4, March 25–31, 1982, 25–26. [Re: *The Issa Valley, Selected Poems*]

Maciuszko, George. Review of *Selected Poems*. *Books Abroad* 49 (1975): 156.

McLean, Hugh. "Czeslaw Milosz Receives the Berkeley Citation." *Polish Review* 23, no. 4 (1978): 71–73.

Mahler, Scott. "A New Introduction to Milosz." *In Print* 11, no. 10 (1982): 4. [Re: *Visions From San Francisco Bay*]

Miller, Jim. "Uneasy Exile." *Newsweek*, October 4, 1982. [Re: *The Seizure of Power, Visions From San Francisco Bay*]

Miller, Stephen. "Writer's Choice." *Partisan Review* 44, no. 2 (1977): 318. [Re: *Selected Poems*]

Miner, Valerie. "In Prose, Too, the Poet Dares to Search for Moral Answers." *Washington Post*, August 15, 1982. [Re: *The Seizure of Power, Visions From San Francisco Bay*]

Możejko, Edward, ed. *Between Anxiety and Hope: The Poetry and Writing of Czeslaw Milosz*. Edmonton: University of Alberta Press, 1988. [Essays by Edward Możejko, Stanisław Bereś, Bogdan Czajkowski, Madeline G. Levine, Paul Coates, and E. D. Blodgett]

Murray, Brian. "The Mind of a Manichean." *Chronicles of Culture* 9, no. 3 (1985): 13–15. [Re: *The Land of Ulro*]

Nathan, Leonard. "Scholars in Exile." *California Monthly*, January-February 1980, 3–4.

———. "The Composing Voice: Reading 'Ars Poetica?' " *Ironwood*, no. 18 (1981): 114–121.

Nordell, Roderick. "Early Milosz Novel of Deceit and Self-Deception." *Christian Science Monitor*, September 10, 1982. [Re: *The Seizure of Power*]

Parkes, Henry B. "The Intelligent Devil." *New Republic*, June 22, 1953, 18. [Re: *The Captive Mind*]

Peck, John. "Last Things." *Ironwood*, no. 18 (1981): 76–86.

Peterson, Virgilia. "Attack on Conformity—East or West." *New York Herald Tribune Book Review*, June 14, 1953, 7. [Re: *The Captive Mind*]

———. "In Poland Survival Meant Degradation." *New York Herald Tribune Book Review*, June 19, 1955, 3. [Re: *The Seizure of Power*]

Quingly, Isabel. "New Novels." *Spectator*, June 24, 1955, 806–807. [Re: *The Seizure of Power*]

Raffel, Burton. Review of *Selected Poems*. *Denver Quarterly* 11, no. 2 (1976): 145–147.

Rudman, Mark. "On Milosz: No Longer in Continuous Time." *Ironwood*, no. 18 (1981): 11–27.

Schenker, Alexander M. "Introduction" to *Utwory poetyckie. Poems*. Ann Arbor: Michigan Slavic Publications, 1976.

Scherer, Olga. "To Ulro Through San Francisco Bay." *World Literature Today* 52, no. 3 (1978): 408–412.

Segel, Harold B. "Czeslaw Milosz and the Landscape of Exile." In *Cross Currents: A Yearbook of Central European Culture*, ed. Ladislav Matejka and Benjamin Stolz, 89–105. Michigan Slavic Materials, no. 20. Ann Arbor: University of Michigan, 1982.

Sell, Jadwiga Zwolska. Review of *Postwar Polish Poetry*. *Polish Review* 10, no. 3 (1965): 82–84.

Sheridan, Alan. "Poland's Poet." *London Review of Books*, December 17, 1981. [Re: *Native Realm, The Issa Valley*]

Sienicka, Marta. "Here and Now in Time and Space." *American Book Review* 7, no. 3 (1985): 22–23. [Re: *The Seizure of Power, Visions From San Francisco Bay*]

Šilbajoris, Rimvydas. Review of *Selected Poems. Journal of Baltic Studies* 5, no. 4 (1974): 421–423.

Sławińska, Irena. "The Image of the Poet and His Estate." *World Literature Today* 52, no. 3 (1978): 395–399.

Spender, Stephen. "The Predatory Jailer." *New Republic*, June 22, 1953, 18–19, 23. [Re: *The Captive Mind*]

Stone, Judy. "Czeslaw Milosz: Child and Man." *New York Times Book Review*, June 28, 1981, 7, 16–19.

Swan, Annalyn. "A Poet of Pity and Anger." *Newsweek*, October 20, 1980, 103.

Thompson, Ewa. "Nobel Laureate Milosz: An Exile's Visions." *Houston-Chronicle*, October 17, 1982. [Re: *Visions From San Francisco Bay, The Seizure of Power*]

Vallee, Lillian. "*The Valley of Issa:* An Interpretation." *World Literature Today* 52, no. 3 (1978): 403–407.

———. Review of *Ogród nauk* (Paris, 1979). *World Literature Today* 55 (1981): 137–138.

———. "What Is 'The World'? (A Naive Essay)." *Ironwood*, no. 18 (1981): 130–139.

Venclova, Tomas. "Czeslaw Milosz: Despair and Grace." *World Literature Today* 52, no. 3 (1978): 391–395.

———. Review of *Emperor of the Earth: Modes of Eccentric Vision. Modern Fiction Studies* 28 (1982): 717–719.

———. "Poetry as Atonement." *Polish Review* 31, no. 4 (1986): 265–271.

Vendler, Helen. "From Fragments a World Perfect at Last." *New Yorker*, March 19, 1984, 138–146. [Re: *The Separate Notebooks*]

———. "Sentences Hammered in Metal." *New Yorker*, October 24, 1988. [Re: *Collected Poems*]

Viereck, Peter. "Red Roots for the Uprooted." *New York Times*, June 7, 1953, 19.

Wasserman, Steve. "American Notes of an 'Incurable European' Haunted by the Tragic Voice of His Homeland." *Los Angeles Times, The Book Review*, August 22, 1982. [Re: *Visions From San Francisco Bay, The Seizure of Power*]

Weintraub, Wiktor. Review of *The History of Polish Literature. Slavic and East European Journal*, 2d ser., 14, no. 2 (1970): 218–224.

———. Review of *Księga psalmów* (The Book of Psalms), translated from the Hebrew by Czeslaw Milosz. *Polish Review* 25, nos. 3–4 (1980): 113–114.

Wilson, John. "The Witness of Poetry." In *Magill's Literary Annual, 1984*, ed. Frank N. Magill, 2: 959–963. Englewood Cliffs, N.J.: Salem Press, 1984.

Wilson, Reuel K. Review of *Postwar Polish Poetry. World Literature Today* 58, no. 2 (1984): 294.

Wirth, Andrzej. Review of *The History of Polish Literature*. *Slavic Review* 29, no. 3 (1970): 561–563.

Wojnicki, Tadeusz. "Ontology of Czeslaw Milosz." *Migrant Echo* (San Francisco) 9, no. 2 (1980): 76–82.

Zaleski, Marek. "The Place of Milosz in Polish Poetry." *Ironwood*, no. 18 (1981): 172–178.

Zweig, Paul. Review of *Selected Poems*. *New York Times Book Review*, July 7, 1974, 6–7, 14.

Index

"The Accuser" ("Oskarżciel"), VI of
"From the Rising of the Sun," 151
Ahumanism, Milosz as poet of, 50
"Album of Dreams" ("Album snów,"
1959), 32
Androgyny, 124–31; divine, 129
Anglo-American literature, nature and
animals, 43–44
Anglo-American poetry, comparisons
with Milosz, 4
Anthropocentrism: Christian, 3; and human image of God, 131; Pascal and,
85; threat to Milosz's, 193; unifier in
Milosz's thought, 85; vision of reality,
50
"Antigone" ("Antygona"), dialogue in,
170
"Anybody" ("Ktokolwiek," 1961), 102–
5
Apocalypse: allusion to in "Elegy for Y.
Z.," 123; in Christian eschatology, 74;
fulfilled in Warsaw ghetto uprising, 45;
hope in Second Coming, 193; images
from Book of Revelation, 77; incomprehensibility of, 79; and Milosz's poetic
universe, 187–88; in "*Oeconomia
Divina*," 80; in "Outskirts," 15; Revelation of Saint John, 139; third phase
of history, 77; in "To Father Ch.," 182.
See also Eden, Garden of
Apokatastasis: definition and tradition,
82; fullness of human existence in,
130; Milosz's attitude toward, 84, 87;
in Orthodoxy, 82, 83
"An Appeal" ("Wezwanie," 1954), 31,
166
Aquinas, Thomas. *See* Thomas Aquinas,
Saint
"*Ars poetica?*" (1968), 153
"Assizes" ("Roki," 1936), 71
Augustine, Saint: creator of soliloquy,
179; and epiphany, 25–27
Avant-garde: late symbolism and Oscar
Milosz, 183; Milosz's assimilation of,

193; Milosz's relation to, 14, 160;
twentieth-century styles in Milosz, 165
Axiology: and childhood drama of initiation, 60; effect of science on, 69–70; in
S. I. Witkiewicz, 72

Baczyński, Krzysztof Kamil, 72
Balcerzan, Edward, on allusion in Milosz,
185
"Ballad" ("Ballada," 1949), 165
Barańczak, Stanisław: on Milosz's poetry,
19–20; on moments of vision in Milosz, 186; on national questions and
Milosz, 100; on oppositions in Milosz
and Zbigniew Herbert, 159; on quotation in Milosz, 183; on stylization in
Milosz, 166
Baroque: imitation in Jerzy Harasymowicz and Stanisław Grochowiak, 168;
metaphysical poetry and romanticism,
193; Milosz's stylization of, 167–68;
silva rerum in Milosz, 166; symbolic
language in, 125
Beckett, Samuel, Milosz on significance
of, 194
Berdyaev, Nikolai: Milosz and, 2; *A New
Middle Ages*, 184
Białoszewski, Miron, interest in the concrete, 17
Bible: associations and references to, 165,
182, 187; civilization and, 84; inspiration for "To Father Ch." and "Dialogue," 157; in "Mid-Twentieth-Century Portrait," 65; Milosz's translation
of, 194–95; quotations from, 184; and
secret of speech, 86; in "So Little,"
187. *See also* Scriptures
Biblical poetics, in Milosz's poetry, 77
Biography, romantic and mythmaking,
158–59
"Birds" ("Ptaki," 1935), 29–30, 77, 137
Birds, in Milosz's poetry, 52–55
Blake, William: *apokatastasis* and, 82,
83; Christian imagination, 2; his

Compositor: Huron Valley Graphics, Inc.
Text: 10/13 Sabon
Display: Sabon
Printer: Braun-Brumfield, Inc.
Binder: Braun-Brumfield, Inc.